The Rise and Fall of Management:

a brief history of practice, theory and context

Gordon Pearson

The Rise and Fall of Management:
a brief history of practice, theory and context
(Pre-publication draft)

Acknowledgements

At time of printing this draft, permissions for the published version are being sought.

This draft will be subject to amendment prior to publication.

Full acknowledgements will be made in the final version.

CONTENTS

FOREWORD

This brief history includes an account of the development of such economic theory as had a significant influence on business and management. That influence has been both benign and malign. No attempt is made to explain the detail of economic theory – it is not a history of economics – but to reveal the impact of economic theory on the practice of management. Repeatedly over the past two hundred and thirty odd years since Smith's *Wealth of Nations*, economists have produced broad general accounts of economic activity which appear logical, stand up to practical scrutiny and seem to work. Then, repeatedly, theorists have delved beneath the surface to examine and explain in detail the foundations of those broad truths and have come up with theories and propositions which appear absurd if not factually wrong. Ricardo's theory of labour value was one such example of absurd detail in support of a broad general truth. Ricardo's theory was grasped by Marx who himself wasted so much time on detailed absurdity that he ran out of steam before completing the later books of *Capital*. Similarly with Keynes' examination of production functions, liquidity preferences etc. The general truth works and is useful; the precise explanations may well be flawed.

This examination of management practice and theory is in sufficient depth to explain what management actually is, rather than accepting the various non-management explanations. Smith referred to managers as 'hired administrators', a definition which Marx was happy to accept as it portrayed them as part of the capitalist conspiracy, merely the 'officers' and 'sergeants' who 'command in the name of the capitalist'. A century later Chandler referred to managers as administrative co-ordinators, a term which singularly fails to capture the essence of management. For economists they were simply 'businessmen' a term which would have been generally accepted by all but management themselves, whether it was expressed with the clinical objectivity of classical theorists or with Galbraith's added veneer of derision. The genuinely autonomous role of management has been generally denied except as an abuse of their privileged position. The examination of management practice and theory here, notably included in chapters six through nine, is intended to explain the role in sufficient depth to substantiate its independent function.

All history is a compromise. Like a fractal, it is always possible to delve into any topic at a further level of detail in order to reveal underlying truths. A brief history is an even greater compromise, leaving out almost all detail in favour of a broad perspective. Moreover, such detail as is included is suspect: it may not have been chosen even handedly, but rather from the point of view of some agenda which remains covert. The agenda here is to be factual or truthful where possible and at least balanced between the half truths where the whole is unavailable.

In its brevity, this history necessarily generalises, for example, in treating management in terms of its emergence, rise, fall and possible renewal. While that may be justified as a moving picture of management generally, some managers have undoubtedly continued to work with competence and integrity for the best long term interests of their organisation and all its stakeholders. Others have explicitly rejected the blandishments of Friedmanite theory to justify their self interested behaviour. But the rise and fall generalisation is nevertheless felt to be a valid picture of the broad trends.

The brevity is further strained by the necessity with this subject to straddle the Atlantic. The initial focus was British, but no account of management's history could be limited to the old world let alone just Britain. Management practice and theory has been dominated by the United States since the late nineteenth century and this history is essentially Anglo-Saxon in its analysis both of the development of management and of economic theory in their political context. The British reality has been closely entwined with the American and that proximity is reflected in these pages which largely exclude non-Anglo-Saxon contributions to the story. The most regrettable omissions are the Japanese and German more technologically oriented contributions, both demonstrably more successful than Britain in their post world war II industrial development.

A final compromise that has to made in a brief history of this kind is the selection and balance between the different strands which make up the history: management practice, management theory, economic theory, the political context and the education of management. The normal respect for chronology is somewhat compromised by this entwining of strands. The first part covers a period from around the beginning of the eighteenth century to somewhere around 1870 when the American economy overtook those of the old world. The second part deals with the following hundred years or so up to the time when 'Keynesian economics' ceased to be the accepted orthodoxy. Part three then takes the story from the late 1970s through to the new millennium, before the current economic doubts began to disturb the public consciousness. Part four is written from a 2008 perspective.

The book is not written from a sociological, nor primarily economic, perspective, but seeks to highlight the main content, influences, themes and theories which have shaped the emergence and development of management practice and theory since the beginnings of industrialisation.

It is, like most history, a story of pendulum swings. In the early stages of industrialisation, labour was exploited by owners and evolved into a politically motivated social class. Inequitable excesses led to legislation which reduced exploitation and empowered labour. From there, politically ambitious and powerful unions exploited their position and, especially in Britain, weakened established industries, in some cases, to the point of destruction. A new pendulum swing against the unions' monopolistic powers commenced around the end of the 1970s with the re-adoption, with variations, of an old economic dogma to justify deregulated markets, small government, low taxes and the conspicuous consumption of a new class of untaxed super-rich, At the time of writing it seems probable a new pendulum swing is beginning, fired by the ultimate failure of extreme Friedmanism.

The subject area is often obscured by contention arising from the unequal distribution of income over which management could exert some influence. It might seem difficult to approach the subject without an underlying political agenda, but that is the intention here. The first twenty years of my working life was in industry as a member of management, followed by almost as long in academia. I envisaged both roles as being disinterested in other than the progress and development of my employing organisation. If an agenda has been brought to this project, that is it.

PROLOGUE

The focus of this brief history is on the management of organisations, primarily of for profit business and commercial organisations, but not exclusively so. Such organisations are important because it is from the fruits of their operations that a nation pays for its, health, education, defence and social services as well as its government. And their management is important because it, or they, largely determine the effectiveness of business operations, usually measured in terms of taxable profitability and growth, and therefore the potential generosity of the national services referred to, which are some measure of the degree to which a society might be regarded as civilised.

Management appears to control the process of capital accumulation and its investment in industrialisation, a process that has always seemed inequitable. Peasant farmers were dispossessed of their meagre strips of land so that it might be enclosed for the economic advantage of tenant farmers and their landlords. Ricardo's later explanation of capital as the accumulated surplus value expropriated from labour clearly had some general justification even if his detailed argument appears somewhat arcane.

The unequal struggle between the waged who regularly became the unemployed, and the owners of capital, has been ever present in the apparently inexorable but unpredictable story of industrial development. And management has presided over the frequently inequitable distribution of the surpluses produced by industry. Whether it is the early mill owners employing children of seven years and less, working through daylight hours on a pittance just sufficient to bring total family income up to subsistence level, or Fred Taylor 'negotiating' with Schmidt, the Dutch immigrant labourer, over how the productivity gains he has achieved should be "shared", or today's super-manager taking millions of pounds from the company in share bonuses as reward for inadequate performance, management has always clearly been at the sharp end of exploitation. From that position management is equally enabled, if it were so minded, to discharge its responsibilities with truth, fairness and frugality, to use Adam Smith's word, eschewing greed and naked self-interest.

During the first half of the 20th century the industrialised world experienced the great depression, two world wars, established collective bargaining rights of workers, and the less divisive impact of Keynesian economics. Consequently there was some closing of the inequitable gap between the waged/unemployed and the owners of capital. But from the late 1970s inequity reasserted itself, informed by the newly incisive version of neo-classical economics promulgated initially by Friedman and colleagues at Chicago. The newly inequitable distribution of wealth and income was not restricted to America and Britain and to a lesser extent Europe and Japan, but crucially also in the developing economies of the South East Asian 'tigers', and China, India, Russia, Brazil, Mexico and an ever widening throng of industrialising nations.

The inequitable gap, sometimes highlighted by the ostentatious consumption of the few in the faces of the insecure many, fuelled continuous aggravation and from time to time open conflict and occasionally bloody revolution. And quite apparently it may do so again.

Now for the first time this conflict of interests is being played out against the realisation that, driven by world population growth and the unceasing quest for better standards of living, the earth's resources are being depleted at an unsustainable rate, its atmosphere polluted and its climate undermined through the industrial activities of the developed and developing world.

In this situation management bears a substantial responsibility. Alfred Chandler started *The Visible Hand,* his account of the twentieth century managerial revolution in American industry, with the assertion that the visible hand of management had replaced Adam Smith's invisible hand of market forces. Modern business enterprise had become *'the most powerful institution in the American economy and its managers the most influential group of economic decision makers'.* [1]

Nevertheless, he noted that economists had excluded management from their theory of the firm: *'Any theory of the firm that defines the enterprise merely as a factory or even a number of factories, and therefore fails to take into account the role of administrative coordination, is far removed from reality.'* [2] And he added: *'Historians as well as economists have failed to consider the implications of the rise of the modern business enterprise. ...*

they have paid almost no notice at all to the managers who ... play a far more central role in the operations of the American economy than did the robber barons, the industrial statesmen, or financiers." [3]   More than thirty years later, the still dominant neo-classical free market economic theory continued to show little comprehension of the role of management. So some assessment in its historical perspective may therefore be overdue.

Important though they are, managements are not completely their own masters. They interact with others, potentially more powerful than themselves, who influence how they behave. Shareholders, customers, employees, suppliers, money lenders, tax authorities, government, their local community and the wider environment which will be the home of future generations, all these demand satisfaction, and management is responsible for achieving at least a tolerable balance of dissatisfactions among them.

Beyond even them there is something more diffuse, altogether less tangible, that dictates behaviour among all those stakeholders and including management.   It is to do with the taken for granted assumptions that people have about 'the way we do things around here'. It is in the culture of organisations, governments and social groups of all kinds. And it is extremely powerful. Over the past two and half centuries, in effect since management began, this culture has been heavily influenced by theory, in this case the economic theory, first identified by Adam Smith,which is based on the simple idea of the rational, self interested, amoral 'economic man' as the foundation stone of economic growth and the 'wealth of nations'.

> *'It is not from the benevolence of the butcher, the brewer, or the baker, that we expect our dinner, but from their regard for their own interest. We address ourselves not to their humanity but to their self-love.'* [4]

The efforts of these many self interested economic men, working purely to maximise their own wealth, would according to the theory, maximise the aggregate wealth of the population. So far the theory has worked better than any alternative in delivering that object. Today the theory dominates business and government alike. But it is not without problems. It not only fails to recognise the role of 'the most influential group of economic decision makers', it requires the destabilising inequity already referred to, and is itself unstable, depending from time to time for its survival on exactly the governmental intervention and regulation the theory proscribes.

Classical economic theory, so named first by Karl Marx, was outlined by Smith before industrialisation and the large scale mills, factories and industrial towns it was to produce. It was a theory for '*the butcher, the brewer, or the baker*' rather than the industrial factory, much less the joint stock, limited liability competitive business with its shares readily bought and sold on the stock market. It was a theory for the owner-manager of small scale operations. It had no place for hired managers.

This same economic theory, with only minor modification of principle, is still promulgated through the academic departments and business schools of research universities, primarily in America, but from there throughout the industrialised and industrialising world. The influence of American business school education is difficult to exaggerate. Leading industrial, political, civil service and academic figures from across the globe gained their post graduate qualifications in American business schools and research departments and this inevitably is a fundamental influence on how they subsequently do their jobs and what they believe works, thereby reinforcing the culture in which managements operate.

This brief history traces firstly the emergence of management as a practice and a body of knowledge and understanding, secondly its development as a crucial and potentially benevolent role in economic progress, thirdly its corruption largely as a result of what Ghoshal referred to as 'bad theory'[5], and finally the possibility of its renewal, enabled by the recognition of its latter day shortcomings and made essential by the finite nature of earth's resources. The Epilogue identifies some of the essential steps which would need to be taken to reverse the decline in management's achievement and to refocus it on higher aims than simply 'making as much money as possible for stockholders'[6]

PART ONE – THE EMERGENCE OF MANAGEMENT

The full history of management might start back in 5000 BC with the
Sumerian temple priests whose tax system involved the amassing of worldly
goods for which records had to be maintained. Or in 4000 BC with the
building of the pyramids which must clearly have involved some
understanding of organisation among the Egyptians. Evidence on Moses
suggests the Hebrews had some management awareness around 1500 BC
and similarly the Chinese from 1100BC. And there are well documented
military antecedents from the fourth century BC in both Greece and China,
with references now included in the modern literature. These may be of
academic interest but the history of management as it is now understood
really starts with the creation of an economic surplus and the subsequent
introduction of industrial manufacturing in eighteenth century England.

This opening part is concerned with that first revolutionary century of
practice and its reflection in the economic theory expounded by Adam Smith
and others. It sees the processes and responsibilities now associated with
management starting to emerge first in the new agriculture and subsequently
in the development of the first transportation infrastructure, the canals and
turnpike roads, and only then in the process of industrialisation itself.
Initially management was indissolubly linked with ownership in the shape of
what was later identified as the 'entrepreneur'.

Smith recognised the revolutionary changes that might be enabled by the
cost reductions that could be achieved by the specialisation of labour. Such
reduced costs would bring what were previously luxury commodities within
the reach of a far greater number. Thus a virtuous cycle would be
established which was limited only by the size of markets. He therefore
argued against the old protectionist systems of trade and commerce in favour
of markets freed from all government intervention.

Industrialisation, based on the division of labour and the accumulation and investment of capital, resulted in an explosion of industrial factory building and the creation of whole new urban populations. It changed everything both for the better and for the worse. It created great wealth and great misery. It supported an explosion in population and established an unprecedented and ever expanding level of consumption simultaneously with the creation of an underclass of paupers and workers who from time to time became the unemployed as the economy progressed through booms and slumps.

Smith did not live to see the poverty and disease of the new industrial towns. It was left to his successors to observe such inequity and consider ways to organise better the industrial system of economics and governance. Some suggested the misery had to be accepted if the increase in wealth was to be achieved. Others violently rejected that proposition. Thus from the beginnings of industrialisation there was a fundamental dichotomy between employers and employed, between rich and poor, capitalists and labour. Management began to emerge as a separate and partly autonomous category, recognised by neither side of industry, labour regarding them simply as the agents of capital, capital suspecting them, as economic theory suggested they should, of seeking to maximise their own self interest at the expense of capital. But management, by definition neither capital nor labour, was in the front line of economic development, and in a position to influence its course for good or ill.

1. THE FIRST ECONOMIC SURPLUS

Industrialisation depended on the prior generation of an economic surplus and the establishment of ways of working for which management, as we now refer to it but didn't then, was primarily responsible. Industrialisation improved the standards of living, health and longevity of industrialising people but it had negative effects as well as positive. Industrialisation created considerable aggravation.

Prior to industrialisation, life in England for the vast majority was fairly short and uncomfortable if not 'brutish'. The English population remained around 5½m through the first half of the eighteenth century, held there by recurrent harsh climatic conditions (1708-10, 1725-29 and 1739-42), poor harvests resulting in famine, poor public hygiene resulting in disease (notably dysentery, smallpox and consumption) as well as much alcoholic excess – output of spirits reached 8 million gallons in 1742-3 six times higher than in the early years of the century and didn't fall till after 1750 when taxes on alcohol were substantially raised. Infant mortality ran at one in fifteen for most of the first half of the century. The population lived in poverty and for the majority life was a struggle against the odds. It was no golden age.

In the last four decades of the century, as industrialization was beginning, conditions overall improved substantially. More productive agriculture resulted in the elimination of famine and improved diet for the masses. Greater supplies of coal for domestic heating, improved ventilation, more soap and washable garments contributing to improved hygiene, improvements in medical practice and surgery with the creation of hospitals and dispensaries and the adoption of smallpox inoculation, all contributed to the reduction and elimination of disease. As a result England's population grew by around two thirds to over 9 million by the end of the century, infant mortality fell almost eightfold to one in 118 and life for the majority became progressively less precarious, though not for all.

The improvements which enabled industrialisation to take off were only achieved by the intelligence, diligence and energy of large numbers of people and perhaps the genius of a small number, all motivated to create something better than had been previously known.

Assuming such people were motivated solely by their own self interest, or greed, is an inadequate proxy for the truth. There had to be something less dismal within man which motivated such heroic achievement.

Human Needs: Engine of Economic Growth

The fundamental idea which underpins much of economic thought is that of 'homo economicus', the utterly rational, amoral, self interested 'economic man' identified by Adam Smith and eternally associated with his name. Writing in 1776, he identified the 'self-love' of producers and tradesmen, rather than their concern for any social ends, as the solid foundation of economic activity and growth:

> *'By pursuing his own interest he frequently promotes that of the society more effectually than when he really intends to promote it. I have never known much good done by those who affected to trade for the public good.'* [7]

This is the simple, direct Adam Smith that survives most explicitly in economic thinking today, but his examination of what motivated people was actually rather more nuanced than just that of economic self-interest.

He recognised that economic growth depended on people being motivated to satisfy certain needs and *'conveniences'*. He suggested a progression of needs, starting from childhood with those arising from hunger and thirst, heat and cold.

> *'The preservation and healthful state of the body seem to be the objects which nature first recommends to the care of every individual ... The first lessons which he is taught by those to whom his childhood is entrusted, tend, the greater part of them, to the same purpose. Their principal object is to teach him to keep out of harm's way.'* [8]

Smith expressed these needs in adulthood as desire, firstly for food (for which desire is *'limited by the size of a man's stomach'*), and then for satisfying

> *'the other wants and fancies of mankind. Cloathing and lodging, household furniture and what is called Equipage'*[9]
> (equipage being identified as articles for personal ornament and use and a carriage etc).

These wants are unlimited, clearly extending to what was later referred to by Thorstein Veblen as *'conspicuous consumption'*.[10] These were the human needs and wants driving economic growth.

Smith also identified the desire to save as the ultimate human need. By saving, rather than consuming all, a person could accumulate capital in order to 'improve' themselves. While others objected that immediate consumption on pleasure, vice and luxury would be the more effective driver of economic progress, Smith argued that 'frugality' was more powerful than vice and luxury. Frugality which enabled people to become

> *'proper objects of this respect, of deserving and obtaining this credit and rank among our equals, is, perhaps, the strongest of all our desires, and our anxiety to obtain the advantages of fortune is accordingly much more excited and irritated by this desire. Than that of supplying all the necessities and conveniences of the body, which are always very easily supplied.'*[2]

Adam Smith therefore had a richer appreciation of human motivation than is now widely assumed. More recent contributors have added to, rather than replaced Smith's model. Maslow proposed a hierarchy of human needs[11] starting with physiological needs (food, sleep, shelter, sex etc) at the lowest level, rising through safety needs, love needs, esteem needs and finally, at the top level, which would be salient once the lower level needs were satisfied, the need for self-actualization (which was exampled as 'a musician must make music'). Maslow's model not only appeals intuitively but seems sound common sense as well as good theory even though it was not based on empirical evidence.

Less elegant approaches may get nearer to the truth. Murray's original work in the 1930s[12], later enhanced by Atkinson[13] and McClelland[14], suggested there were more than twenty intrinsic human needs, any one or more of which might be potent at any one time. There was not necessarily a hierarchical relationship between needs, no structured progression from one need to the next and no indication that the various needs were necessarily of equal importance. This less structured account offers some diversity and flexibility as well as the messiness of reality.

Alderfer[15] produced a simplified model suggesting just three basic human needs: existence, relatedness and growth. Existence can be taken as similar to Maslow's physiological and safety needs. Relatedness is similar to Maslow's love and esteem needs and also to McClelland's need for affiliation. Alderfer's growth need is equivalent to Maslow's self-actualization and McClelland's needs for achievement or as Smith suggested the need to become a 'proper object of respect'.

There is therefore some basic consistency among many theoreticians, more or less independent of their era, about the human needs which might motivate behaviour: basic needs (existence, food, shelter, clothing, safety etc), social needs (love, esteem, affiliation, relatedness, 'wants and fancies' etc) and growth needs (achievement, self-actualization, 'frugality', etc).

Adams' equity theory[16] sheds further light by adding the concept of fairness and justice. This is not an absolute measure, but comparative. An individual perceives his or her own treatment and compares it with the apparent treatment of others and so assesses the equity of their own treatment.

Growth needs appear to be the most powerful motivators once the basic needs have been satisfied. But growth means different things to different individuals. For example, growth may, as Maslow indicated, lead certain individuals to making music, or painting or poetry. These creative outlets are recognisable as satisfying the need for self actualisation. Others may feel more motivated to the achievement of quite different outcomes, such as great buildings, or feats of civil engineering, such as the bridges and tunnels of railway lines, or even the lines themselves. For others the creation and development of a new enterprise, which contributes directly to, and involves in many various ways, the lives of other people.

Any such projects may be the focus of the growth needs for some individuals. For others the focus may be rather less heroic. Smith's amoral, self-interested 'economic men' certainly exist and for them the focus will be on the acquisition of money and power. And as Smith suggested with some disdain, they may well be motivated by the ability to display their power or money in front of a wide audience with the expectation that they will be accorded respect, if not love, for their celebrity.

Lower level needs, including the need for equity, are likely to fall into the category of what Herzberg called hygiene factors which do not themselves motivate behaviour, but could well demotivate, even aggravate, if unsatisfied.

Using this simple model as the backdrop it seems clear that, initially at least, as Adam Smith suggested, it was the basic set of human needs which led people to initiate and accept the developments in agriculture which resulted not only in the population being more reliably fed but also the generation of an agricultural surplus simultaneously with the disadvantaging of some. Similarly, social needs, including the need for esteem from peers, would explain the unlimited market potential for all kinds of commodities, while growth needs among some sections of the population must have driven the accumulation of capital and the process of industrialisation. At the same time, the lack of satisfaction of basic and social needs among other sections, and the obvious lack of equity, was clearly the cause of considerable discontent.

The rational, amoral, self interested 'economic man' was always an inadequate substitute for this richly varied reality which encompasses human beings who also exhibit courage, generosity and kindness, characteristics which economics is simply not equipped to address and therefore excludes from its analysis.

Agricultural Development

Prior to industrialisation the main purpose of economic activity was to satisfy man's basic needs, that is to provide food, shelter and clothing to support a subsistence society. Most activity was essentially localised, with each village being largely self sufficient having little need for long distance communications. One of the critical prerequisites to breaking out of this subsistence economy was the creation of an agricultural surplus. Formerly the dominant notion had been that a farm should be just big enough to support a family, ie in motivational terms would satisfy basic survival or subsistence needs. Such a unit would achieve satisfaction except in dearth years when poor harvests might result in hunger and disease or even famine. There would therefore be some motivation for the farmer to achieve an additional surplus and accumulate it as capital against more needy times.

The transition of the peasant subsistence farmer to the landless waged agricultural labourer appeared to be the inevitable result of capital accumulation by the few to invest in new scientifically based methods which through systematic management would substantially raise productivity.

England's experience of this process was different from that on continental Europe, where the ancient rights of the peasant farmer were protected and still influence today's Common Agricultural Policy. The process in England was more ruthless. Though it culminated in the eighteenth century with larger landlords dispossessing the peasant by enclosing his land, the process of dispossession had actually started much earlier.

The breakdown of the old manorial system whereby the peasant worked his few strips of land and shared in labouring for the lord of the manor had started in England before 1348-9 when the Black Death gave it further impetus by killing off more than a third of the population. After the Black Death the lord of the manor was left without tenants to work his land and if he tried to buy in labour to do the job he found it in short supply and expensive, despite the Statute of Labourers which was intended, but failed, to fix wages at pre Black Death rates. Without tenants and labour the lords of the manor were driven to give up agriculture themselves and to lease their land for what they could get. By the fifteenth century, English agriculture was based to a significant extent on lease holding tenant farmers and their labourers.

Major changes followed in English agriculture in the sixteenth century with sheep farming significantly replacing arable. The price obtainable for corn was controlled by the State in the interests of the consumer and its export was similarly restricted so returns to the farmer were limited and beyond his control. On the other hand there was a ready market for English wool which was long fibred and suitable for making into fine cloth for which there was also an unregulated and buoyant export market. Moreover sheep farming was less labour intensive than arable, making it viable when labour was in short supply, so it subsequently contributed to the re-emergence of a labour surplus. However, it could not be conducted on the old manorial system of scattered strips of land, requiring instead the creation of large sheep runs. This could be achieved by rationalising and consolidating land holdings and enclosing them behind fences, walls, hedges and ditches.

The sixteenth century enclosure movement dispossessed many of the remaining peasant farmers who joined the bands of unemployed roaming the countryside seeking work or begging. The eighteenth century enclosure movement, though significant, was therefore only the final completion of the process which turned the English peasant farmer into an agricultural labourer.

The dispossession of the peasantry was not achieved without aggravation. Sporadic outbreaks included the Peasants' Revolt of 1381, the Pilgrimage of Grace in 1536 and Ket's Rising in 1549 plus innumerable riots and disturbances against enclosures plus a multitude of minor aggravations.

In the eighteenth century, with increasing population, the growth of towns, and the early development of larger scale manufacture, the prices of agricultural produce rose making it feasible for waste land to be brought under cultivation and for that common land which had not previously been enclosed and was still being used for peasant farmer subsistence, to be enclosed to grow food for the market.   From 1760 to 1800 there were 2000 enclosures by Act of parliament whereas in the previous sixty years there had been very few. The enclosure movement was significant in its economic effects but even more important as a rallying symbol of the dispossession of England's yeoman farmer.

Common land could be enclosed either by buying up the rights of common right holders or by Act of Parliament, either of which was expensive. Sometimes such enclosure, for example, by an estate owner reasserting ancient rights which had been long ignored, could cause great aggravation. Defoe in his 1722 *'Tour through England and Wales'* reported one such case, a Buckinghamshire landowner,

> *'presuming upon his power, set up his pales, and took in a
> large parcel of land call'd Wiggington common ... the cottagers
> and farmers opposed it, by their complaints a great while; but
> finding he went on with his work, and resolv'd to do it, they
> rose upon him, pulled down his banks, and forced up his pales,
> and carried away the wood, or set it on a heap and burnt it;
> and this they did several times ...'* [17]

Such aggravated action was widespread.

In addition to the enclosure movement there had also been a marked decline in small farms.

> *'The land tax evidence ... shows ... The major decline of small
> owners and of small farmers in general must have occurred
> before 1760, probably between about 1660 and 1750.* [18]

The reasons for that decline of small ownership were various: low prices and high taxes led to some mixed farms failing; alternative occupations in trade, industry and the professions were growing making small farms less attractive both as an occupation and as an investment; many such small farms and land holdings were bought up by larger land owners. These effects applied unevenly across the country with small farms remaining strong in some areas where incomes were augmented by industrial earnings.

The symbolic dispossession of the yeoman farmer peasantry by the land owners and their tenants through the later eighteenth century enclosure movement was therefore only a part of the march of capital in English agriculture.

By mid eighteenth century tenant farmers were managing bigger farm units that could benefit from the division of labour as well as various technical innovations some of which required the application of more capital. For example, fertility was increased dramatically through the application of inventions such as the deep plough, the drill sower and machine hoe. Also a new crop rotation system was introduced based on the alternation of cereal crops with artificial grasses and winter roots such as turnips, swedes etc, replacing the old system which required the land to be left fallow every third year. Not only did the new system effectively increase the land under cultivation by a third, but the root crops also provided winter feed for livestock so the autumn cull of surplus animals, which had previously taken place on all farms across the country, became unnecessary. Livestock breeding was also hugely improved by a more scientific approach. The development of breeds of sheep and cattle, enabled by enclosures, saw the doubling in weight of the main breeds in not much more than half a century. Such 'scientific' inputs to farming dramatically increased the efficiency and overall output of agriculture.

The main produce was in grain-stuffs and livestock which were the staple food, and barley which was the staple drink. Rye and oats were used to make bread and meal for the poor as well as feed for cattle and horses. With a surplus production over and above subsistence needs, agriculture was also able to support the development of other industries. For example, wheat was supplied to corn millers, bakers, distillers and starch makers. The corn millers supplied not only bakers but stationers, bookbinders, linen printers, trunk makers and paper hangers. Similarly, barley was supplied to distillers and brewers for the production of beer, and ale and rye meal was supplied to the leather tanning industry.

Livestock supplied similarly broad end markets. Sheep supplied the wool textile industry and cattle supplied hides for tanners and various leather based industries. Fat from sheep and cattle supplied soap boilers and candle makers. Horns were used by cutlers and bones by glue manufacturers.

The development of agriculture demonstrated much that was good and bad about capital accumulation as well as some early examples of what might be referred to as commercial management. A whole class of people were dispossessed of their original land birthright but were compensated as wage earners so that, initially at least, they were significantly better off, though it was from their ranks that the homeless unemployed emerged and were often treated rather more as criminals than victims.

The immediate and long term beneficiaries, the landlords and tenant farmers, were able to invest some of their surplus in improving their land and holdings, sometimes with a long term perspective from which they themselves would be unable to benefit, for example the long term plantation of trees on which the British navy depended up to and beyond the Battle of Trafalgar. Others becoming the newly rich land owning class became major investors in the new capital projects, including the transportation systems and newly emerging manufactures. These sections of the population, motivated by growth, addressed themselves to the management problems of forecasting and planning, command and control. Their success produced the surplus to invest without which the ensuing benefits could never have accrued.

Transportation Infrastructure

Another strand in the pre-industrial change, and a vital prerequisite to industrialisation, was focused on internal travel and transportation: the development of the turnpike road system and canals, the turnpikes for personal transport and higher value goods, the canals for industrial freight, such as coal, stone, slate, clay and grain, which were all low cost, heavy items uneconomic to transport by road.

Previously, the chief highway of England had been the sea, but travel was a long slow process. Ashton quotes an example of a pig iron load being delivered from Horsehay in Shropshire to Chester.[19] Its journey started by being transported by road a few miles to the river Severn. It was then loaded onto a barge and sent down river to Bristol where it was unloaded and put on a freight coaster ship to go round the Welsh coast to the river Dee where it was loaded onto a river barge and thence up stream to Chester. The journey was around 250 miles, involved four loadings and unloadings and took many weeks to accomplish even if the weather conditions remained fair. Many cargoes were lost as ships foundered in storms at sea and sometimes even in the rivers. Opening up the canals reduced the journey to 50 miles, eliminated any interference by bad weather, cut out most of the double handling and reduced the time in transit from an average of up to three months to five days. This was not only much cheaper but also freed up huge amounts of cash tied up in goods in transit that could be invested in fixed capital.

Few of the English rivers were naturally navigable and most were also blocked by corn mill dams and other obstacles to shipping which charged for their opening. In the 17th century a number of rivers had been 'improved' and made navigable and this process continued apace in the early 18th century by the formation of navigation companies largely financed by merchants who stood to gain from their development. Improvements included the removal of weirs and dams, the deepening of channels, the building of locks and also the shortening of routes by digging new 'cuts'. From this it was a short step to the great capital consuming enterprise of canal building which started in the 1750s.

Canals were not new. The Romans built the Fossdyke from Lincoln to the River Trent, for both drainage and navigation, in around AD 50. The Grand Canal of China was completed in the tenth century and the 150 mile long Canal du Midi in France which connected the Mediterranean to the Atlantic via the Garonne River was completed in 1681. Nor was canal lock technology new. The pound lock was invented by the Chinese in 983 and the still familiar V shaped mitre gate held together by the water pressure is generally attributed to Leonardo da Vinci. What was new was the creation of a whole system of canals.

The Duke of Bridgewater started the canal mania when he employed James Brindley to build a canal connecting his coal mines at Worsley to the coal consuming city of Manchester. The project involved building both an aqueduct and various tunnels into the mines. The reduced cost of delivery to the end users in Manchester substantially lowered the price of coal and demonstrated the viability of canal transport. There followed a number of long distance navigations, with Brindley as the leading canal engineer of his time. He largely built the so-called "Grand Cross" of canals which linked the four great river basins of England: the Thames, Severn, Humber and Mersey.

Building major infrastructure projects like this involved facing a number of what we would now refer to as management problems that had not been previously confronted. The canal engineers faced all the practical details of surveying the route and estimating the costs likely to be involved. It was necessary also to draw up a petition for an Act of Parliament to be passed approving the project. This was expensive as was bribing objectors to the proposed canal and compensating private land owners through whose territory the canal would go, as well as sometimes compensating navigation owners for their loss of toll income. Funds had to be raised to finance the project, mainly by the sale of company shares. It usually took several years for a canal to be completed and so companies necessarily raised further funds by mortgages and issues of bonds or promissory notes. The ingenuity with which capital funding was raised was one of the major contributions of the canal movement to the capital accumulation and industrialisation project.

In addition the engineers, either resident engineer or clerk of works, had to procure supplies of material and equipment, assemble large numbers of 'navvies' (short for navigation labourers, ie pick and shovel men) often in remote places, arrange their board and lodging and supervise their work. Managing 500 or so unskilled hard drinking men scattered over miles of countryside no doubt presented some new problems for the engineer. Brindley's approach was to devolve responsibility for specific projects such as locks or bridges, down to contractors who were paid a fixed price for each item. For the main cuts it was normal to agree with groups of men a price per cubic yard of earth and stone removed. As well as pick and shovel labourers there were large numbers of brick makers, quarrymen, bricklayers, miners and tunnellers as well as different groups of skilled artisans. The division of labour between different specialisations considerably exceeded that required in agriculture. In addition canal building involved many specialised tools and items of equipment. Bridgewater had barges fitted out as mason's, carpenters and blacksmiths shops so that work could proceed as the project progressed. From the start of the project to its completion and the commencement of its ability to earn and pay back, a substantial investment of capital was absorbed, far in excess of that required by any earlier enterprises such as the overseas trading companies.

Similar problems were confronted with the building of turnpikes. Previously the road system had just about been good enough for the local farmer, or pedlar or for a packhorse laden with woollen or linen goods. But they didn't serve satisfactorily as main roads between major cities. Their foundations were weak, drainage extremely limited, the narrow wheels of carriages made deep ruts and cattle further damaged the surface in wet weather. Personal transport by road, other than on horseback, was extremely slow. Ashton reports a Mr Roderick Random wishing to go from Newcastle to London first looked for passage by ship[20]. He was persuaded by the perils of the sea to go by road on foot and overtook a wagon that had set out on the same journey two days before him.

The problem was largely one of organisation. Maintenance and upkeep of roads was legally the responsibility of each local parish who generally employed out of work and unpaid paupers on road maintenance. National legislation was mainly focused on defining the sorts of traffic allowed which was largely concerned with the width of wheels, and the relative tolls that could be charged. Wider wheels were less damaging to the road, but narrower wheels faster and more comfortable for the traveller. By mid eighteenth century, however, it was clear that attention should be focused on the road itself rather than its traffic.

Improvements were initially achieved following enclosures of agricultural land permitting new routes to be established and often paid for by the proprietors of coal mines and other burgeoning industrial enterprises in order to improve the transport of their goods to market. The turnpikes, established by Acts of Parliament, transferred responsibility for the maintenance of roads from the parishes to trusts which took responsibility for the whole length of a road through many parishes and which charged the road's users for its building and maintenance. The new turnpikes were established with gates at each end where users were charged tolls and with fences or walls at the side of the road to ensure users were not able to avoid the toll gates.

Building the new turnpikes involved many processes similar to those of canal building. They were major projects involving substantial investment and a prolonged time delay before they were able to generate any income in return. The engineers involved, such as Telford and Macadam, faced many of the same issues confronting the canal builders, planning the routes, estimating the costs, solving the engineering problems presented by the particular terrain, negotiating with parliament and local landlords and authorities, managing large teams of navvies, semi-skilled and skilled workers and artisans as well as raising the funds for the whole project.

Canals and turnpikes were great infrastructural projects which absorbed huge amounts of capital. The roads had to be supplied with fences, gates, bridges and tollhouses and canals with reservoirs, locks, sluices, towpaths, bridges and quays. All of which building needed not only labour and skilled craftsmen, but also new tools and equipment. New types of craft and vehicles were needed, as well as new inns, stables and warehouses. They added nothing immediately to the supply of goods for consumption. But they created substantial employment for others including the satisfaction of the navvies' demands for food, drink, clothing and shelter.

These new infrastructural projects, as the new agriculture had also, substituted capital for labour. Phillips noted how, for example, standing at Brindley's Barton aqueduct over the Irwell navigation, you could see at the same time

> 'seven or eight stout fellows labouring like slaves to drag a boat slowly up the Irwell, and one horse or mule, or sometimes two men at the most, drawing five or six of the Duke's barges linked together, at a great rate upon the canal.' [21]

The substitution of capital had consolidated the dispossession of the peasantry into an unskilled waged or unemployed pool of labour. Whilst a long way short of the deployment of robots in modern manufacture, it was the beginning of the process which first created the pool of labour and then displaced that labour from the process of manufacture. Nevertheless the process of capital accumulation and labour substitution improved immeasurably the degree to which most people were able to satisfy their basic needs, as can be seen in the records of mortality, health and population growth previously cited.

Pre-industrial and Domestic Manufacturing

At the start of the eighteenth century manufacturing all over England was only accomplished through small scale operations as had been done for preceding centuries. There were no large scale manufacturing operations and no large units of employment. Coal getting, for example, was by shallow bell pits employing only small numbers, typically no more than thirty, and usually aiming only to provide for local consumption rather than sending to more distant markets. There were no large scale deep coal mines and the application of capital in mining was limited. The same was true of brick manufacture and also for iron founding. Abraham Darby's foundry and forges at Coalbrookdale had worked on a small scale through the early eighteenth century making domestic iron pans. But it was not till the last two to three decades of the century that significant expansion was achieved following the successful development of coke iron-making. And it was not till 1795 that Matthew Boulton and James Watt commenced construction of the Soho Foundry which was to establish the precision and accuracy of metal finishing that enabled them to produce the reliably working pistons and cylinders, critical components of steam engine manufacture.

It was that other basic of a subsistence society, clothing, which led the industrialisation process. The textile industries had long been major employers, but most of the enterprises were small with only a few employing large numbers of workers. Even among the larger employers, nearly all the employees worked from their own homes where they operated domestic scale equipment. The machinery had to be small enough to be sited in the kitchen or possibly in purpose built spinsters' cottage lofts. Overall the capital involved in the textile industries was not substantial by later standards and its ownership was spread thinly. The acquisition of a spinning machine or loom was not completely out of reach of the one who operated it though mostly they were owned by the employer.

The textile industry employed many supply chain middle men. For example, a fustian dealer, fustian being the basic coarse cotton fabric, might employ a country manufacturer to put out raw cotton and yarn to carders, spinners and weavers. The country manufacturer would be charged for the materials and he paid for the wages of the people he put the work out to and he was then repaid for the completed materials plus a commission for his own expertise and labour in organising, putting out the work, paying of wages and collecting finished materials at depots rather than the cottage door. Raw fibre was collected by spinsters (traditionally women and girls) from the depot and they took it home and spun it into yarn, returned it to the depot and were paid by the piece. Similarly, yarn was collected by the weavers (usually male) who took it home and wove it into fabric before returning it to the depot for payment.

The country manufacturer, who also played a limited role as owner at least of working capital, had no responsibilities for employing people or keeping them in work. There was no need for large central premises and overhead costs beyond the setting up of a small depot for the distribution and collection of material.

The dealer's prime task was to sell the finished product and to be an effective buyer and seller of materials so that a reasonable margin could be earned between the two transactions. He could expand his business simply by buying more raw fibre and having it distributed it to more spinners and weavers so long as he had a ready market for the product he was handling.

Superficially at least there were considerable advantages for the home workers in this domestic system of production. They had greater control over their lives, over when and how fast they worked, and their children working at home were less susceptible to the abuse and exploitation they later experienced under the factory system. But there were downsides. Because the output from the system was so small the workers were paid very little and were not far above the breadline even when working full time. There are many contemporary accounts from Defoe and others which suggest their lives were far from idyllic.

This flexible way of organising business required the dealer to focus on three issues which we now recognise as problems of management. Firstly, it was vital to manage logistics efficiently so as to eliminate any cash being tied up unnecessarily in work in progress. He would require the manufacturer to operate timely collection by, and delivery from, the spinners and weavers which would have played a significant part in the manufacturer's controllable costs. Secondly, the dealer, and therefore also his manufacturer, would also be responsible for ensuring the work was completed at the required quality of workmanship which meant developing close relationships of trust with the highly skilled independent spinners and weavers. Finally, it was also vital for the dealer and manufacturer to create and maintain effective relationships with the various other parties to the business such as customers and suppliers as well as the spinners and weavers. All these relationships determined the quality, cost, price and availability of finished product. If they were not well managed the dealer and his manufacturer would fail. If they were well managed then any or all the middle men would be able to earn a surplus profit and be able to accumulate some capital for future investment and growth.

Elements of Management

Economic activities generally entail some aspects of management. Farming, once it had progressed beyond simple subsistence, required the accumulation of some capital to invest in new equipment and machinery, the development of new and better ways of doing things and the identification of how to sell the surplus produce for wider food markets or new industrial uses.

The development of the internal transport infrastructure with canals and turnpikes produced a whole new set of management problems. The canal and road engineers needed to be accomplished managers, envisaging a completely new scale of project and having to plan their profitable completion as well as control their actual implementation. The scale of the projects and therefore of the funding required for their completion was completely new, as was the long term delay before the commencement of any income and therefore return to the providers of capital. In addition they had to arrange the procurement of all the necessary materials and other resources including, most importantly of all, the people who would do the actual work building the canal or road. And they had to devise practical ways of recruiting, organising and rewarding that new form of migrant labour and controlling their work so that it was completed in conformity with required quality standards and on time. The technical engineering problem that had to be overcome along the way was completely without precedent. The funding of such projects required detailed planning and close control over costs and timing in order to generate returns to the providers of funds.

The entrepreneur was the key role in pre-industrial textile manufacture. It was the French economist, Jean Baptiste Say, who introduced the term 'entrepreneur' to describe the role which combined management with some element of ownership in the creative, developmental role understood today. The element of ownership might start off quite small, but from that toehold in ownership the entrepreneur would seek to grow and accumulate an increasing share of the surplus and consolidate their position in ownership. Identification with the best long term interests of the business was crucial to the entrepreneur concept. It was a quite different role from that of, for example, the travelling salesman who was not expecting to visit the same territory ever again. Such an individual, being an amoral 'economic man', would naturally seek, by fair means or foul, to squeeze every ounce of advantage for himself out of every sale. The entrepreneur, on the other hand, would focus on a continuing relationship with customers and be concerned to demonstrate his worthiness of their trust.

In pre-jndustrial textiles the entrepreneur might have been the dealer who started the process in motion and who sold finished product, or the country manufacturer who was the one with direct contact with the spinners and weavers. His task required foresight and planning as well as some command and control in achieving an essentially innovative and profitable result.

Logistics and quality control, as well as stakeholder relations, were key to the entrepreneur's success. Profitability was also of crucial importance as without it there would be no surplus to reinvest to ensure the organisation's survival and future prosperity. But the necessary retention of surplus could only be achieved by strictly controlling all costs including, most importantly of all, the wages paid to the workers.

All these problems were to present themselves when the development of the factory system of manufacturing was undertaken, but by then they were not completely new. They had already been confronted and means of their solution identified.

2. A THEORY OF INDUSTRY AND COMMERCE

The generation of an economic surplus came after millennia of, at best, subsistence living. The explanation of why it happened when and where it did remains incomplete, though theories abound. Adam Smith, wrote 'An Inquiry into the Nature and Causes of the Wealth of Nations' just as the very first examples of industrial development were being established. His theory of economics was developed further as a consequence of industrialisation and became in its turn influential on governments in shaping that process. More recently economic theory has played an overwhelmingly influential role in shaping the job of management itself.

Smith probably started his investigations prior to 1760; his experience in France up to 1766 clearly added a cosmopolite flavour to his work and especially informed his attack on mercantilism. He finally published in 1776. He did not live to see the impoverishment and misery of life in the factories, mills and mill towns of nineteenth century England. That was left to his successors, Ricardo, Malthus, Say and others. Nevertheless, he acknowledged aspects of the dehumanising impact of the division of labour.

Smith laid out the territory of economic theory and established its basic logic. The innovations and changes to the main thrust of his model have been relatively minor even though the industrial and economic world the model seeks to explain has changed beyond recognition.

The emergence and development of what came to be known as classical theory had substantial influence on the development of management though it was not immediately obvious. The early industrialisers were probably unaware of economic theory, though the importance of Smith's work was publicly acknowledged in 1792 by Pitt the Younger addressing parliament:

(Smith's) *'extensive knowledge of detail and depth of philosophical research will, I believe, furnish the best solution to every question connected with the history of commerce and with the question of political economy.'* [22]

Economic theory and political and industrial practice were interdependent from the beginning of industrialisation and remain so today, perhaps more powerfully than ever.

Mercantilism and Trade Protection

During the period of achieving an economic surplus and its initial investment in infrastructure and manufacturing, government's role in those economic activities was essentially piece-meal and discontinuous. It was more concerned with the matter of trade and commerce. England had long seen itself as competing with the other European states, especially France and Spain, for a finite amount of trade with Africa, Asia and America. Governments sought to regulate that trade through tariffs and subsidies so as to enrich themselves and become more powerful.

Spain acquired precious metals through its South American colonies and its accumulated bullion was accepted as a measure of that nation's wealth. This led to a rather curious exaggeration of the importance of bullion which still persists in some quarters today. To compete, in the absence of gold and silver mines, England had to accumulate a surplus of exports over imports. This favourable balance of trade was seen as crucial. So government's aim was simply to impose tariffs to limit imports and offer subsidies to stimulate exports.

Domestic industries and agriculture were protected from overseas competition and subsidies were paid to producers who made a surplus for export. Initially these trade balances were considered for the individual industry but later it was agreed that what mattered was the overall balance of trade, with imbalances allowed in particular industries. The simple belief, which was later referred to as mercantilism, was that governments had a duty to intervene in trade so as to grow the national wealth at the expense of 'competing' nations.

By late seventeenth century the wool trade, for example, was protected by heavy import tariffs and wearing certain imported cloths was forbidden by law. Laws were also passed to make use of English cloth mandatory for some uniforms and even, a law in 1667, which ordered the dead to be buried wrapped in English wool cloth. Moreover the emigration of skilled artisans was forbidden in case they should give any industrial secrets away to foreign competitors and the export of machinery was made similarly illegal.

Foreign trade was also directly forbidden in some instances. Import of French wines, brandies, linen and paper was illegal, while trade with Portugal, which was thought to be in favourable balance, was encouraged. Transporting goods between England and overseas possessions had to use English ships. The colonial trade produced significant surpluses, with the English heavily involved in trade in spices and also slaves kidnapped in Africa and sold in America.

Government also involved itself in awarding monopolies in commodities and in geographical areas to the great trading enterprises which were set up as joint stock companies, initially with stock-holders acquiring a share of the financial responsibility and profits of individual expeditions. These were risky projects, many such expeditions were unprofitable and in some cases the ships simply did not return. Protection in the form of a royal charter granting monopoly rights provided some compensation for the assumption of such risk.

This interventionist approach to trade, which had long informed government policy, was firmly in place when industrialisation first began. Although there had been some energetic objections to various individual trade limitations, notably the prohibitions on French trade, especially wine and brandy, there had been no assault on the mercantilist system itself until Adam Smith pressed the argument in favour of free trade.

Accumulation of Capital

Smith's prime concern was with the progress of society and he saw industrialisation and the wealth it created as a key turning point. At the same time he recognised the inequality industrialisation caused and the fundamental need to do something to alleviate it. He expounded a simplistic model of society's progress, identifying four ages of man defined according to how they earned their subsistence.

First, the age of the hunter-gatherer who was innocent of the notion of private property and government.

Second, the age of the shepherd who necessarily owned property in the form of flocks and herds and so had some simple notions of property, justice and government.

Third, the age of agricultural man who owned private property and had a relatively complex legal system to protect it and government to enact and oversee the law. Justice was corrective in that it punished those who harmed another person, their property or their reputation, rather than being distributive, that is ensuring an equitable distribution of riches.

Finally the age of commercial man which was the phase then being entered. The growth of capital and inequality raised the question of why citizens should be obedient to government or respect authority acquired through wealth.[23]

Smith's crude fable emphasised the progression of inequality as the consequence of economic progress with the property owners developing government and a protective legal system to permit continued economic development and further inequality.

Such a model might accept that society may always have been hierarchical – hierarchy exists even in animal groups – but a critical development was when the hierarchy became based on the ownership of property, the distribution of which generally had little to do with justice. The old aristocracy and landed gentry usually came by their possessions for no better reason than that they happened to be on the winning side. When land was plentiful it was cheap and of limited use beyond subsistence. It was owned but it was not energetically exploited because there was no market for surplus produce. Over the centuries landed and landless had co-existed in a generally accepted inequitable interdependence.

However, when the economy stirred, some of the landed gentry discovered they had untold wealth under their feet. The Duke of Bridgewater, for example, found he was the owner of rich seams of coal and built his canal to get it cheaply to market. Others of the old aristocracy enjoyed similar riches, but in aggregate their wealth was wholly insufficient to fuel industrialisation. That had to be funded from within the industrial process itself

Richard Arkwright, for example, who built the world's first cotton mill, was the son of a small tailor, youngest of seven children, without the funds even to pay for schooling. He was trained as a barber and subsequently a wig maker. With no money to invest in industrial development, he learned about the possibilities of a new spinning machine, joined forces with some of the inventors, managed to borrow the money to invest in a prototype machine, perfected it and then managed to engage the interest of other investors to finance the building and equipping of the first cotton spinning mill.

Borrowing by entrepreneurs such as Arkwright was duly made easier by the establishment of banks. Initially banks were merely safe places for the deposit of money in its various forms and all the money so deposited was kept solely for the disposal of the depositor. Payment of a debt would be accomplished by the movement of money from one deposit to the other. Bankers were therefore holding deposits of money which were largely inactive and in due course they began to lend a proportion of those deposits to borrowers who wanted to invest in projects which would otherwise have been far beyond their reach. It was unlikely that all depositors would require their money back at the same time, unless of course word got out that the bank was insecure. So the proportion of deposits that banks could afford to lend out was a matter of fine judgment: lending too large a proportion might be too risky, but lending too little meant they would be turning down opportunities to do good business and, more importantly, restricting the amount of new funds available for investment.

Investors in an industrial project had to be persuaded of its viability and the likelihood of it generating a sufficient return to make their investment worthwhile. The project had to earn a surplus having paid all its expenses including its employees' wages. Wages were ever in contention both in practice and in the curious theories developed to justify them being kept at subsistence levels. Beyond these expense items the firm needed to earn a surplus for the entrepreneur to either retain or to invest in the firm's future development. From this retained profit, entrepreneurs like Arkwright accumulated considerable personal wealth, which capital was a prime source of funding for the new industries.

Division of Labour

Human beings have always divided work so that different individuals specialise in particular jobs and become more proficient at their completion. Without speculating into the ways of the hunter-gatherers of pre-history, at least as early as ancient Greece specialisation was a well established way of life. Plato not only refers to the system, but justifies it on the grounds that

> 'no two of us are born exactly alike. We have different
> natural aptitudes which fit us for different jobs.'[24]

He goes on to describe division of labour between the farmer, the weaver and the shoe maker and the smiths and craftsmen needed to make their various tools and equipment.

Nevertheless the degree of specialisation did increase as economies developed and an increasing surplus was produced. Petty, born 100 years before Adam Smith, noted the division of labour used in Dutch shipyards. In English shipyards workers would build ships in sequence, finishing one before starting the next. The Dutch used several groups of workers, completing the same specialised tasks on each ship. He subsequently applied the same principles in his Irish survey splitting the workload into skilled and unskilled jobs, passing the unskilled to untrained workers[25]. He also gave the example of watch manufacture in which the division of labour between the various watch components reduced the cost, enabling the price of watches to be reduced thereby increasing demand. The principle is quoted as applying quite generally to all trades.

> *'The Labourer will still have as much wages, and will consequently be enabled to purchase more Conveniences of Life; so that every interest in the Nation would receive a Benefit from an Increase of our working People.'* [26]

Similarly Mandeville in 1728:

> *'if one will wholly apply himself to the making of Bows and Arrows, whilst another provides Food, a third builds Huts, a fourth makes Garments, and a fifth Utensils, they not only become useful to one another, but the Callings and Employments themselves will in the same Number of Years receive much greater Improvements, than if all had been promiscuously follow'd by every one of the Five...'* [27]

Hume also refers to the *'partition of employments'* drawing attention to the benefits on a broader front, including not only the increase in manpower and skills, but also to reduced exposure to accidents.

> *''Tis by this additional force, ability, and security, that society becomes advantageous'*.[28]

The ideas of specialisation and its many benefits were clearly well understood by 1776 when Smith famously elaborated it in 'Wealth of Nations' . His first sentence reads:

> *'The greatest improvement in the productive powers of labour, and the greater part of the skill, dexterity, and judgment with which it is anywhere directed, or applied, seem to have been the effects of the division of labour.'* [5]

His particular example was pin making, which he himself described as a 'very trifling manufacture'. Smith emphasised the benefits from specialisation of labour separately from those from the application of capital which had not then become so decisive as it was later to become. Whereas one man making a pin from beginning to end would perhaps make one a day, *'and certainly could not make twenty.'* By the division of labour, ten men could make *'upwards of 48,000 pins in a day'*.

> *'One man draws out the wire, another straights it, a third cuts it, a fourth points it, a fifth grinds it at the top for receiving the head'* [29]

and so forth.

The benefits in terms of output and cost were clear. The further benefits for society at large in terms of reduced prices and therefore raised living standards were also obvious. But that was only the beginning. Benefits accrued in terms of increasing expertise and matching that expertise with specialised tools and equipment. The more specialised a job could be defined, the greater the specialised expertise that could be developed leading to technical innovations in the form of more efficient and sophisticated tools and equipment as well as improved methods of working.

Smith, as others before him, recognised the universal applicability of the benefits of specialisation across all human activity, including even *'philosophy or speculation'*, in which, as in every other sphere, the result would be improving *'dexterity and saving time'*. Somewhere between pin making and philosophy, the idea of specialisation could also be applied to the labour of management itself.

A consequence of even the most primitive forms of division of labour was that individuals reduced their own self sufficiency and therefore needed to trade and barter. As specialisation increased and with it the benefits in terms of productivity, reduced prices and raised standards of living, so the degree of self-sufficiency diminished and thus the areas over which people needed to trade increased, so markets became more important. Markets, initially physical locations where trade and barter took place, developed and diffused so that the term market came to have a less specific, more abstract meaning.

Regulation, or interference in the free operation of markets, as was done by governments under the mercantilist system, only served to constrain and inhibit their development and ultimately limit their size and therefore restrict the degree to which labour could be specialised and the cost of production reduced. Thus, classical theory derived from Smith rejected the idea of regulation or interference with markets since that could only reduce the rate of economic growth.

However, the division of labour was not automatic; labour did not necessarily specialise in particular tasks, or do so by mutual consent or by some democratic process. The process and the consequent investment in, and application of, specialised tools and equipment provided from accumulated capital, had to be initiated and directed by those responsible. Moreover, those responsible were also in a position to see that the division of labour and the distribution of its benefits were accomplished equitably.

Smith himself was concerned by some of the ill effects of the division of labour, warning that it leads to a *'mental mutilation'* in workers:

> *'The man whose whole life is spent in performing a few simple operations, of which the effects are perhaps always the same, or very nearly the same, has no occasion to exert his understanding or to exercise his invention in finding out expedients for removing difficulties which never occur. He naturally loses, therefore, the habit of such exertion, and generally becomes as stupid and ignorant as it is possible for a human creature to become. The torpor of his mind renders him not only incapable of relishing or bearing a part in any rational conversation, but of conceiving any generous, noble, or tender sentiment, and consequently of forming any just judgment concerning many even of the ordinary duties of private life. Of the great and extensive interests of his country he is altogether incapable of judging, and unless very particular pains have been taken to render him otherwise, he is equally incapable of defending his country in war. The uniformity of his stationary life naturally corrupts the courage of his mind, and makes him regard with abhorrence the irregular, uncertain, and adventurous life of a soldier. It corrupts even the activity of his body, and renders him incapable of exerting his strength with vigour and perseverance in any other employment than that to which he has been bred. His dexterity at his own particular trade seems, in this manner, to be acquired at the expense of his intellectual, social, and martial virtues. But in every improved and civilised society this is the state into which the labouring poor, that is, the great body of the people, must necessarily fall, unless government takes some pains to prevent it.'* [30]

Smith's proposal was to counterbalance these effects of such work by attending to the education of the workers, an ideal adopted later by Robert Owen and others. He had previously explained his basic sympathy:

> 'How SELFISH soever man may be supposed, there are evidently some principles in his nature, which interest him in the fortune of others, and render their happiness necessary to him, though he derives nothing from it, except the pleasure of seeing it. Of this kind is pity or compassion, the emotion which we feel for the misery of others, when we either see it, or are made to conceive it in a very lively manner.'[31]

The conflict of interest between those who accumulated capital and those who were dispossessed of what little they had was multiplied many times over by the industrialisation process. Whilst citing the citizens' pure self-interest as the solid foundation of economic progress Smith nevertheless acknowledged, and had sympathy for, all humanity including especially those who were inevitably disadvantaged by industrialisation.

While he counselled against governments interfering directly in free markets, he nevertheless advocated a progressive taxation system whereby the rich pay proportionately more of their wealth and income than the less rich and the taxation be deployed to benefit the poor, for example, through their education.

> 'The subjects of every state ought to contribute towards the support of the government, as nearly as possible, in proportion to their respective abilities; that is, in proportion to the revenue which they respectively enjoy under the protection of the state ... It is not very unreasonable that the rich should contribute to the public expense, not only in proportion to their revenue, but something more than in that proportion.'[32]

The neo-classical version of Smith's theory which widely pervades government thinking today and which is used to justify low and non-progressive taxation is clearly in contravention of Smith's approach.

Markets, Trade and Comparative Advantage

The division of labour resulted in reduced prices and consequently increased the amount of goods that could be bought. The resultant diversified economy depended for its prosperity on an increasing level of trading between its members, each, according to the theory, acting from self-interest to achieve the most favourable outcome for themselves. As productive output grew, so the size of markets also had to grow if they were to absorb the increased output. The growth in markets could only be maintained by reducing prices that was made possible by increased division of labour and the application of accumulated capital to the newly specialised tasks. The lower the price of a product, the more that would be bought. The more that could be produced and sold, the greater the justified investment in plant and equipment and thus the feasible extent of the specialisation of labour and the greater the resultant cost savings.

Such a virtuous cycle was limited only by the size of markets. The bigger the market, the greater the investment that could be justified and the consequent opportunity to specialise. Therefore it was crucial to eliminate anything which inhibited or restricted the freedom to trade or distorted the effect of market forces. Thus Smith's advocacy of unrestricted free trade, both domestically and internationally, and his direct attack on mercantilism and its tariffs and protections which interfered directly with open markets.

Free-market economics, based on the 'homo economicus' assumption, proved perhaps to be the most influential of Smith's contributions. It suggested that the combined efforts of many amoral 'economic men', working purely to maximise their own wealth in competition with each other, served to maximise the aggregate wealth of the population.

Freedom was essential to enable the unrestricted competition to produce cost reductions and the means by which prices would be forced to a minimum for the benefit of the general population. But Smith was mindful of the fact that those self interested competitors would seek to place limitations on competition:

> *'People of the same trade seldom meet together, even for merriment and diversion, but the conversation ends in a conspiracy against the public, or in some contrivance to raise prices. It is impossible indeed to prevent such meetings, by any law which either could be executed, or would be consistent with liberty and justice. But though the law cannot hinder people of the same trade from sometimes assembling together, it ought to*

do nothing to facilitate such assemblies; much less to render them necessary.' [33]

Any associations that might result in fixing prices, or any cartel arrangements, were anathema to Smith. And he was profoundly opposed to monopoly which was the extreme case of such limitations on competition. Under mercantilism monopolies were routinely granted by government as charters to the trading companies, granting unique legal rights to trade in particular commodities or defined regions. Not only did such monopolies limit the development of markets, but they were also disadvantageous to the monopolising nation which thus cut itself off from the real source of economic success which was competition. The only economically justifiable grounds for monopoly was of a limited term such as when a new and dangerous overseas trade was being opened up. The argument for that was exactly similar to the justification for a limited term patent protection. But when the limited term was completed, free market competition should ensue for the benefit of the general population.

There is some incoherence within Smith's work. What survives most powerfully today is the clear and simple 'greed is good', amoral philosophy which proscribes interference with or hindrance of market forces and seeks to protect the total freedom to compete and trade on the grounds that such a system ensures maximum economic growth and aggregate wealth. What has survived less securely is his recognition of inequality as an inevitable result of economic growth and his argument that its worst effects should be offset by a more than proportionately progressive system of taxation which could fund further social progress of the poor.

Further understanding of how markets worked was achieved by Smith's successors, David Ricardo and Jean-Baptiste Say both born as Wealth of Nations was being published. They had the great advantage of living through the industrialisation process and seeing the immense changes to the economy and to society that resulted.

Say was a fearless advocate of free markets and his famous contribution to economic theory was a 'law of markets' which stated that there would always be demand for any level of supply. This was because every item produced and sold would provide a return to the producer which would have to be spent or saved, and if saved it would be invested and subsequently spent. Thus the supply of goods would create the funds to satisfy its own demand. There could never be an oversupply of goods.

From time to time there was clear evidence of oversupply in particular industries, with the resulting discontinuities, increases in unemployment and consequent further reductions in demand. However, Say's law was applied at the level of the whole economy: in aggregate there could be no shortage of demand for products and full employment would therefore be maintained. When there appeared to be general oversupply and the resulting unemployment appeared to exist across the whole economy, it was explained away as a temporary situation to which there would be a natural adjustment after which normal supply and demand rules would again apply. Thus business cycles became part of the generic economic model. Say's law clearly did not work out in practice, but it nevertheless remained a key concept of classical economics till well into the twentieth century.

The importance of Say's law of markets was that it suggested the economic system was self regulating and therefore it served to reinforce the classical idea of unrestricted free markets. The free market had within it the means of its own optimisation. If sufficient demand was assured, then attempts to interfere or regulate markets would merely produce a sub-optimal result.

Ricardo elaborated the treatment of monopolistic markets and the dangers they posed to the common good. He distinguished between resources which were reproducible (ie copiable) which would be priced according to their labour value, and those that were not, which would be priced according to their scarcity value. The non-copiable resources were the basis of monopolistic markets in which the monopolist could achieve higher prices and rates of profit at lower levels of output than would be achieved in a competitive market. Ricardo noted that in fact almost everything was reproducible and so the evils of monopoly were limited. The only exceptions he noted were

> *"rare statues and pictures, scarce books and coins and wines of a peculiar quality which can be made only from grapes grown on a particular soil."* [Ricardo, 1817, p12]

These concepts of monopoly were rather different from the simple idea of monopoly granted and protected by law. The creation of monopolistic markets, or at least the limitation of free competition, as referred to by Ricardo, is familiar in today's markets with their emphasis on differentiated and branded products which command a premium price.

Ricardo broadened the theory of competitive markets to international trade, focusing on the comparative costs enjoyed in different countries and the gains that could be made from trade between countries with different inherent costs. He used the example of Anglo-Portuguese trade. Portugal could produce wine cheaper than England, ie it had a comparative advantage, while England had a comparative advantage in the production of woollen cloth. It would therefore be profitable for Portugal to specialise in the supply of wine and sell some to England for less than it would cost England to produce it, while England could supply cloth to Portugal for less than it would cost to produce in Portugal. Thus both nations benefit from the trade. If all countries specialised in the goods where they enjoyed a comparative advantage, the generation of wealth across the world would increase.

Thus Ricardo's law of comparative advantage, like Says law, reinforced the argument in favour of free unregulated trade.

Alternative views did exist. Malthus, for example, challenged Say's Law that supply would create its own demand and regarded markets as naturally unstable. Producers may well focus on securely establishing their businesses rather than consuming all, which would reduce funds available for demand. Thus over production and subsequent economic recession was perfectly feasible, if not inevitable from time to time.

The theoretical model of competitive markets with competitors seeking only their own profit, would result in aggregate social welfare being maximised. However the theory did not address the distribution of social welfares, which in practice was quite obviously unequal. If participants adhered to the self interested model, as theory taught them they should, the theoretical result would inevitably be that the strong would exploit the weak. And that was also the practical outcome.

Remunerating Labour and Capital

The division of labour and the consequent need to barter and trade, the inequitable accumulation of capital and its subsequent investment which multiplied the inequity, and the unedifying portrayal of man as amoral, eternally self-interested and competitive are all aspects of classical economic theory. On this foundation, the classical model sought to explain how prices and wages should be established and justified.

Smith initially struggled with a labour theory of value which asserted that the value of a commodity was equal to the amount of labour involved in its production. A commodity's price was therefore dependent on the cost of its production, but Smith was less than definitive about how costs were to be identified. They were incurred on labour, capital and land, agriculture being yet a dominant economic activity, the rent returned to the landlord still loomed large in their considerations. Each of these had to be remunerated.

Subsistence theory held that wages should be just sufficient to maintain the labour force in existence, sufficient to pay for the labourer and his family at simple subsistence level. The remuneration of capital and land was less straightforward for Smith. Having identified the labour theory of value – that the value of anything was equal to the labour incurred in its production - he left the obvious inference for others to pick up that the returns to the owner of capital were in effect wages withheld from labour. He left the question of rent open, being undecided whether it was a cost or a residual item after other costs had been paid for.

Ricardo, Malthus and others tightened up the theory and defended it from attack. Malthus further examined the subsistence theory of wages. He saw that population depended on the means of its subsistence, that it would grow when the means of subsistence permitted and it would grow geometrically while food supplies would only grow arithmetically, and therefore population would ultimately be limited by hunger and starvation, unless previously limited by war, plague, or disease. Thus subsistence was all that the labouring classes could hope for unless, he later added, they would exercise 'moral constraint'. Any benign attempt to improve the lot of the labouring masses would simply result in an excess of procreation which would drag them back to subsistence level. This was a powerful argument against any such benevolence.

Ricardo reinforced the subsistence theory, arguing that wages would be naturally at a level

> 'which is necessary to enable the labourers, one with another,
> to subsist and to perpetuate their race, without either increase
> or diminution.' [34]

Thus it was inevitable - an 'iron law' - that workers would remain living at subsistence level. Their continued misery was an essential of the system.

How capital should be remunerated was less clear. The distinction between risk free investment remunerated by interest and risky investment rewarded by uncertain levels of profit was not fully made till the twentieth century. Ricardo like Smith had recourse to the labour theory of value, which could be applied equally to the capital items required for production so they were similarly valued as equal to the labour involved in their production. Thus any surplus value that accrued when a commodity was sold, value which was taken by the provider of capital, was in truth the value that should have been paid to labour including those previous generations who produced the capital items.

To this potentially explosive idea, Sismondi[35] added the notion of two quite separate social classes: the rich and the poor or as later termed: the bourgeoisie and the proletariat.

The early theorists who developed this system which was apparently clinical in its objectivity, accepted that achieving the greatest degree of economic advancement would inevitably result in the unfair treatment of some. The theoreticians themselves recognised the unfairness of the system and sought in different ways to ameliorate its worst effects. For example, Smith's advocacy of a redistributive taxation system with the tax revenue deployed to benefit the poor. And Ricardo sought to soften the interpretation of subsistence by including 'conveniences' which became a habitual part of life, so that the labouring class might justify an improving standard of living, as the economy grew, which he foresaw continuing indefinitely.

Classical theory is prescriptive about how businesses and governments should behave, but there were clearly differences of view as to how the obvious unfairness of the classical system should be offset. It was widely recognised that the unfairness was unsustainable in the long term and such recognition suggests a vulnerability in the system which might bring about its downfall with a reduction of benefit to all. The system worked but it was unfair and the unfairness needed to be ameliorated. Such amelioration was partly in the hands of government and partly in the hands of those on the ground who determined the balance in the employer : employee relationship, ie management.

Management and Classical Theory

The many practical examples and anecdotal evidence included in Adam Smith's account suggest his inclination was to be, as far as possible, empirical. However, as he predated the worst excesses of industrial misery, the evidence for his observation was incomplete. The large scale mills and mill towns only emerged three or four decades later, to be observed by Ricardo and Malthus and then to become a stage further grotesque when reported by Engels.

The pin factory was a nice example of a small scale workshop of the time which made use of worker specialisation without much capital investment in specialised plant and equipment. For Smith, it had to suffice as the example of industrial development on which economic growth depended. New wealth was created through the aggregate activities of all such workshops competing against each other in free, unregulated markets for the benefit of the consumer. These small scale enterprises were for the most part owner managed, which was the organisational form espoused by classical theory. The idea of professional managers controlling a business, but not owning it, was unacceptable to Smith and the classical theorists.

> *'The directors of such companies, however, being the managers rather of other people's money than of their own, it cannot well be expected, that they should watch over it with the same anxious vigilance with which the partners in a private copartnery frequently watch over their own. ... Negligence and profusion therefore must always prevail, more or less, in the management of the affairs of such a company.'*[36]

Smith could not have been more wrong in his assessment of hired management as subsequently shown by their achievement in terms of productivity, innovation and efficiency. Galbraith, writing in 1987, commented:

> *'Returning today, he* (Smith) *would be appalled at a world where, as in the United States, a thousand corporations dominate the industrial, commercial and financial landscape and are controlled by their hired management.'* [37]

Maybe he would have been appalled; maybe he would have been surprised and fascinated. His suspicion of the corporation controlled by hired management was a symptom of the era in which he lived. At that time the leading examples of such corporations were the trading companies legally set up and protected as monopolies of which he was duly sceptical. He did not give much credit to the major infrastructural projects such as the canals and turnpikes which were effectively managed by the engineers rather than the shareholder owners. And he was, of course, innocent of the publicly owned, management controlled, limited liability competitive business which came to be dominant in the later nineteenth century.

Smith's successors were also more fully informed as to the inequity industrialisation caused, but their responses were largely justifications of the established system. Malthus' argument was that the working class, if circumstance ever let them escape poverty, would always breed their way back to subsistence living, so the subsistence level of wage was inescapable. Ricardo accepted a similar analysis and even pointed out that the working classes were being dispossessed of their fair wages by the owners of capital.

The decisions as to what might be done about this inequity were in reality in the hands of the management who controlled how the factors of production were to be deployed to generate wealth and how the surpluses generated were to be distributed.

Although economic theory may not initially have impinged greatly on how management worked, it was nevertheless contributing to the culture of the times. It was probably not pure coincidence that, though there were exceptions, the exploitation of workers by the mill owners and industrialists accorded so precisely with the archetype defined by classical theory. Moreover this archetype was subsequently justified by utilitarian moral philosophers such as Bentham and Mill, arguing that though economic progress involved considerable hardship for some, the aggregate was an increase in 'happiness' – which economists necessarily interpreted as wealth – and the hardships must therefore be borne in order to achieve the greatest happiness for the greatest number.

Industrial management in those early days, largely the entrepreneur owner-managers, may or may not have been susceptible to such arguments. They may or may not have seen themselves as 'economic men' with the duty to seek only to maximise their own self interest, so that the greater good could result. Or they may have been motivated to act in the best interests of their business organisation, concerned for its survival and long term prosperity and so to preside over a just and equitable distribution of benefits. Both breeds of management have existed from the beginning of industrialisation.

Management was neither capital nor labour and classical economic theory had some difficulty accounting for its peculiar position.

3. INDUSTRIALISATION and MANAGEMENT

The textile industries were at the forefront of industrialisation and the first to establish factory units employing large numbers of people in the same plant. Other industries quickly followed. Metal working, brick making and coal getting were already beginning to expand by mid eighteenth century, establishing small factories and workshops which were rapidly to grow in scale following the precedent set in textiles. Industrialisation quickly extended beyond the subsistence industries related to food, shelter and clothing

Smith's pin factory bore little resemblance to these industrial factories. It made little use of capital equipment and none of power driven machinery. There was no requirement for the essential discipline of factory working, only some recognition of the mind deadening effects of the simple repetitive tasks defined by the division of labour.

Smith set out his theory of industry ahead of the practice being established, unaware of the unforeseen consequences of industrialisation: its misery and despair. For him, the inevitable inequalities were largely theoretical and necessarily justified by theoretical argument. Succeeding generations of economic theorists saw the negative impacts of industrialisation as well as the positive, and were in a position to develop a means of offsetting the one against the other. However, their general approach was less progressive than Smith's advocacy of redistributive taxation.

Those responsible for industrial management were in a position to implement the industrial process with fairness and justice even if many failed, at least initially, to do so. By mid to late nineteenth century, when management became recognised as an autonomous category, their practice had improved for the benefit of employees, customers, suppliers and the local community as well as stockholders.

The Industrial Factory System

The first industrial scale textile factory was built by Thomas Lombe in Derby, England, in 1717. Lombe had taken out patents for winding, spinning and twisting fine raw silk and built a number of such machines for the Derby factory. He was the first of many textile machinery 'inventors' accused of stealing their ideas, in his case from an Italian machine invented around a hundred years before. The whole truth of that accusation remains unclear. Lombe predated Arkwright by almost fifty years though literature accords Arkwright the accolade 'father of the factory system', possibly because of the greater importance of the cotton industry in the subsequent industrial revolution. During that fifty year period the great infrastructural projects were forging ahead devising new ways of raising capital and managing large scale employment. Arkwright had the benefit of that prior experience, but Lombe had to pioneer his own way forward.

Lombe's mill employed around 300 people working at machines driven by a massive water wheel turned by the River Derwent. No such had ever been built before. To be first to build such a *'manufactory'* required some innovative and courageous commitments. The power of water wheels to drive large numbers of machines was well understood. Such power could not be exploited driving domestic machinery sited in cottages spread around the area. Bringing them all together on one site would clearly enable water power to be used efficiently. Lombe had to confront the problems of management: he needed to estimate the costs involved in this new sort of building, in equipping it with the newly devised machinery, estimating how long it would take before it could be brought into production, raising the necessary funds to support the development, recruiting the necessary skilled workers including a core from Italy who spoke no English, training the others, investigating the market opportunities in terms of volume and price and making some estimates of the eventual profitability of the enterprise.

The project was revolutionary and if it had failed Lombe would have been finished. But he got it right. The silk mill was a success and others followed in England as well as overseas in Europe and America. It is surprising that it was the impecunious son of a Norfolk weaver who foresaw the potential for this enterprise. Perhaps it was that the basic economics were so overwhelmingly favourable that had Lombe not done it when he did then someone else would very soon afterwards have done so on the basis of the most crude calculations.

If that were so, the case for building Arkwright's cotton mill in Cromford was even more timely. The agricultural surplus was already achieved and development of the internal transport infrastructure, canals and turnpikes, was well underway by 1771 when Arkwright's first mill opened. Unlike silk, cotton was in practically limitless supply from America, already being shipped into Liverpool from where it could be brought to Cromford in Derbyshire initially by packhorse but planned shortly to utilize the new canal system.

Like Lombe, Arkwright equipped his cotton spinning mill with newly invented machinery, in his case the water frame spinning machine which in effect mass produced cotton thread. The true provenance of the water frame is in doubt, Arkwright, Samuel Crompton and Thomas Highs probably all contributed but Arkwright gained the patent and made the effective modifications to bring the machine to production performance. Compared to domestic spinning wheels the output of standard thread was revolutionary in terms of both quantity and consistent high quality.

But Arkwright, like Lombe before him, had more to contend with than the simple matter of invention and innovation. To raise the finance to build the first large scale cotton mill he had to estimate the capital cost of building and equipping the mill, forecast the amount of cotton thread he could sell at the price he estimated he could afford as well as how much he could produce at the cost for which he could produce it, under market conditions substantially influenced by his proposed new factory system. His estimations must have been that the cost reductions from mass producing would create new mass markets for cotton textile justifying the cost of building and equipping the new mill. Similar issues were faced a hundred and fifty years later by Henry Ford planning the mass production of his Model T. Arkwright also faced problems of location – there were no people in the areas where climatic conditions were most suitable, so he had to build a company village to accommodate them.

Having no money himself, he had to borrow what he could and also persuade those with money to invest in his hair-raising scheme. Arkwright's problem was not merely the formulation of his plan, though given its ground breaking nature that was problem enough. He also had to deal with what is now recognised as the much greater problem of implementation: developing new machines, getting them to work efficiently, building the mill, recruiting and housing the people, sourcing the raw materials and finding new markets for finished product.

Whether Arkwright was an inventor is in doubt, but certainly he was an innovator, bringing inventions to commercial fruition and innovating new ways of doing things. Water power made it feasible to use large scale machinery rather than simple manually operated domestic equipment, and technological developments revolutionised the productivity and output of machines. The dealers, manufacturers, entrepreneurs and newly enriched land owners had progressively accumulated surplus profits to invest in these new capital projects. With water power it was as cheap to drive a bank of large scale machines as to drive a single machine and so factories were built in which large numbers of people were employed. In a few short years the scale and nature of business organisation had been changed for ever.

Arkwright's forecasting and planning, no matter how informal or crude, are nevertheless apparent in his building the Cromford mill. Having had his initial projections confirmed or, more likely, far exceeded, he moved quickly to replicate that success. Within a few short years he and his partner, Strutt, had built more than a dozen much bigger mills employing many times the 300 strong original workforce, using hundreds of machines initially driven by waterpower and then by Watt's greatly improved rotary drive steam engine, and creating whole new communities, mill towns, as well as the infrastructure to move bulk materials. His success was quickly copied by many others across Britain, Europe and America.

Arkwright's main legacy, the factory system, gave the employer control over the product and the means and cost of production as well as the organisation and command of labour in one specialised workplace. Under the domestic system, though their hours were long and their pay extremely poor, workers had some control over when they worked and when they took breaks. With the factories came the necessity for rules and regulations. The machinery would necessarily all start and finish working at the same time, so times were set each day and workers began to be subservient to machines.

Moreover, there had to be rules which achieved consistency in the quality of work produced. There had to be at least some rudimentary rules related to the safety of working. And there had to be people responsible for seeing the rules were obeyed. Arkwright's organisation and co-ordination in the first mill are apparent in the way the mill was designed not only as to its internal specialised departments but also the physical disposition of his own house from where he had a clear view overlooking the mill's main entrance and mill-yard and from where it was thought he exercised a high degree of command and control.

In addition, with the creation of the factories the nature of the work itself changed. The new steam power driven machinery resulted in new jobs being created. Traditional highly skilled work was replaced by semi-skilled jobs and an ever increasing number of unskilled. Each generation of new machinery removed the requirement for some element of personal skill by the operator and progressively even craft work became de-skilled. Unskilled labour, often largely concerned with moving material from one work place to the next, involved large numbers of people.

Arkwright himself appears to have been a relatively enlightened employer, providing his workers with good quality housing, allotments and other facilities and in return his work-force showed some loyalty standing by to defend the mill against the threat from Luddite machine breakers. But there were many employers who were less benign, whose workforces were more exploited and abused.

Arkwright has been adjudged by more recent commentators. Mantoux characterised him as *'neither an engineer, nor a merchant, but adding to the main characteristic of both, qualifications peculiar to himself: those of a founder of great concerns, an organiser of production and a leader of men.'*[38] And to a historian of management theory, his factory system innovated *'continuous production, plant site planning, co-ordination of machines, materials, men and capital, factory discipline, and division of labour'.*[39].

The factory system saw the establishment of semi-autonomous manufacturing 'states' where the employer's power was more or less absolute and defended by laws primarily designed to protect private property. Under such circumstances the industrialist, acting from pure self-interest, could abuse his position of power and mercilessly exploit those less powerful, the workers, who were legally prevented from acting in concert, in combinations, till the Trade Union Act of 1871. Exploitation of labour was the rule, including women and children. It was 1847 before the Ten Hours Act, for example, protected them from being forced to work all daylight hours.

Moreover the employer had the personal right to hire and fire any of his employees at any time for any reason. And for the worker the worst of all situations was to be unemployed without income or relief of any kind. For them life was precarious with starvation a continuous and very real threat. Engels recorded that,

*'During my residence in England at least twenty or thirty
persons have died of simple starvation under the most revolting
circumstances, and a jury has rarely been found possessed of
the courage to speak the plain truth in the matter. Let the
testimony of the witnesses be never so clear and unequivocal,
the bourgeoisie from which the jury is selected, always find
some back door through which to escape the frightful verdict,
death from starvation. The bourgeoisie dare not speak the truth
in these cases, for it would speak its own condemnation.'* [40]

Acceptance of this extreme of inequality stabilised the industrial system and
kept the wages of the employed sufficiently low that capital could be further
accumulated by those who needed it least and could therefore afford to
invest it in further development.

Outcomes from Industrialisation

The speed with which industrialisation took off was remarkable, rightly
earning the label 'revolution'. The British cotton industry, for example,
imported 4,760,000lbs of raw cotton in 1771, a figure which had been
roughly stable for decades. Over the next thirty years imports multiplied
more than twelve times to 60,500,000lbs. Such economic growth was not
restricted to the cotton and it was clearly not just a blip, but the start of a
fundamentally different way of life.

It created concentrations of working people in the new industrial towns
located adjacent to the main deposits of coal. And despite the rapid growth
of population their standard of living after several decades of ups and downs,
progressively improved so that the lasting result was one of advance for all,
apart perhaps for the unemployed underclass which was largely ignored till
the later decades of the nineteenth century.

Whole industries were adopting the factory system, not just individual
entrepreneurs. The woollen industry, silk, cotton, coal, iron and
transportation all experienced the same massive growth from adopting
industrial scale operations and the technological innovations industrialisation
enabled. Also trade which had traditionally been localised round mainly
small market towns, was opened up to whole regions and to export and
import. And the capital accumulation which was required to finance this
explosion gave rise to a revolution in banking which in effect enabled the
creation of new money for further investment. Simultaneously the

development of joint stock companies facilitated wider corporate ownership than previously available.

The inequality between employer and employee was repeated throughout the economy. Inequity, sometimes imposed by exploitative and abusive employers, was endemic, if not absolutely essential, to the industrial system.

Rural populations, rendered landless and unemployed by the changes in agriculture, migrated to the new mill towns which provided the desperately needed employment. But there were other consequences. As work became further specialised and deskilled the workers suffered, as Smith had suggested they would, from the dehumanised work and became, though he didn't use the word, alienated. It was the start of the process which much later was depicted in the Charlie Chaplin film 'Modern Times' showing work on the mass production line.

The factories became places of hardship and despair, exploiting women and children through the imposition of long hours, low wages, and often dangerous working conditions. Working hours were typically from dawn to dusk, six days per week. Wages were set at a level that entire families, father, mother and children, had to work in order that the family might survive at a bare subsistence level. Even Arkwright's relatively enlightened partner, Strutt, employed children. In 1774 he told a committee of the House of Commons that he employed children from the age of seven but preferred them to be over ten. He criticised those employers who took children as soon as they were *'able to crawl'*.

An empirical account of early English industrial working life was provided by the young Friedrich Engels, son of a German textiles magnate, who was sent to England for work experience. He provides a graphic account of the appalling life experiences in the new industrial towns and of the horrendous living and working conditions in the mills, foundries and factories.[41] The following are extracted from his study of 'The Condition of the Working Class in England':

> *'On the occasion of an inquest held November 14th 1843, by Mr Carter, coroner for Surrey, upon the body of Ann Galway, aged 45 years, the newspapers related the following particulars concerning the deceased: She had lived ... with her husband and nineteen year old son in a little room, in which neither bedstead nor any other furniture was to be seen. She lay dead beside her son upon a heap of feathers which were scattered over her almost naked body, there being neither sheet nor*

coverlet. The feathers stuck so fast over the whole body that the physician could not examine the corpse till it was cleansed, and then found it starved and scarred from the bites of vermin. Part of the floor of the room was torn up, and the hole used by the family as a privy.' (p63)

'... the filth, debris, and offal heaps and the pools in the streets are common to both quarters, and in the district now under discussion, another feature most injurious to the cleanliness of the inhabitants, is the multitude of pigs walking about in all the alleys, rooting into the offal heaps, or kept imprisoned in small pens. Here, as in most of the working-men's quarters of Manchester, the pork raisers rent the courts and build pig pens in them. In almost every court one or even several such pens may be found, into which the inhabitants of the court throw all refuse and offal, whence the swine grow fat; and the atmosphere, confined on all four sides, is utterly corrupted by putrefying animal and vegetable substances. ... on rereading my description, I am forced to admit that instead of being exaggerated, it is far from black enough to convey a true impression of the filth, ruin, and uninhabitableness, the defiance of all considerations of cleanliness, ventilation and health which characterise the construction of this single district, containing at least twenty to thirty thousand inhabitants.' (p86)

'On Monday, January 15th 1844, two boys were brought before the police magistrate because, being in a starving condition they had stolen and immediately devoured a half cooked calf's foot from a shop. The magistrate felt called upon to investigate the case further, and received the following details from the policeman: the mother of the two boys was the widow of an ex-soldier, afterwards policeman, who had had a very hard time since the death of her husband, to provide for her nine children. ... When the policeman came to her he found her with six of her children literally huddled together in a little back room, with no furniture but two old rush-bottom chairs with the seats gone, a small table with two legs broken, a broken cup and a small dish. ... The poor woman told him she had been forced to sell her bedstead the year before to buy food. Her bedding she had

pawned with the victualler for food. In short everything had gone for food.' (p63/4)

Engels made early use of the official blue book statistics and reliable secondary sources as well as his own observations. But the outcomes he described were not permanent. His own preface to the 1892 English edition of his book included the following:

> '... *the repeated visitations of cholera, typhus, small-pox, and other epidemics have shown the British bourgeois the urgent necessity of sanitation in his towns and cities, if he wishes to save himself and family from falling victims to such diseases. Accordingly, the most crying abuses described in this book have either disappeared or have been made less conspicuous...*'

Engels clearly implies that such improvements by the '*bourgeois*' were not made from any concern for their fellow humans, but purely for their own preservation as would be the case if they were conforming to classical economic theory. Working conditions were also progressively improved, hours reduced and the very worst exploitations largely eliminated. The suggestion was frequently offered that such improvements were made in order to achieve the higher productivity that could be obtained from a healthy workforce. Such interpretations of motive are irrelevant to the economic case. In the early years of industrialisation conditions were appalling and inhuman and later they were improved. Whether the original conditions resulted from a conspiracy of employers to exploit their workers or whether it was ignorance of how industrialisation would develop without intervention must remain conjecture. Undoubtedly there were mercilessly exploitative employers and there were also some who were more benign and enlightened. There is no universal truth.

It is clear that the employers who were rapidly, like Arkwright, becoming themselves owners of capital, increasingly seen by government as the source of new national wealth, were gaining political power and influence. By contrast the workers had no political power. When they tried to organize into the first labour unions, they were often outlawed by fearful governments actively supporting the ever increasing inequality. This aggravation was the seed bed of English socialism and the reform movement which later was to focus on the achievement of universal suffrage.

Accounting for Profit and Capital

The focus of much aggravation has been on the concepts of profit and capital. For some, profit is what has been sequestered from labour's rightful wage and set aside to be accumulated as capital. Profit and capital are sometimes dealt with by theoreticians as though the terms are unambiguous, clear and simple, but their meaning is not without complication. Both profit and capital are published in a company's accounting schedules, balance sheet and profit and loss account, and their calculation has long been required to be true and fair, with their truth and fairness audited by professionally qualified third parties. They nevertheless both involve matters of judgment in their valuation and are by no means as clinically precise as they might on the surface appear.

The purpose of the accounting schedules is to provide a public account of management's stewardship of the company over the previous year. The balance sheet provides a picture of the company's net worth, what it owns less what it owes, at the end of the year, while the profit and loss shows how much surplus the company made during the year and how that surplus has been deployed.

Profit is a term which appears several times on the profit and loss account schedule. There is a calculation of profit which is the surplus of the firms sales revenue less the direct costs of making those items sold. By direct costs is meant the cost of materials and wages involved in production. That calculation is referred to as gross profit. There are other expenses which have to be paid, items which are not attributable directly to production, such things as the rent and rates of buildings, the wear and tear on machinery, the costs of administration, sales staff, office staff and management. The remaining amount, the net profit, has to cover the interest to be paid on borrowings, the tax to be paid on any profits earned, and the dividends which are paid to shareholders. The remaining amount, if there is any, is the profit which is retained and reinvested in the company.

It is not easy to identify in the above what Ricardo identified as the profit which is the surplus sequestered from labour's wages. Out of the items referred to, dividends are the only items which are not bound to be paid and which do not explicitly and directly contribute to the company's financial strength and viability. Yet if dividends were to be reduced the value of the company's shares may well be affected and the future security of the company threatened and along with it the livelihood of workers. The position is by no means clear cut.

Capital is the other concept which needs some clarification. For some, capital is regarded as simply the accumulation of whatever has been stolen over the years from labour. But the balance sheet has a more objective perspective, though not completely so. Capital appears on the balance sheet in two forms. Firstly it is the amount of money originally put into the business and subsequently accumulated from its operations. Secondly capital is also shown on the balance sheet as the assets which have been acquired by the business to make its operations more productive and efficient, such items as specialised machinery and equipment. These are the capital assets on which industrialisation depends. They were traditionally separated into two categories: land and buildings which tended not to lose their value and to wear out only slowly, and plant and machinery which tended to wear out more quickly. Latterly motor vehicles were added as a separate even more rapidly wearing category of 'fixed' capital.

There seems to be little ambiguity in such items and little to cause aggravation. Such capital items are essential to industry and there is nothing inherent in them which denotes any particular form of ownership or the means by which ownership has been achieved.

The valuation of such capital items, particularly land and buildings, can be problematic. Far from wearing out, property, over the long term, has substantially appreciated in value and for many companies its valuation has been critical to the overall value of the company. Moreover, it is perfectly possible within the law for the value of such assets to be understated, or overstated, inadvertently or deliberately, which can be of critical importance especially in situations of merger and acquisition.

The company owns the assets already referred to plus it may also own cash and other quickly realisable assets as well as raw materials and consumable items and it may be owed money by its customers. These are its current assets. And the firm will probably owe money to its suppliers, its current liabilities. Current assets less current liabilities are referred to as working capital.

The total net value of all these assets, fixed and working capital, is 'balanced' by the sources of its long term funding. These sources include the money its shareholders contributed originally when the company was formed and the value they have since accumulated as a result of the company's operations, plus any money borrowed on a long term basis. The providers of this debt are paid a fixed amount of interest each year irrespective of how well the company has performed, while the shareholders receive a dividend which may vary according to how profitable the company has been. Loan stock therefore carries relatively little risk, it normally being given preferential treatment in the event of the firm being wound up. Shareholders, on the other hand, accept a level of risk; if the firm performs badly they may receive no dividend and the value of their shares may fall substantially and if the firm is bankrupt they may lose the whole of their original investment.

This broadly is how industrialisation was financed from the beginning and how the great enabling infrastructural projects, the turnpikes and canals, were also financed. There is nothing inherent to the system of capital ownership which determines the nature or motivation of capital owners. They are many and various. Some may be idealists bent on supporting the purpose of the company, others may be other firms, they may be small investors who have put their meagre savings into a company they admire, or they may be super rich individuals seeking to maximise their take. Today, among the biggest shareholders are the pension funds and other financial institutions which achieve their investing power from, and discharge their management responsibilities to, a wide spread of relatively small members and investors.

Even from this brief review it is clear that the treatment of profit and capital in economic theory is somewhat simplified. An economic theory, such as the labour theory of value, suggested that a proportion of profit earned by labour was not paid to them and must therefore be regarded as stolen from them. This wrong, if such it is, should surely be righted, but it is not at all clear how this can be done in practice. What proportion of profit could be identified as stolen wage? And is it part of the profit distributed to shareholders, or is it part of the profit retained within the company? If it is to be taken back from shareholders it would mean reducing or eliminating dividend payments, but this would immediately impact on the share price. And if that fell, would the company become vulnerable to take-over and would that be in the best interests of the employees? Or if it is to be taken from retained profit, how could that be realised without selling off some part of the company with similarly dubious impacts on employees? Decisions would then have to be taken as to how to reduce investment in the company's future development and would that be in the employee's best interests?

Economic theory appears to sidestep practical realities. But these investment and distribution decisions cannot be sidestepped by the management responsible.

Management, Labour and Capital

The remuneration of labour is one important aspect of the relationship between management and labour, but it is by no means the whole story. It is a personal relationship between parties with unequal power. Such conspicuous inequality invited correction by enlightened employers and considerable attention was paid to their efforts, which were exampled by local acts of paternalism. David Dale was one such relatively enlightened employer. He set up textile mills at New Lanark outside Glasgow and employed Glaswegian orphans who he accommodated in his mill village. No doubt their lot was improved but they still worked thirteen hour days for six days a week till hours were somewhat reduced when the plant was taken over by Robert Owen.

Owen had seen the grim environment in fast industrialising Manchester: its bad housing, bad factory conditions, labour exploitation, cyclical unemployment and gross poverty. His meteoric rise commenced at age 20 when he managed a mill employing 500. At 25 he became managing partner of Chorlton Twist Co which in 1799 took over the New Lanark Mills from Dale. There he established a benign, if paternalistic, company culture which was at the same time commercially profitable.

Owen himself put his success down to a unique understanding of working people.

> (I) *'produced such effects over the workpeople in the factory in the first six months of my management, that I had the most complete influence over them, and their order and discipline exceeded that of any other in or near Manchester; and for regularity and sobriety they were an example which none could then imitate.'* [42]

Though allowance must be made for the different language of that era, this neverthteless sounds as though it might be dangerously self-deluding. Some put such statements down to Owen's undoubted intellectual insecurity. However it was not mere talk; Owen took various practical initiatives in relation to the New Lanark workforce. For example, at that time it was common practice for employers to pay wages at least in part in the form of tokens exchangeable only at the company shop where prices were kept artificially high and quality low. But Owen's New Lanark shop sold high quality goods at little more than cost and he passed on the savings from bulk purchases to the workers, which idea later formed the basis of the co-operative movement. Under Owen the New Lanark village was much the same as under Dale except that there were some new public initiatives, such as the school and playground as well as the company shop. Alcohol was limited in supply with neighbouring sources progressively closed down, and higher standards of hygiene were generally enforced.

Owen's most notable innovation was in worker education, especially of the young and he established the company school to provide free education for employees and their children.

In the preamble to his articles which comprised '*A New View of Society*' Owen wrote:

> '*To the superintendents of manufactories, and to those individuals generally, who, by giving employment to an aggregated population, may easily adopt the means to form the sentiments and manners of such a population*

> *Like you, I am a manufacturer for pecuniary profit, but having for many years acted on principles the reverse in many respects of those in which you have been instructed, and having found my procedure beneficial to others and to myself, even in a pecuniary point of view, I am anxious to explain such valuable principles, that you and those under your influence may equally partake of their advantages.*'

Owen was motivated to make a profit by fair means. He was not driven by any religious conviction which he energetically rejected. The principles he referred to were based on the idea that a person's character is formed by the effects of environment. Education was therefore central to the formation of a rational and benign human being. The educator should therefore provide a benevolent environment, in which a child could develop; corporal punishment was prohibited and child labor limited.

Owen's management approach was shaped 150 years before McGregor's Theory Y assertion that

> '*the limits on human collaboration in the organizational setting are not limits of human nature but of management's ingenuity in discovering how to realize the potential represented by its human resources.*' [43]

He was successful at New Lanark. Clearly the mills had to be viable as businesses in a competitive world, but he demonstrated that management, which was enlightened from the point of view of workers, could also be successful from a business point of view. The way the company shop operated helped to raise real wages. And the infant school enabled mothers to return to work when their children reached the age of one year. The operation created its own self perpetuating momentum.

But he was not a life time manager. His report to the County of Lanark, though informed by his experience at the industrial village was focused on social development rather than management and industry.

His 'new view of society' was in effect an attempt to recreate the imagined old English rural society of supposedly contented interdependence, which he took some steps to recreate in the modern industrial society at New Lanark. His subsequent experiments, such as New Harmony, Indiana, were failures.

Many other enlightened employers in the nineteenth century were motivated by religious scruple stirred by the obvious and extreme inequality created by industrialisation. Notable among these were many Quakers, successful in starting and developing various businesses, notably in chocolate manufacture, soap, metal industries and retailing. There approach to management was similar, both in their underlying sympathy and in practical implementation, to Owen's New Lanark model. Many of these were highly successful businesses for many generations some surviving through to the twenty first century.

The wealth unleashed by industrialization was orders of magnitude greater than had ever been seen previously and in the main it came into the hands of the entrepreneurs and new industrialists. When Arkwright set up his first large scale mill it was possible for him to do it without money of his own. For a generation, new factories were established and managed by people without prior wealth. Owen had no money of his own when he set out on his mill management career, yet he was enabled to make substantial investment in New Lanark and in due course become a relatively wealthy man before retiring as a practitioner.

By mid-nineteenth century such entrepreneurial innovation and achievement was becoming more difficult. The scale of viable manufacturing operations had grown so that the required investment was beyond the scope of individuals with no funding of their own. By the end of the century such enterprises were being run by professional managers reporting on their stewardship through an annual general meeting to their increasingly diffuse owners: the shareholders. Such a progression has been seen more recently with internet based organizations where for a period of perhaps less than two decades it was possible for individuals without funding to create innovative businesses which rapidly acquired substantial value. But such opportunities subsequently became more limited requiring substantial investment even to achieve a satisfactory launch.

Financing industrialisation was fundamental to its birth and survival. The land and buildings, tools and equipment and the raw materials and wages all had to be paid for before the customer paid for the goods they had received. The details of raising finance and subsequent financial control were a particular management responsibility that had to be well understood by the early industrialists

Responsibility for all these areas of decision were management's, neither as worker nor as owner, but mediated between the two, ensuring at least some minimum level of justice and equity without frustrating the process of economic growth. Perhaps it was inevitable when management's role became explicit, that it be seen by workers merely as the tools of owners, and by owners as individuals interested only in feathering their own nests at the owners' expense. Such suspicion, and denial even of the possibility of higher motives, spring naturally from the ingestion of classical economic theory.

4. ECONOMICS, POLITICS AND INDUSTRY

Since the eighteenth century economic theory has shaped the development of industry and its management, both directly and through its pervasive influence on the industrial-political context. Though it has undoubtedly been effective in promoting economic growth, it has been criticised for its concomitant unfairness and from time to time it has appeared to be dangerously unstable.

Defenders of the system recognised its unfairness, but rather than seeking to interfere with its simple logic, their approach was to attempt its justification on various grounds. This defence included some surprising contributions from those whose primary concern was moral and ethical rather than purely economic.

Marx acknowledged the economic effectiveness of the system but regarded its exploitation of labour as indefensible. Moreover, he predicted the capitalist system would destroy itself when it culminated in monopolistic markets dominated by a small number of super rich capitalists brazenly exploiting the labouring masses. In this he significantly contributed to the counter theoretic legislation and regulation which moderated the basic system and limited its worst excesses.

Simultaneously with the moderating industrial legislation, capital ownership was becoming less concentrated in the hands of individual owners and more diffuse among many small shareholders, which diffusion also saw the recognised emergence of management as an autonomous and potentially enlightened category.

Defence of Classical Theory

The exercise of classical economics produced both great pleasure and great pain. A fundamental question was whether the one could justify the other.

The keystones of the theory, established by Smith and his immediate successors, were 'economic man', open competition and free markets with minimal government regulation or interference. Under these circumstances the engagement of business people, acting purely out of amoral self interest, competing against each other, would, through the operation of free market forces, reduce prices of products and increase the quantities produced so that the population as a whole would benefit. Moreover this beneficial system was stabilised around the natural wage rate for labour which was at the level of its subsistence. The unequal distribution of the surplus generated was acknowledged but not addressed other than through Smith's proposal for a more than proportionate redistributive system of taxation of income and wealth. This, however, was not universally accepted as an essential of the classical system.

Classical economic theory did not address the fundamental unfairnesses of the system. Capital accumulation by the few and dispossession of the many, protected by law that had been shaped and implemented by the few, was acknowledged and explained with attempts made for its justification rather than its rectification. Malthus had argued that it was inevitable: the working classes, should they ever escape poverty's clutches, would always breed themselves back to the bread line.

Smith had himself speculated as to why 'the great body of the people' should tolerate such inequalities. One possibility appeared to be that though inequality increased, the absolute standard of living of all sectors, including the workers, also increased. That may have been a plausible explanation so long as the unemployed underclass, Marx's 'industrial reserve army', was excluded from consideration.

However, inequality and injustice were not simply matters of economics, but also of morality. Bentham, writing not much more than a decade after publication of 'The *Wealth of Nations*', advocated a utilitarian approach to assessing the morality of a situation and developing legislation accordingly.

> *'Nature has placed mankind under the governance of two*
> *sovereign masters, pleasure and pain ... The principle of utility*
> *recognises this subjection and ... approves or disapproves of*
> *every action whatsoever according to the tendency which it*
> *appears to have to augment or diminish the happiness of the*
> *party whose interest is in question.'* [44]

To apply this principle, 'the party whose interest is in question' had first to be identified. From the point of view of the accumulator of capital the utility of the system might have appeared to be high; from the perspective of the worker it might not. The Mills, James and his son John Stuart, generalised the utilitarian approach to what was widely quoted as 'the greatest happiness for the greatest number'. Utilitarianism, an influential idea through the nineteenth century, was identified by J. S. Mill as

> *'the creed which accepts as the foundation of morals, utility, or the Greatest Happiness Principle, (which) holds that actions are right in proportion as they tend to produce happiness, wrong as they tend to produce the reverse of happiness. By happiness is intended pleasure and the absence of pain; by unhappiness, pain, and the privation of pleasure.'* [45]

At the same time he accepted Malthus' argument regarding the fecundity of the working class, and added in his *'Principles of Political Economy'* the immutable idea of diminishing returns to labour as their numbers increased. Their poverty, even if not morally justified, therefore seemed inescapable.

The principle of the greatest happiness for the greatest number was widely accepted as a way of assessing the moral justification for actions, until the practical difficulties were confronted in measuring happiness or pain and pleasure. J. S. Mill, philosopher and economist, had no difficulty equating happiness with consumption. So he identified as good the reducing prices and more ready availability of products for the general population made possible by industrialisation. And that 'happiness' for the great number benefiting, outweighed the pain being born by those labouring in its production. Thus the inequality and unfairness caused by industrialisation were morally justified!

The conflation of economics and moral philosophy achieved a curious but significant principle. By equating utility with consumption, utility became simply measurable in monetary terms, the value of money being fixed and not dependent on whose money is being considered. Orthodox theory therefore established that the marginal utility of money was fixed, unlike the marginal utility of other commodities which declined as supply increased. This device therefore denied the obvious, common sense fact that the utility of an additional pound, ie the marginal pound, was much greater for the poor than it was for the rich. Theory's necessary assumption that the marginal utility of money was fixed worked as yet another justification for the inequities of the free market economy.

Moreover, Mill argued that outcomes would become progressively more benign over time; working conditions would improve; work would become easier; standards of living would rise; even employers would become more enlightened. To some extent these were already happening. The utilitarians lent the inequities resulting from classical theory a cloak of moral respectability.

Much of the happiness, as well as the pain, arising from the workings of the classical model resulted from unregulated competition. Smith acknowledged that employers such as the butcher and baker (ie the co-partneries) would, given half a chance, conspire against the public to fix prices so as to increase their profit. Such challenge to the working of classical theory was real enough. However, Smith could not envisage that laws would ever be passed to prevent such conspiracy.

His suspicions that business people would incline to avoid competition where possible and otherwise minimise its effects, may have proved broadly correct. But his doubts as to the possibility of legislation against such anti-competitive actions were less well founded, though it was not till the monopolistic enterprises became over-powerful that competition law resulted in their reduction. The potential weakness in the classical system was recognised and governments were sensitised to the need for vigilance which eventually produced antitrust and competition legislation to limit the natural outcomes of unregulated markets without destroying the effectiveness of free market forces.

A further justification of the inequities caused by free market economics was provided by the social Darwinist argument of Herbert Spencer: the survival of the fittest made it respectable, even desirable, to resist both taxes and charity; poverty and insecurity were necessary, if regrettable, in liberal systems. Though Spencer was British, his approach was more readily accepted and influential in America than at home.

With these defences, despite all its shortcomings, classical theory remained the dominant explanation of how the economic world worked. And the industrialisation process it reflected, and helped to shape, was hugely successful in terms of economic growth and wealth generation. Among its limitations, in this brief history of management it is apt to repeat the model's explicit omission of management as a valid and significant autonomous actor. The theory denied management's role as a separate entity within the industrial process, with responsibility for managing both capital and labour and with the opportunity to do so in a way which was fair and equitable as well as effective. Instead classical theory saw the process as simply pitting capital against labour, accepting that power rested with capital and that it would therefore necessarily always win.

Marx's Assault

A fundamental difference between classical theory and Marx's economics was their opposing views as to the economic system being stable around an equilibrium position. Marx rejected equilibrium, recognising that economic forces were in continuous flux with no necessary stability or equilibrium state. He predicted that the 'capitalist' system defined by classical theory contained within it the seeds of its own extinction, which process he and Engels had prophesied in 1848 with *The Communist Manifesto* which famously opened:

> *'A spectre is haunting Europe -- the spectre of communism. All the powers of old Europe have entered into a holy alliance to exorcise this spectre: Pope and Tsar, Metternich and Guizot, French Radicals and German police-spies.'*

The manifesto advocated a broad programme of political initiatives such as the progressive abolition of private property, heavily progressive income tax, abolition of inheritance rights, centralisation of banking, communications media and transport, the central control of industry and agriculture, provision of free education for all and the abolition of child labour in industry. Marx's aim was for a laissez faire system far in excess of Ricardo's, for government was required primarily to protect private property. Under Marx's communism there would be 'no further need to police the masses or curb the larceny of acquisitive modes of thought', so the state could progressively 'wither away'.[46]   But first had to come the revolution which would initially see the proletarians taking over from the capitalist bourgeoisie, but with a classless society being the longer term aim.

Where communist revolution was achieved the subsequent stage of the state withering away never followed. Communism was found not to work as effectively as the capitalist system, with failure being widely put down to the limitations of central planning, as against market forces, in creating economic dynamic, the loss of individual autonomy resulting in a lack of personal motivation and the corruptibility of the 'new proletarian tzars' who exercised absolute power.

Marx's 'Capital', published twenty years later, contained the more reasoned critique of the then orthodox economic theory. He accepted that the 'capitalistic' system worked well in terms of productivity and wealth generation, it having

> 'created more massive and more colossal productive forces than have all preceding generations together.' [47]

He was primarily motivated by its extreme lack of equity which he recognised as an essential underpinning of the system:

> "Accumulation of wealth at one pole is therefore at the same time an accumulation of misery, agony, of toil, slavery, ignorance, brutality and mental degradation at the opposite pole." [48]

Marx rejected Ricardo's argument that the working class would inevitably be locked into poverty because of their fecundity. Instead he held that poverty was the result of the wage negotiation which was not a bargain between equals: employer and labourer. Labour was

> 'no free agent ... the vampire will not loose its hold on him 'so long as there is a muscle, a nerve, a drop of blood to be exploited'. For protection against 'the serpent of their agonies' the labourers must put their heads together, and, as a class, compel the passing of a law, ... that shall prevent the very workers from selling ... themselves and their families into slavery and death.' [49]

He identified the negotiation between the employer / 'capitalist', who he personalised as 'Mr Moneybags', and the possessor of labour power, as the critical stage in capital accumulation, the actual act of theft of surplus value. He introduced it with heavy irony and then went on to refer to the unequal wage negotiation on completion of which

> 'He, who before was the money-owner, now strides in front as capitalist; the possessor of labour power follows as his labourer. The one with an air of importance, smirking, intent on business; the other, timid and holding back, like one who is bringing his own hide to market and has nothing to expect but - a hiding.' [50]

Marx gave the analysis a historical foundation going back to feudal, aristocratic and landowning classes which had largely been displaced by the industrial 'capitalist'. He would probably be surprised that the old hierarchies, even in some cases extending to monarchy, were still tolerated 150 years after 'Capital'.

Marx had total confidence in the moral rightness of his critique. He also offered some detailed analysis of classical theory as well as an empirical review of its effects. His explanation of the production and accumulation of capital was a mixture of obscure Ricardian theory of value plus overt anger at the injustice of the workers' treatment within the 'capitalist' system. Theory seems to have been the necessary justification of the anger which was itself essential to the implementation of a solution.

The accumulation of capital was only achieved by the 'capitalist', 'Mr Moneybags', expropriating the surplus value produced by the worker, which Marx discussed at length in terms of use value and exchange value. Marx's 'Mr Moneybags' accumulated the surplus value as further capital which he reinvested in

> *'the technical necessities of Modern Industry ...(which) ...*
> *dispels all fixity and security in the situation of the labourer.'*
> (The consequent) *'antagonism vents its rage in the creation of*
> *that monstrosity, an industrial reserve army, kept in misery in*
> *order to be always at the disposal of capital; in the incessant*
> *human sacrifices from among the working class, in the most*
> *reckless squandering of labour-power; and in the devastation*
> *caused by a social anarchy which turns every economic*
> *progress into a social calamity.'* [51]

Marx foresaw the fundamental paradox in the free market 'capitalist' system: the natural consequence of an unregulated competitive market being a monopoly. In any market the most successful competitor will in the end defeat the rest. This process would lead to the extinction of the middle class and the concentration of capital in the hands of a very small number confronting the massed and growing ranks of workers and their comrades in the 'industrial reserve army'. This concentration has been acknowledged in standard text books: as industries mature the number of competitors declines and oligopoly emerges as the natural state of industry in advanced economies.

For Marx, the dichotomy between the few capitalists and the massed ranks of labour excludes consideration of any autonomous role for management, it being merely the officer rank reporting direct to 'Mr Moneybags'. Having seen the early development of publicly owned companies and predicted the development of monopolistic corporations Marx might also have recognised the role of management had his agenda not been focused elsewhere:

*'this despotism takes form peculiar to itself. Just as at first the
capitalist is relieved from actual labour so soon as his capital
has reached that minimum amount with which capitalist
production, as such, begins, so now, he hands over the work of
direct and constant supervision of the individual workmen, and
groups of workmen, to a special kind of wage-labourer. An
industrial army of workmen, under the command of the
capitalist, requires, like a real army, officers (managers), and
sergeants (foremen, overlookers), who, while the work is being
done, command in the name of the capitalist ... It is not because
he is a leader of industry that a man is a capitalist; on the
contrary, he is a leader of industry because he is a capitalist.
The leadership of industry is an attribute of capital. Just as in
feudal times the functions of general and judge, were attributes
of landed property.'* [52]

Marx's critique was about the unequal distribution of power and income and
the 'capitalist' crisis of depression and unemployment which he predicted in
denial of Say's Law that production would always create its own demand.
Say's Law is now consigned to history, so in this at least Marx was right as
he was that the natural outcome of unregulated competition is monopoly.
Possibly he was right about much else as well, though the demise of
'capitalism' has been a long time coming. It may well have been that this
miscalculation arose at least in part because Marx mistakenly accepted
classical theory's denial of the role of management independent of
ownership.

Mitigating Legislation

A Marxist revolution was probably avoided in most of Europe because the
great injustices done to working people were recognized and attempts made
to limit those wrongs. Laws were passed in England relating to working
conditions and hours of work, to public health and to the rights of workers to
combine in unions

Disease and ill health had been rife in the early cotton mills and mill towns
of Lancashire and had resulted in a series of Factory Acts and other
associated legislation to improve the worker's lot.

The first of these, in 1802, laid down that no parish apprentice (ie pauper
child) employed in cotton or woollen mills should work for more than
twelve hours a day and night working was forbidden. Ventilation was

enforced, sanitation improved and apprentices were to be provided with proper sleeping accommodation and adequately clothed. Some provision was also to be made for apprentice education And a system of inspection and enforcement was instituted. The terms of the Act serve as a reminder of the working arrangements and conditions then existing. It had little practical impact and was widely ignored. Nevertheless it was a first step. Other Acts followed, in 1819, 1825 and 1831. These Acts fixed a twelve hour maximum day for 'free' children and minimum working age as nine, but they were not energetically enforced. Substantive progress was not really made till the 1833 Act which followed publication of a Commission of enquiry report earlier that year which

> *'disclosed a frightful state of affairs. The worst of the population had been gathered from all parts of the country and collected in the north country towns. A factory type had grown up, often weak and even deformed, often with hereditary diseases, deficient in mind, and doubtful as to morals. In the early years of the century the term "factory hand" was almost one of disgrace. ... England no longer depended on its yeomanry, but upon pauper workers. "*[53]

The 1833 Act outlawed the employment of children under nine, those under thirteen were limited to a working week of forty eight hours maximum and working day to a maximum of nine hours and importantly the first factory inspectors were appointed. At first the factory inspectors were viewed with suspicion by workers and employers alike, but they nevertheless dedicated themselves to the task of

> *'correcting the great moral evils that had taken root and extensively spread in ... industry.'* [54]

Further Acts in 1844 and 1847 set the maximum working day for women and children at ten hours, finally followed in 1850 and 1853 by similar limitations which applied to all workers. From 1880 onwards legislation established workers' rights to compensation for injury or fatality at work, levels of compensation being set as weekly amounts for injury and lump sum payments to dependants in the case of death. Previously an employer could escape liability if the cause could be shown to arise from the victim's own negligence or that of a fellow worker. These loopholes were closed and most employers took out insurance against such liabilities though it was not obligatory.

These legal limitations had been hard fought and won against vehement opposition from hard line employers and their parliamentary representatives. The battle for social justice was initially focused on efforts to establish the right to form a combination or trades union.

Smith had noted the disparity of treatment between employers and employed on the question of combinations:

> *'We rarely hear, it has been said, of the combinations of masters, though frequently of those of workmen. But whoever imagines, upon this account, that masters rarely combine, is as ignorant of the world as of the subject. Masters are always and everywhere in a sort of tacit, but constant and uniform combination, not to raise the wages of labour above their actual rate... Such combinations, however are frequently resisted by a contrary defensive combination of the workmen, who ... are desperate, and act with the folly and extravagance of desperate men, ... The masters upon these occasions are just as clamorous ... and never cease to call aloud for the assistance of the civil magistrate, and the rigorous execution of those laws which have been enacted with so much severity against the combinations of servants, labourers, and journeymen.'* [55]

Legislation outlawing worker combination and representation were difficult to make effective and were finally repealed in 1824, making trade unions no longer illegal. Joining them and becoming active nevertheless remained perilous. In 1832 the 'Tolpuddle martyrs' formed the *Friendly Society of Agricultural Labourers* to protest against a one third reduction of their wages. Legal action was brought against them under, of all things, the Mutiny Act of 1797 and they were found guilty and transported, but the public outcry was such that the rights of trade unionism and collective bargaining were accepted thereafter.

The ongoing struggle for social justice contributed to the politicization of labour which from time to time was expressed as open rebellion as in the Luddite riots of 1812 and the Chartist rebellions of 1839 and 1842. And in due course it led to the formation of the Labour Party and the realignment of the Tory landowning interest with the new rich free market Whig radicals to form the twentieth century left : right political divide.

Some of the fire was undoubtedly taken out of industrial relations by the improving working hours and conditions and the more permissive legislation regarding unions and the ability for workers to make their voice heard. At the same time, the prediction that free market 'capitalism' would destroy itself by its monopolistic tendency was not fulfilled. Again legislation mitigated the otherwise probable monopolistic outcomes, even though the laws to limit monopoly were slow being enacted. And even when it was enacted its real effect on competition was uncertain, though the existence of anti-trust law, together with the means of it being vigorously implemented, no doubt provided some protection against 'conspiracy' to fix prices or otherwise limit competition.

Further pressure was released from Marxist revolutionary fervour by the rising standards of living, provided by industrialisation. And where Marx's reserve industrial army of unemployed might have been expected to suffer continued poverty, its worst effects were offset by public expenditure on various nascent components of a 'welfare state' being first established in late 1880s Germany and subsequently in Britain. These served to reduce the anger and violence which Marx had anticipated would be unleashed by the failure of the 'capitalist' system.

By the time *'Capital'* was published it was clear that Marx's 'spectre' of revolution had already lost some of its potency in the industrialised economies. But reducing hardship was not the only reason Marx's predictions did not work out in Europe. He had been most exercised over the iniquities of 'Mr Moneybags', the personal beneficiary of capitalist monopoly power. But 'Mr Moneybags'' position was radically changed by the company formation law in mid nineteenth century. Ownership of large scale enterprise was becoming less the charge of a wealthy individual and more the aggregate of many smaller shareholders.

Ownership and Management

The first shareholders in business enterprise were those who invested in overseas trading expeditions. Originally, each expedition had been financed separately. Investors put up the money to pay for an expedition and waited, powerless but committed, for news of their particular expedition's progress. They were necessarily locked in to their investment till their ship should come safely home and the contents of its holds be unloaded and sold. Only then were the investors rewarded with a share of the proceeds which, if the expedition was successful, might be substantial.

However ownership of such stock was not without risk, liability being without limit. An expedition might simply not be as profitable as hoped so the returns might be meagre. Or the ship might not return at all, being lost with all hands, when the stockholder might not only lose the value of their initial investment but be required also to provide some compensation as well. Moreover, investors were not able to reverse their investment or dispose of it, there being no open market for such stocks.

Ownership had already become separated from management in such enterprises. Management sailed away with the expedition and were responsible for its economic success. Management had total control of operations. Ownership's participation was limited to a share of the profits.

The trading companies which organised these expeditions gradually accumulated permanent capital. So the 'terminable stocks' – shares relating to individual expeditions - became inappropriate. By mid seventeenth century the practice of dividing the capital, as apart from profits, among shareholders was ended and from then on the companies traded as single units with a permanent indivisible capital fund which incorporated the interests of many shareholders in the formation of a joint stock company.

This was the organisational form, protected by a royal charter granting monopoly rights, which Adam Smith had in mind when he suggested it was not to be expected that managers *'of other people's money'* would *'watch over it with the same anxious vigilance'* as if it were their own. He was not referring to the expeditionary seamen, but the permanent staff at the administrative headquarters. He was certainly right to make the distinction between those 'managers' and the risk taking stockholders. But it is less clear whether there is any similarity between them and the managers and shareholders of a modern limited liability publicly quoted competitive corporation.

Joint stock organisation with unlimited liability was then also adopted for the major infrastructural projects such as canals and turnpikes. Stockholders in these enormous projects remained responsible for the whole of a company's debts, just as they would as partners. And there was still no ready market for the purchase and sale of shares, so they remained effectively committed to their original investment and shared totally the risks involved in the enterprise which usually took several years before commencing to earn any sort of return.

The formation of such joint stock companies remained both expensive and cumbersome until the Joint Stock Companies Act of 1844 greatly simplified company formation as independent legal entities. The Act brought to an end the costly and hazardous method of seeking incorporation by royal charter, letters patent or special Act of Parliament,[56] replacing it with a relatively simple registration process.

Limited liability had been long debated in the British parliament and was finally accepted in the Act of 1855. This brought company ownership to a wider section of the public, applying as it did to companies with more than 25 shareholders. By that time the small owner managed workshops and factories such as Adam Smith's pin factory, were still in aggregate the major employers, but the successful enterprises which Marx envisaged as the developing monopolies, were joint stock companies with an increasingly widespread share ownership. The personalisation of the capitalist as 'Mr Moneybags' had already become an inappropriate metaphor.

The entrepreneur owner-manager, was nevertheless depicted as the ideal type. Smith had dismissed the concept of hired management and classical theory fully endorsed that dismissal in idealising the owner-manager entrepreneur who latterly became famous for quick decision taking and lack of bureaucracy, being flexible, innovative and risk accepting. The entrepreneur set the very best example. As an owner, the entrepreneur was locked in and personally took all the financial risks. As a manager the entrepreneur fought on what Sun Tzu referred to as 'death ground'[57] where you either win or die. The owner-manager could be relied on to act energetically in their own self-interest.

The rewards for successful entrepreneurship could be considerable, though the prospects for success for new start-up businesses have never been much more than a one in ten chance of surviving the first five years. The rewards were not necessarily restricted to maximised self-interest expressed solely in monetary terms. They might also include the intrinsic satisfaction of creating a prosperous and lasting enterprise that supplied some valued new product or service, which also provided employment which could be made congenial, as well as playing a valued role in the wider economy. The model entrepreneur may be motivated more by the possibility of that creative achievement than by the chance of making quick money.

Divergent Economics

Classical economic theory attracted critics from the start, notably because of its careless treatment of industrialised workers who it appeared content to exploit without restraint. It survived more or less without serious challenge so long as it worked. And that it appeared to do, generating great wealth some of which was deployed to offset and compensate its worst effects on the underprivileged.

But classical theory contained some curiosities: the elaborate and unreal assumptions required to breath life into its model of a competitive market; the illusory nature of competitive equilibrium; the fact that real markets were neither purely competitive nor monopolistic, but were at some intermediate oligopolistic state where the classical model lost precision; that agriculture was the nearest thing to a real competitive market, but in that market above all others it was necessary for governments to intervene and regulate prices and quotas. And there was also Say's law which gave the curious assurance that production created its own demand and that therefore the whole economic system was stable. This failed to explain the boom and bust reality which persisted throughout the nineteenth century and beyond, and was anything but a stable equilibrium. Each such curiosity was received by theoreticians as a challenge to provide an explanation which preserved classical theory more or less intact.

But the theoreticians themselves were less than convincing as to the theory's validity. Malthus and Ricardo both argued that in a progressive society, by which they meant one with a growing population, the beneficiaries of economic growth would be the small number of wealth owners. The economic position of all other members of society would merely remain the same or could even worsen. Malthus' argument that only 'moral restraint', by which he meant later marriage, could rescue the working class from poverty was widely accepted, and Malthus himself recognised that the likelihood of 'moral restraint' was slight.

J S Mill recognised the problems of the classical approach and having justified them with the utilitarian argument, proposed the taxation of rent, the limitation of inheritance and the development of what he referred to as 'co-operative production'. His final contributions were those of an Owenite socialist, a form of idealism without great hope of practical enactment.

Since the start of industrialisation economies were subject to the periodic production of more commodities than were demanded. The consequent cut back in production created large scale unemployment which reduced the amount of money available to buy commodities. Thus demand for commodities was further reduced. Such a vicious cycle of events was clearly unstable.

Despite this, the classical theorists developed their defensive theories to explain the booms and slumps of business cycles. For some speculation was the problem, for others the cause was sun spot activity, while others cited waves of technological innovation. Whatever the cause, it was clear that Say might be wrong: production did not appear to create its own demand.

Alfred Marshal in his 1890 'Principles of Economics' emphasised continuity from the classical tradition of Smith and Ricardo. Though a mathematician, he was concerned with the moral contribution of economic theory, for example, in resolving the long term problem of poverty and the inequitable distribution of economic benefits. His contemporary, the Austrian economist, Carl Menger, also a mathematician, focused on mathematical modelling, describing relationships between economic phenomena in terms of simultaneous equations. With Jevons and Walras, Menger developed the mathematical expression of classical theory which became labelled as 'neo-classical'. It opened up a rich new seam of quantitative theoretical analysis which became a primary focus of academic interest for itself, rather than its practical application to real world situations.

Marshall's concept of marginal analysis was a significant step in theory development. Using this idea it was asserted that the value of a commodity was equal to the utility provided by the last incremental unit in its supply, ie the marginal unit. This marginal utility approach was generalised across economic analysis and effectively disposed of Ricardo's arcane labour theory of value which had been subsequently adopted by Marx.

Marshall was concerned with the practical relevance and effect of theory. He recognised that different circumstances presented in different industries at different times required different solutions. For him there was no one best way applicable to the economy as a whole and readily expressible by a mathematical formula. This more empirical approach led him to analysis in terms of partial equilibrium, with each industry having its own distinctive situation regarding resources, technology, geography and economy. Were the general equilibrium model applicable to the whole economy at a particular point in time it would merely be a happy coincidence of many partial equilibria.

Additionally Marshall acknowledged the time dependence of economic theory: in the short run very little could be changed whereas in the long run most things were changeable and problems, such as poverty and inequity, could be open to solution. However neo-classical theory's mathematical analysis was unable convincingly to accommodate time dependence.

Marshall's partial equilibrium approach disposed of Say's law in theory, but it was not until the great depression of the 1930s that it was finally ditched in practice. In the interim it was the workers who were forced to shoulder the main burden of economic slumps and recessions. This energised early manifestations of the British socialist movement. Trade unions, Fabianism, Guild Socialism, the co-operative movement and the British brand of Marxist communism, were all firmly aligned with the lot of the industrial worker and correcting the inequitable divide of the gains from industrial activity.

These various initiatives added pressure on government to ameliorate the workers' lot and led in due course to the establishment of various components of what became known as the welfare state. The first elements of welfarism involved the payment by the state of a benefit for the unemployed. This not only relieved its recipients of the worst effects of economic deprivation but at a macro level assisted the general economic recovery. Similarly investment in public works, primarily of economic infrastructure such as transportation and communication systems, also served to initiate economic recovery.

Such initiatives which were widely adopted before the first world war in most European economies, including Britain, were largely the result of pragmatic common sense rather than economic theory. The theory did not come till 1936 with the publication of Keynes '*General Theory of Employment, Interest and Money*'. Keynes himself was influential on both sides of the Atlantic but the model of the state managed economy promulgated by his followers was never accepted with much enthusiasm in America while in Britain and Europe it became the new orthodox wisdom.

During the nineteenth century America's higher growth rate insulated it from the very worst effects of the booms and slumps of business cycles. Its dedication to classical theory was not therefore challenged to the same degree as in Europe. That remained the case until the great depression of the 1930s, when government intervention in markets was found to be essential to the economy's survival and, ironically, to preserving the capitalist system intact.

By then America had achieved world leadership in economic and business affairs. Initially it did not develop any uniquely American explanations of economic and business development which differed significantly from the old European models. Yet America's situation, with practically infinite resources, especially land, and the rapid expansion this facilitated, was quite different from that of the old world. And in due course the development of theory followed practice across the Atlantic.

PART TWO – THE RISE OF MANAGEMENT

Management, though clearly apparent as a practice, was not formally recognised till around a century after Arkwright's first cotton spinning mill and Smith's 'Wealth of Nations'. By then the size of companies had grown substantially and their ownership was becoming more fragmented among large numbers of shareholders. The hired managers, so distrusted by Smith as not having the 'anxious vigilance' of owners to prevent 'negligence and profusion', were becoming powerful, hugely effective and largely autonomous.

During the mid 19th century the centre of gravity of management, practice and theory, started to move across the Atlantic to America. There the world's biggest and most successful corporations prospered in the freely competitive domestic markets which were orders of magnitude bigger than any in the old world. Not only did they enjoy substantial economies of scale, but more importantly from the business perspective, American markets were growing more rapidly than those of the old world. The greater scale and more rapid growth of markets justified substantially greater investment in new capacities, technologies and methods. So America became the world's leading industrial producer, creator of what was referred to as the 'mass production society'.

The big business which developed in America required new functions and roles to be undertaken by management and these were consolidated into a body of professional expertise, specific to different tasks but coalescing into a consistent management approach. Researches into industrial organisation, particularly the management of people, were adopted as general systems of management, each successive system adding new knowledge and understanding.

America's management advance was not restricted simply to industrial practice. It also led the old world in terms of education and in particular the development of a management curriculum capable of being taught in specialist colleges. Management education programmes developed in

American universities around the turn of the twentieth century, long before their equivalents elsewhere and American business schools and their MBA degrees, became the ubiquitous standard of management professionalism.

Over the eighty years or so up to the late 1960s, professional management saw business and industry grow and prosper and become more enlightened in its understanding and treatment of its people. This was the period of management's rise. Theories of management emerged from academic studies of practice, and practice benefited from the lessons learned.

By the end of the 1960s management though it had become the dominant industrial actor, nurtured by governments, was being seriously challenged by organised labour which had prospered in the more benign environment which followed the 1930s depression. Industrial ownership had over that same period become fragmented and weakened both within companies and in its relationship with governments. Management was unique in being a power group which was not founded on the traditional base of private property. Nevertheless theirs was, as Chandler expressed it in 1977, the key role in twentieth century wealth creation.

This second part looks at the development of management in the new American context of big business, the division of its labour, its practices and responsibilities as an autonomous category addressing the opportunities and problems presented by mass industrialisation. And the development of theories of management, again predominantly shaped from observation of big business practices.

Initially management had been promulgated as a putative profession and early American educators had sought to invest it with the social and public ideals of the older professions. But management was not a closed shop profession and its ranks contained all sorts. Progress was far from even.

Classical free market economics which failed to foresee and deal with the great depression was modified by Keynes who targeted the achievement and maintenance of full employment. 'Keynesian economics', though there were some sceptics, became the new dominant orthodoxy through till the late 1970s when the combination of inflation and slow economic growth defeated government interventions and when the divisions between employer and employed warranted a political solution.

This part of the story ends around 1977 when Chandler's 'The Visible Hand' was published and before the re-adoption by governments of free market economic practice had crystallised in the shape of the Reaganomics and Thatcherism of the 1980s.

5. NEW WORLD – NEW MANAGEMENT

The American colonies declared their independence from Britain in the same decade as Arkwright opened the first cotton mill and Smith published *Wealth of Nations*. Within around 60 years the American population at over 17 million had overtaken Britain's. Over the following twenty five years it almost doubled, and doubled again in the following three decades. By 1880 America's gross national product was already one and a half times that of Britain. By 1900 it was double Britain's and by 1920 three times.

Such economic success may have been a sufficient defence of classical economic theory which had been accepted with only minor modification. American capital accumulation and investment produced inequalities just as it had in Europe, but in America the workers enjoyed a more comfortable and continually improving standard of living and the unemployed 'reserve army' was a smaller proportion of the population.

The inequalities inherent in the classical system were nevertheless defended, as they were in Europe, and with the added weight of Herbert Spencer's social Darwinism which could be used to justify even slavery, the greatest inequality of all, which the economy of the south was based on till the end of the civil war in 1865.

The greatest differences between the American economy and those in the old industrialised world were those of scale and growth. By 1890 the domestic American market was substantially bigger than any in the old world, encouraging ever larger scale businesses to become established with the clear threat of monopolisation. It was only then that the Sherman Act was passed in America stating that,

> *'Every contract, combination in the form of trust or otherwise, or conspiracy, in restraint of trade or commerce among the several States, or with foreign nations, is declared to be illegal'*

The size of the domestic markets and their urgent and continuous growth enabled profitable investment in industrial operations of a scale never before contemplated. The earlier British experience of Lombe, Arkwright and others, individuals with no capital enabled to pioneer completely new industrial activities, was repeated in America.

A generation of such entrepreneurial individuals emerged to lead the railroad, steel, ship building, shipping, real estate, oil and finance industries in America during the growth phases of their development.

Such 'captains of industry', sometimes referred to as 'robber barons' because of their amoral, exploitative business methods, subsequently became notable philanthropists, funding among other things the establishment of management education.

As American industries matured and their growth slowed down there was generally a period of 'shake out' and concentration. Some competitors ceased business while others joined forces through mergers and acquisitions to form even more massive organisations which required a new form of administration to achieve the necessary effectiveness and efficiency of operations. Such administration exercised control quite separately from any questions of ownership. And the education and training required for this new form of administration was pioneered in America to create a new category in society: professional management.

The Affluent Economy

H C Carey, America's leading economist of the 1830s and 40s, pointed out the American difference from Europe was one of fundamental abundance. He noted that Ricardo

> *'had never seen from his window the progress of a new settlement; had he done so he would have had a different view of the prospects for mankind ... with the passage of time, men were not forced as Ricardo claimed to poorer and poorer land with ever lower return to their labour and, for any land that was better than the worst, ever higher rents to the landlords. On the contrary they first cultivated the thin but unencumbered soil on the top of the hills. Then at a later period they tackled the thick vegetation in the valleys; having cleared away the trees they proceeded to work this richer alluvial soil. The returns to their toils were not less but more.'* [58]

America was then still largely agricultural with farms being worked by their owners, quite differently from Britain where landlords and tenant farmers employed waged labour. There being no shortage of undeveloped land in America, holdings were vast by European standards, later confirmed by The Homestead Acts which set out 160 acres as enough to support a family. In such circumstances every man was able to earn a rich living from his own industry. The same was true in the south where the cotton industry prospered on the back of the slave system.

Slavery apart, the American experience was of growth and rapidly improving standards of living which included the working class. The old world's experience on the other hand was of rising affluence for the owners of capital but continuing misery and insecurity for the working people and unemployed. The classical economic ideas may not have been appropriate for America and while Carey argued strongly for domestic *laissez-faire* on the grounds that interference by government could only stifle initiative, he was a staunch tariff protector of foreign trade.

The early American economic idea was simply to develop industry in line with agriculture and for infant industries to be tariff protected from European competition in the north with the south to enjoy free trade with Europe so as to expand exports of cotton and in return import cheap European manufactured goods.

By around the middle of the nineteenth century world economic leadership had migrated across the Atlantic. The economic infrastructure in communications and transportation was being developed to open up ever more territory adding further to the size of domestic markets. Economic progress in America, though not completely continuous, far exceeded the European achievement. Nevertheless, great inequalities resulted and in a land strongly espousing Christian values these had to be justified. The Malthusian argument that the workers would always breed themselves back to poverty, should they ever escape it, was clearly untrue in America. The utilitarian argument that the greatest good for the greatest number could justify the misery of some was deployed in defence of classical theory's unequal outcome.

Moreover, the generally positive economic opportunities in America would have made it more easy to accept that anyone who failed did so because of their own shortcomings. Clearly, in Britain, such failure was the result of any number of causes which had nothing to do with the individual concerned. Social Darwinism did not therefore attract much support in the old world, but it was influential in America. Spencer's phrase 'the survival of the fittest' not only justified not supporting the weakest members of society, but actually their 'weeding out'. For Spencer and his followers, the process of natural selection was inevitable and unavoidable. Thus any governmental intervention or charitable works intended to reverse the process could only result in prolonging the agony of the 'unfittest'. Moreover, at the other end of the social scale, as one of his supporters put it:

> *'the millionaires are a product of natural selection ... the naturally selected agents of society for certain work. They get high wages and live in luxury, but the bargain is a good one for society.'*[59]

John D Rockefeller of the Standard Oil Company which was subsequently broken up as a result of anti-trust law offered this further explanation:

> *'The growth of a large business is merely the survival of the fittest ... The American Beauty rose can be produced in splendour and fragrance which bring cheer to its beholder only by sacrificing the early buds which grow around it. ... 'This is not an evil tendency in business. It is merely the working-out of a law of nature and a law of God.'*[60]

Thus the affluent need not feel guilty over the hardships and inequalities suffered by those less fortunate. In addition, the same arguments were used to enable, with the same guilt free conscience, the hereditary passage of riches down the generations, such hereditary advantage being a matter of genes from which the species gained.

Such a curiously elaborate argument promulgated by some fascist dictator might have been roundly condemned as evil, but social Darwinism held considerable sway in America through the second half of the nineteenth century.

An alternative American perspective on the inequalities produced by the accumulation and investment of capital was provided by Thorstein Veblen who held up to considerable amusement the 'conspicuous consumption' and 'conspicuous waste' of the 'leisure class'.

> *'No one finds difficulty in assenting to the commonplace that the greatest part of the expenditure incurred by all classes for apparel is incurred for the sake of a respectable appearance rather than for the protection of the person. And probably at no other point is the shabbiness so keenly felt as it is if we fall*

short of the standard set by social usage in this matter of dress.
... people will undergo a very considerable degree of privation
in the comforts or the necessaries of life in order to afford what
is considered a decent amount of wasteful consumption; so ...it
is by no means ... uncommon ... in an inclement climate, for
people to go ill clad in order to appear well dressed.[61]

'The ostentation, waste, idleness, and immorality of the rich
were all purposeful: they were advertisements of success in the
pecuniary culture. Work by contrast, was merely a caste mark
of inferiority.[62]

The point was serious: 'conspicuous consumption' and 'conspicuous waste', had already become a significant part of aggregate demand when Veblen was writing more than a hundred years ago. And so they remain, provoked by corporate marketing and promotion.

Galbraith pointed out the conventional economic wisdom was developed in and for a world of poverty where the emphasis was wholly on production because it was through production that wealth was created and the standards of living of everyone was raised. But in an affluent economy the production of goods was not so important as the employment it provided. The goods themselves might be, as Veblen pointed out, utterly frivolous, but the work involved in their production and sale as well as its remuneration, was necessary for the maintenance of a stable economy. Therefore it would make sense to engage people in more useful employment, rather than in the production of goods for which there was no need and no natural want unless energetically promoted, in the production of goods for which there was a general desire, such as

'better schools, hospitals ... urban development, sanitation, ...
police and a thousand other things ... The economy is geared to
the least urgent set of human wants. It would be far more
secure if it were based on the whole range of need.[63]

That debate continued, but the argument had to assume that private production of goods was profitable and therefore paid the taxes to provide the public employments to which Galbraith referred. But first, firms must continue to be competitive if they were to survive and make profits. And this was what American business achieved supremely well.

Birth of Big Business

Chandler's account of the railroads which he described as *'the nation's first big business'* identified their role in the development of management practice capable of controlling and developing a scale of business hitherto not experienced.

America had followed Britain in establishing a transportation infrastructure, first with canals and subsequently railroads. Major canal building projects started with the construction of the Erie Canal which connected the Hudson River with Lake Erie and was completed in 1825. By 1890 America had built around 4000 miles of canal, almost twice the length of the British system. Furthermore the American builders had to contend with more mountainous terrain, severer weather conditions and sparser population as well as far greater distances over which to manage the manual labour force. The potential profitability of the American canals was less apparent than the British though the benefits to States in opening up territory were real enough. Consequently public funding played an important role in American canal building, the Erie Canal, for example, being funded by New York state.

The initial reduction in costs achieved by canal transport, as compared with wagon haulage, was decisive in establishing trade between the east and west and opening up the American interior. However their economic life span was short before they were overtaken by railroad transportation.

Railroads were not new. In Britain, a 'wagon way' carrying coal from Newcastle to the river Tyne had been used since the mid 1500s. In 1767 iron rails were adopted at Coalbrookdale on its 'wagon way' carrying iron ore and coal. An early but unsuccessful steam engine devised by Trescothick was used to replace horses pulling coal at Merthyr Tydfil in 1804. More successful coal moving attempts were made at Leeds in 1811 and Newcastle in 1813. Stephenson built his first steam engine in 1814, got authorisation for the twenty six mile long Stockton and Darlington Railway in 1921 and four years later the railway opened with the immediate result that the price of coal at Darlington dropped from 18 shillings a ton to 8 shillings, some measure of the economic impact of fairly short distance railway transport in a system already served by canals.

Following the success of these lines major British railway developments got under way, only briefly interrupted by a financial crisis in 1847 caused by wildly speculative and disastrous investments in rail projects. By 1850 there were 6,600 miles of railway line in Britain. By 1860 there were 10,000 miles and by 1870 15,000 miles after which further development slowed.

America's railroad building started a little later than the British system but quickly overtook it in terms of miles of track having around 9000 miles laid by 1850. Ten years later this had grown to over 30,000 miles and continued to expand rapidly till by 1890 there were over 166,000 miles of track laid, far in excess of any other country. It had a massive impact on the American economy. One contemporary commentator describing the opening up of the West by the railways as follows:

> *'The pioneer, as he moves forward over the prairie of the west, carries with him the railway – as necessary to his life as are the axe and the plough. The railway keeps pace with the frontier line of settlement; so that the crop of this year of a frontier farm, in the great march of civilization, has only to be held to the next, to be sent whizzing to the Eastern market at a speed of thirty miles to the hour.'* [64]

Railroads quickly opened up the new agricultural areas of Illinois, Indiana and Wisconsin to the markets of the Eastern seaboard. Moreover, concurrent with the new railroads, developments in shipping, the iron hull and steam driven screw propulsion, increased the scale, speed and efficiency of overseas transportation thus opening up European markets to American produce. American registered steam shipping tonnage grew from 5,631 in 1847 to 97,296 in 1860.[65] Cunard's transatlantic steam packet line from New York to Liverpool, began in 1848 quickly followed by others, cutting the crossing time from an average of 35 days to less than two weeks.

The carrying capacity of ships and railways to both domestic and export markets grew continuously. But their impact was not restricted simply to opening up new markets for the 'frontier farm'. The new means of distribution for manufactured goods to all parts of the new American market made it feasible to produce on a large scale. Previously, only in textiles had factories employing more than two hundred been viable; other manufacturing had been accomplished through small work shops and a system of subcontracting work. Now, large scale production units became the norm, manufacturing such things as 'shoes, clothing, clocks, watches, sewing machines, agricultural implements, machine tools, and small arms for the civilian market as well as such basic materials as iron and brass.'[66] All these began to be mass produced.

Both the impact and the scale of the American railroad development was without precedent. By the 1850s American railroads had become the biggest market in the world for coal, wood, machinery, felt, glass, rubber and brass. The requirement for capital investment caused a revolution in banking and the scale of employment of workers and managers caused a revolution in the practice and theory of management.

Unlike the canals, most of the investment in railroads was obtained from non-public sources. Initially individuals at termini towns or along the route of a proposed railroad would invest as they stood to gain from such developments. But these investments were insufficient to meet the needs of the railroad companies and so further investment was sought from Eastern cities or even from Europe, such investors' sole interests being in the returns they stood to gain from their stock given the risks involved. These distant investors often were attracted to bonds and preference stock rather than full risk bearing shares and their need for professional advice led to the formation of many investment banks for this purpose. This in turn led to the New York stock exchange becoming the dominant national exchange, gaining precedence over Boston and Philadelphia largely because of its commercial port and communications with the capital exporting countries of Europe. Wall Street being the main exchange for railroad securities its position as the nation's leading stock exchange was further consolidated after the 1850s.

Railroad managements were of course not only concerned with the raising of finance. Running the railroads was as expensive as building them. In the 1850s the largest American manufacturer, the textile mills of the Pepperell Manufacturing Company, had operating costs of around $300,000 and employed around 800 people. The New York and Erie Railroad cost almost $3m per annum to run in 1855 and employed over 4000. The Pennsylvania railroad cost well over $2m to run in 1855 and by 1862 costs were almost $5.5m.

But the scale of the railroad operations was only part of their management problem. Unlike manufacturing operations their activities were spread over hundreds of miles and included rail tracks, telegraph lines, rolling stock, shops, terminals, stations, warehouses, offices, bridges etc. Management had responsibility not only for the overall profitability of operations but for the safety and time keeping of their customers and the safety and condition of freight. Routinely decisions had to be taken as to the numbers of cars to be scheduled to meet constantly changing requirements and the determination of charges and prices. Management had also to be concerned with the longer term decisions as to expansion, maintenance and/or replacement of tracks, terminals, cars and freight wagons, equipment and other facilities and how to finance such developments.

These decisions, being confronted on a scale of operation that had not previously been faced, required new methods of corporate management to be devised. Management of the Baltimore and Ohio Railroad were the first to separate accounting and finance from those of the railroad operations. The accounting department kept track of all the company's financial transactions and the treasurer's section was concerned with raising finance and controlling the allocation of funds to maintenance and replacement of assets. Management of the Erie and the Pennsylvania railroads initiated the setting down of line responsibilities and what became known as the chains of command and communication. The Pennsylvania also pioneered the setting up of a separate traffic management function responsible for obtaining and processing freight and passengers.

By the 1870s the focus of railroad management had ceased to be on expansion and more on competition which was destroying profitability and a consequent concern with costs and pricing. This focus led to federations between railroad companies and consolidation by mergers and acquisitions into a smaller number of integrated railroad systems with New York's financiers played a leading role in this rationalization process, not just arranging finance but importantly being involved in the achievement of greater efficiency and effectiveness.

Some managements of these newly created complex organisations introduced a decentralised structure with regional managements being responsible for the profitable operation of their regional system. This sort of structure foreshadowed the famous decentralisation of manufacturing led by General Motors some fifty years later.

Clearly railroad management was not an optional extra addition to the costs of running a railroad, they were an unavoidable part of the organisation and one which pioneered effective and efficient ways of doing things without which the railroads, and subsequent large scale business organisations, could not have prospered.

The precedent set by the railroads was the big business model. There was no question of the small workshop building and operating an entrepreneurial railroad. To build and operate a railroad from New York to Chicago was a large scale operation from the beginning; it clearly couldn't achieve the necessary scale by organic growth. The management of such an enterprise was forced to pioneer new ways of doing things. Equally, the financing of such a project could not be achieved by the progressive accumulation of capital and its incremental investment in further track extension; it had to be financed from the outset as a whole entity. As in Britain financing was achieved by selling the stock of a limited liability company, but in America the scale of such projects meant the stock ownership was substantially more fragmented and complex.

For such projects management and ownership were necessarily separated. It was not an option; there was no other way such projects could have been planned and executed. The days when an Arkwright could arrange the financing of a whole new factory business among a small number of individuals were over.

Control without Ownership
The separation of ownership from control of the large American railroad companies was followed by similar separation of big business manufacturers and distributors.

Such separation was widely held to be more democratic than the tyranny of owner control and was achieved among the vast majority of big American businesses, Ford being one of the few exceptions. While Henry Ford retained ownership and management control of his motor company and was initially pioneering and successful, his retention of personal control resulted in the near disastrous collapse in company fortunes which was only rectified by his grandson establishing a professional management regime to run the company.

The separation of ownership and control was effective in enabling large business to be financed and it was successful in permitting such large scale businesses to be run effectively and efficiently. It was widely regarded as preferable to the ownership and control being in the hands of a single individual such as had been envisaged by Marx with 'Mr Moneybags'. But it was controversial. Western democratic government and the legal system it had developed was largely based around the notion of protecting private property rights and classical economic theory had identified the divergence of interest between company owners and its hired managers.

Though the interests of enterprise and owner might coincide in the entrepreneur role it was not necessarily true for businesses which had developed beyond the entrepreneurial stage. For such business the distinction between management and ownership was fundamental. Whatever form its ownership took, business decisions which had direct profit implications were taken by those in control of the business, its management. But economic theory taught that management without ownership would seek to maximise their own self interest. Smith had suggested they simply wouldn't be vigilant while later theoreticians held that they would develop what they referred to as 'slack' which they would deploy for their own personal benefit. Separation therefore involved not only a distinction between management and ownership, but a direct conflict of interest.

Berle and Means studied this divergence of interest. They identified three distinct functions: business ownership, business control and participation in action on behalf of the business. They noted that in the nineteenth century the owners fulfilled the first two and hired managers fulfilled the third:

> *'the owners ... were in a position (their emphasis) both to manage an enterprise or delegate its management and to receive any profits or benefits which might accrue. The managers on the other hand ... operated an enterprise, presumably in the interests of the owners.'* [67]

With the growth of big business towards the end of the nineteenth century they noted that the position of owners had been reduced and management advanced. For Berle and Means owners had three main interests:

> *'first that the company should be made to earn maximum profit compatible with a reasonable degree of risk; second that as large a proportion of these profits should be distributed as the best interests of the business permit ...; and, finally, that his stock should remain freely marketable at a fair price.'* [68]

These interests were couched in measured terms. There was no simplistic assertion that the company should just maximise profit or dividend payments, or therefore, shareholder wealth. Nor was there any explicit assertion of the interests of management though they did conjecture about their possible interest in personal profit, or in prestige or power or perhaps in the gratification of 'professional zeal'.

The theory's assertion that company management might exercise their natural desire to maximise their own self interest by usurping profit for their personal use, comes close to a suspicion of management criminality. Company law specified the duties of directors. While non-conformance may be difficult to identify and prove it was nevertheless binding on management to conform. The British Companies Act of 1844 provided the first legal identification of a company director's responsibilities as *'the direction, conduct, management, or superintendence'* of the company's affairs. This was important as it specified the directors' duty as being to the company itself, which was established as an independent legal entity, rather than to its shareholders, or indeed allowing self-interest to pervert that prime duty.

The shareholders had a separate contract with the company, based on their purchase of share certificates which entitled them to a potential receipt of dividends and benefit of capital growth, both of which being at risk. Beyond that shareholders were established with the right to appoint directors (or confirm their previous appointment, or not, at a company general meeting) and were able to vote for resolutions raised at company general meetings. The shareholders owed no duty to the company or its employees, having discharged it in full when they paid for their shares. Thereafter the relationship between the shareholders and the company is one of risk and reward.

Management's responsibility to the company as a separate legal entity, rather than its shareholders, was explicit from 1844 on. Management had no statutory contract with shareholders, despite Smith's enthusiasm for *co-partneries* and suspicion of hired managers.

Nevertheless, management had a clear responsibility for providing shareholders with a return in terms of dividends and the prospect of capital growth which would be sufficient to ensure the company's survival and long term prosperity.

The separation of ownership from management may have first occurred with the creation of limited liability and ready access to stock markets and the establishment of big business. But it also occurs anew when any successful business start-up progresses through the several intermediate stages to becoming a publicly quoted corporation. The change may be more real than apparent. From a start up the typical successful business goes through a stage of entrepreneur management, then a family business, family managed with wider ownership, publicly quoted company and possibly becoming in due course a wholly owned subsidiary of a larger corporation. At each such stage of development management becomes further remote from ownership, though retaining all control and responsibility.[69]

Management Education and Neo-Classical Theory

America's pioneering large scale business and the consequent necessity for competent management led it to establish suitable training and education for those specialists. Business colleges, around 130,000 of them established by 1895,[70] were teaching skills such as book keeping, typing, clerical and secretarial work.

Professional engineering education had been provided at the U.S. Military Academy at West Point since its founding in 1802. The University of Michigan offered courses in engineering from 1854, to be followed by others. But there was no provision of management training or education, though the increasing numbers of university graduates going into business did not go unnoticed. The president of Harvard University reported that even in his year of graduation, 1853, more graduates were going into business than any other calling and that by 1900 the figure had grown to more than half. The need for Harvard to provide suitable education had become pressing. He noted that

> *"thorough mental training must give a man an advantage in any business which requires strong mental work."[71]*

However, the precise nature of that 'mental training' remained unspecified. A relevant debate had been raging in England following publication in 1854 of Newman's *'The idea of a University'*. Newman supported the idea of liberal education being a training of the mind which would fit a person for any purpose:

> *'This process of training, by which the intellect, instead of being formed or sacrificed to some particular or accidental purpose, some specific trade or profession, or study or science, is disciplined for its own sake, for the perception of its own proper object, and for its own highest culture, is called Liberal Education.'[72]*

John Locke's rejoinder quoted below in Newman's text makes the case for more specific practical training:

> *"Tis a matter of astonishment ...that men of quality and parts should suffer themselves to be so far misled by custom and implicit faith. Reason, if consulted with, would advise, that their children's time should be spent in acquiring what might be useful to them, when they come to be men, rather than that their heads should be stuffed with a deal of trash, a great part*

*whereof they usually never do ('tis certain they never need to)
think on again as long as they live; and so much of it as does
stick by them they are only the worse for.'*

This argument still surrounds the management education curriculum, part of
which is undoubtedly mental training or liberal education with the specific
management focus being secondary, and other parts which cover particular
technical aspects of the management task.

The first businesses schools at Pennsylvania, Dartmouth and Harvard
pioneered education for the new big business management, instilling them
with a sense of social obligation, typical of the accepted professions of the
day. This may well have been in reaction against the worst excesses of the
'robber barons' who had grown up with their new industries, as exploitative
of their workers as the worst kind of mill owners recorded by Engels had
ever been, no matter that some few of them later turned into major
philanthropists financing among other things, private business school
education.

The leading university academics and the industrialists who provided much
of the funding, shared a view as to the values which they thought industry
should espouse. They included a belief in scientific rationality, a politically
liberal perspective, a view of education as formative of character as well as
technical competence, and a commitment to meritocracy.

The American civil war spurred the development of science and technology
and the scientific method which was revolutionising engineering, medicine
and agriculture. In due course it was also to revolutionise management.

Professional education had been pioneered at Harvard, with its Medical
School being established as early as 1782 and its Law School in 1817 long
before those professions were themselves firmly established. The American
Medical Association (AMA) was established in 1847 and the legal
profession founded with the American Bar Association in 1878. Previously
practitioners had been trained under a system of articles or apprenticeship
with no nationally recognized standards of competence or codes of practice
and no national association or organization to act as gatekeeper to the
professions.

The AMA was established at the Academy of Natural Sciences in
Philadelphia when the AMA Committee on medical education was
appointed and standards for preliminary medical education were established
for the degree of MD and the AMA Code of Medical Ethics was published.

Article 1 of Chapter 1 of the code encapsulated some of the essence of what distinguished a profession from other callings:

> *'A Physician should not only be ever ready to obey the calls of the sick, but his mind ought also to be imbued with the greatness of his mission, and the responsibility he habitually incurs in its discharge. Those obligations are the more deep and enduring, because there is no tribunal other than his own conscience, to adjudge penalties for carelessness or neglect. Physicians should therefore, minister to the sick with due impressions of the importance of their office; reflecting that the ease, the health, and the lives of those committed to their charge, depend on their skill, attention and fidelity. The should study, also, in their deportment, so to unite* tenderness *with* firmness, *and* condescension *with* authority, *as to inspire the minds of their patients with gratitude, respect and confidence.'*

This emphasis on the ever ready willingness to provide competent and honourable service to their clients, in that case patients, totally without regard to pecuniary reward, required the professional person to be a totally different sort of human being from the 'homo economicus' assumed to inhabit all other walks of life.

The professions were becoming established at the turn of the century with the number of professional schools increasing rapidly and including dentistry, pharmacy and veterinary medicine all recognised as professions by 1910.

The distinguishing characteristics of the professions included professional knowledge and credentialed expertise with the espousal of values and codes of practice protected by a central national association acting as gate keeper.

As the American research university became more important and influential it became the natural home for the education of the professions and research university growth was accompanied by the establishment of an increasing number of professional schools which won support not only from public sources but increasingly from private donors such as the Carnegie, Stanford and Ford foundations. The conviction grew that professional managers not only could, but should, be trained in universities.

The problem for management education was firstly that it was clearly not a profession. There could be no central gate-keeper to management jobs demanding specific professional qualifications since a substantial number of successful managers might have evolved, as did many captains of industry /

robber barons / great philanthropists, from entrepreneurial or purely practical backgrounds. That being the case there could be no universally recognised management body equivalent to the American Medical Association. Nor could there be an ethical code of practice to which all recognised managers must subscribe. And there could be no universally held management ideal relating the job to its positive contribution to the greater good of society.

Anyone could become a manager with no particular knowledge, training or qualification. The eighteenth and nineteenth century industrial entrepreneurs were blazing completely new trails. There were no rules telling them what they should do. It was within them that they created something new, worthwhile and lasting from which others could benefit either directly or indirectly.

So the aims of the early business school academics and their industrial sponsors, of establishing management as a profession, were frustrated. Moreover, the question of a coherent management curriculum was not satisfactorily resolved. It was not so much a single subject in itself but a composite of fragments of professional training such as finance, accounting and law, plus other accepted academic disciplines such as applied mathematics and statistics, social psychology and, most critical of all, economics. From this assortment of subjects with the addition of new learning methods such as the case study, a management curriculum did emerge and form the core of most business school degrees.

By 1914 there were twenty five American business schools and by then they were teaching what was referred to as the science of management, which was to be distinguished both from scientific management and management science. The science of management was an approach which made use of the scientific method, was analytical, avowedly objective and where possible quantitative. The quantitative approach also informed the revised version of economic theory, the neo-classical, which became dominant in most American research universities and business schools.

The application of mathematics in neo-classical theory added a further layer of justification to that body of orthodox wisdom. Its significance was not that it changed theory in any substantive way but that it confirmed the rightness of the theory from this more 'scientific' perspective.

The application of calculus enabled theoreticians to create models of the economic world which appeared to deliver the truth with quantitative precision, defining how firm managements decided such critical issues as the prices of products and the amounts to produce. For these models to work according to their own logic, they required various assumptions to be made about markets, products and competitors. The basic assumption was that businesses sought always to maximise profits. The model considered the immediate profit effects of particular pricing and quantity of output decisions. It was not sensitive to the difference between short or long term effects of those decisions. The concept of long term profit maximisation had no operational meaning within the theoretic model.

To make such a crude and simple theoretical model operative it was necessary to assume that the market was clearly defined with its boundaries unambiguous, that all products in the market were identical, that all producers had exactly the same costs, and all producers were unable to influence the market price for products, that suppliers and buyers in a market all had total information as to products and prices, that there were no barriers to entry to and exit from the market and so on and so forth. With these assumptions in place, and feeding cost and price information into the model, the producer would, according to the theory, supply that quantity of product which would result in its marginal cost being equal to the market price. One item more or less would only result in a reduction in profit. Such was the curious nature of economic theory of the firm in a competitive market.

No assertion was made that the model reflected reality. Clearly it did not. But if it was not a model of reality what was it a model of? The instrumentalist argument, borrowed from natural science though with spurious logic in its application to the uncertain world of a social science, was raised in its defense: that the model should not be assessed as to whether it depicted reality, but by how effective it was at predicting phenomena. Many argued that it failed in this as well. What it did was offer a mathematical version of the classical theory, which might serve some academic purpose, but which if it explained anything, only appeared to explain the limitations of the theory itself. However, the instrumentalist argument was accepted by theoreticians even though it was never truly tested, or indeed was capable of being put to the test in the way that natural science models were. There was a general broad truth in the classical theory, but not a precise one.

The theory identified both competitive markets and monopolies, competitive markets operating for the common good, monopolies for the benefit of the monopolist against the common good. In a perfectly competitive market it might be proposed that one participant managed to achieve some innovative progress which either allowed a cost reduction and therefore reduction in price or a product enhancement at no additional cost. Then according to all the remaining arcane assumptions about competitive markets, that innovator would be able to sell whatever quantity they wanted. In due course they would become a more powerful supplier, able to influence or even dictate market prices and in the end such dominant supplier would, so long as there was no external constraint, achieve a monopoly position. The almost inevitable paradoxical result of an unregulated perfectly competitive market would therefore be a monopoly.

An alternative outcome might be argued on the basis that the assumptions required for a perfectly competitive market include zero barriers to entry. Therefore, through perfect information, others would see the higher profits being earned by the successful competitor and enter the market to enjoy those higher profits. The new entrants would thus drive prices down, eliminating profit, so that a new competitive equilibrium would be achieved. It was not explained how newcomers to the market would achieve the level of competitiveness which had eluded all but one of the existing competitors.

The only alternative to the monopolistic outcome of competitive markets would be that the market was controlled and regulated so as to prevent a monopoly being established, which was what became regarded as necessary in the real world, though abhorred by theoretical purists.

The general truth of neo-classical theory, for example that competition drives prices down and that usually increases demand, required no mathematical modelling. The precise truth, elaborated by calculus, was more or less spurious, not just in the obvious way, that outputs and prices were not set on the basis of marginal costs etc, but in its simplistic modelling of both competition and monopoly which betrayed little understanding of the conditions governing actual management decisions in an industrialised world.

Nevertheless this was the economic theory which was taught and learned in American research university departments and business schools and which was to have a dominant influence on the conduct of business and its relations with government through much of the twentieth century and beyond. The unreality of neo-classical theory and the curiosities it contained, referred to in the previous chapter, were to come under direct challenge with its failure to foresee, avoid and reverse the great 1930s depression.

Economics of Depression

The depression was announced by Wall Street share values almost halving during the Autumn of 1929. A 25% drop was recorded in just two days trading on 28th and 29th October. Shares had lost almost 90% of their value by July of 1932 when industrial production was at its lowest ebb and American unemployment was reaching 25%. The economy remained at this disastrously low ebb through the following summer after which it commenced a slow recovery, interrupted by a recession in 1937-9, but finally complete after America entered the second world war.

The causes of this depression have been put down to a careless expansion of the money supply through the 1920s leading to a reckless credit-driven boom that inevitably bust in the shape of the Wall St crash, the effect of which in the real economy was magnified by the initially strict contraction of the money supply by federal authorities which sparked off numerous bank failures and industrial bankruptcies.

It was not just an American affair. It was experienced through all industrialised economies, the brunt of its worst effects being experienced by industrial workers across the world. Responses to the depression led to changes of government in America with the inauguration of F D Roosevelt as President and in Britain with the collapse of the first Labour government and its replacement with a Conservative dominated coalition. The question was what should governments do to revive the economies when market forces failed to do the job.

The solution that appeared to work was a mixture of pragmatic economic action from Roosevelt apparently motivated more by a desire to achieve some social justice rather than following the promptings of any economic theory. This produced short term benefits. In the longer term such initiatives had to be given some explanation and rationale if they were to have lasting effect and this was provided by one of Marshall's students, J M Keynes, whose *'The General Theory of Employment, Interest and Money'* was published in 1936 . Keynes provided the justification and support for initiatives taken under Roosevelt's New Deal, some of which were still operative more than seven decades on.

The New Deal saw massive government investment in the economy intended both to ameliorate hardships by creating employment to stimulate economic growth and also to prevent the economy falling victim of future depression. It established a system of universal retirement pensions, unemployment insurance, and welfare benefits for poor families and the handicapped all paid for by a payroll tax.

In terms of job creation the New Deal included a public works administration set up to instigate large public projects providing mass employment; a civil works administration offering temporary jobs to millions of unemployed; a works progress administration to employ more millions across the country, mainly in rural and western mountain regions; and a civilian conservation corps created to employ young men doing unskilled work in rural areas under army supervision.

Roosevelt took particular interest in farming believing agriculture to be a litmus test for the whole economy. The Agricultural Adjustment Act raised farm prices both by cutting total farm output of major crops and livestock and also providing a system of subsidies.

On the financial front legislation was passed to insure bank deposits, the aim being to restore confidence in the banking system. The Securities and Exchange Commission was established in 1933 to establish and control stock exchange operations including for example the requirement for transparency regarding investment risk. Also the gold standard was abandoned so bullion reserves were no longer required to support the currency.

There were also several initiatives aimed at protecting the interests of labor. The National Labor Relations Board was established to supervise labor-management relations, protecting the rights and interests of trade unionists. A maximum normal working week of 40 hours and a minimum wage were established and most forms of child labor were outlawed.

Though the main aim of the New Deal was to address the short term problems of the depression, various of its components were of a permanent nature. This dichotomy between short and long term was present in the theory as well as practice.

For Keynes an economic slump was a short-run problem of a lack of demand. If the normal action of market forces did not stimulate the required increase in demand then government should be prepared to spend - investing in public works to create employment or by reducing taxes to add to spending power - in order to boost demand and to do this by running a budget deficit in the short term. When the economy recovered, as surely it would, then normal market forces would resume and the government could reduce its spending and pay off the debts accumulated during the recessionary times. Keynes proposed a balanced budget in the medium term. But not in the short run. As he famously pointed out in regard to the long term: 'In the long run we're all dead.'

Keynes' main criticism of classical theory was its *'failure to provide for full employment and its arbitrary and inequitable distribution of wealth and incomes.'*[73] In addition to improving the short term problem of unemployment the New Deal also went some considerable way to solving Keynes' long term problem of inequitable distribution of wealth and incomes.

During the twentieth century significant progress had been made, especially in Britain, *'towards the removal of very great disparities of wealth and income ... through the instrument of income tax, surtax and death duties'* and he suggested that the accumulation of capital on which an industrialized economy depended would not be restricted if those forms of taxation were increased. Classical theory held that increases in taxation would hinder the accumulation of capital whereas Keynes argued that more progressive taxation would assist the accumulation of capital since redistribution to the less well off would have the beneficial effect of increasing aggregate demand and thus economic growth.

Keynes was no revolutionary. He thought of classical economic theory as merely a special case of his general theory which applied only at times of full employment. Others would argue that Keynes' theory was but a special case of the classical model valid only in times of depression. The essential point was that, given a Marshallian sensitivity to circumstances, the two models were not wholly incompatible.

As Keynes himself pointed out:

> *'Our criticism of the accepted classical theory of economics has consisted not so much in finding logical flaws in its analysis as in pointing out that its tacit assumptions are seldom or never satisfied, with the result that it cannot solve the economic problems of the actual world. But if our central controls succeed in establishing an aggregate volume of output corresponding to full employment as nearly as is practicable, the classical theory comes into its own again from this point onwards.'*[74]

During the years up to the second world war the Keynesian focus on full employment became the new orthodoxy, justifying the New Deal initiatives. They were only partially successful, it being the second world war which finally eliminated the last vestiges of depression. Federal expenditure rose from its 1929 level of 3% of GNP to over 40% by 1944. With the American military employing around 12 million men, unemployment was ended and employers found great difficulty recruiting sufficient workers. Wages rose sharply reducing the inequitable gap between rich and poor, with food rationing and price controls ensuring a healthy diet at reasonable cost for everyone.

Keynes focus on the achievement of full employment did not make him an enthusiast for government intervention in any other circumstance than an economic slump causing unemployment. He in fact argued that

> 'the important thing for government is not to do things which individuals are doing already ... but to do those things which at present are not done at all'. [75]

The only government department he ever proposed new duties for was the British Treasury, a department which had an administrative staff, amazing though it may seem now, of just over twenty when he joined it during the first world war.[76]

Keynes' followers – he died in 1946 – developed the model further so that what became known as 'Keynesian economics' was something which the man himself would almost certainly have disowned. R F Harrod critically extended the Keynesian model from one of short term adjustment to minimise unemployment to a long run model of government intervention to achieve a self-sustaining economic growth at an acceptable level of inflation. This was the theory which dominated post war university departments and business schools and was the approach adopted whole-heartedly in Britain and briefly and with less enthusiasm in America.

In America there was some disagreement over the New Deal reforms as to whether they were intended solely to achieve short term recovery, as Keynes proposed, or whether they were aimed at permanent reforms as the Keynesian disciples would have intended. In the event, after the war, America chose to reassert its rugged individualist commitment to private enterprise by reversing most of the New Deal reforms with the Taft-Hartley Act of 1947. In Britain the Keynesians were joined by a genuinely democratic socialist government establishing a truly mixed economy, which was a substantial step beyond anything Keynes himself would have supported. Thus America and Britain provided substantially different industrial contexts for post war management.

6. DIVISION OF MANAGEMENT LABOUR

A sociological approach to understanding the role of management might be to view it, without prior conception, as a class of individuals. They have no democratically won authority, being merely appointees. Yet within their own organisation they appear to have more or less absolute power. Their authority is not legitimated by any obvious means. They are not in post as a result of the application of rational-legal rules and procedures. Nor are they for the most part appointed as a result of an agreed hereditary succession or any other traditional process, and the legitimacy of those that are is dubious. Their authority appears to lack any moral justification, yet they exercise moral discretion over all manner of significant decisions affecting not only those employed in their company but on a much wider front, for example including their suppliers, customers, local community and the world at large. They decide, on whatever grounds they choose, how the surplus their company generates will be distributed. They are all powerful but with no apparently valid claims to legitimacy.

Such an analysis might raise interesting questions about management. But industrial management itself has not been much concerned with making claims for its own legitimacy. Management was drawn into existence by sheer necessity. The most obvious fact about management was that it cost money. While it did not itself make anything, or sell anything, it nevertheless had to be paid a salary and provided with a space in which to work. Such additional cost, without apparent profit, would not be attractive to *'the butcher, the brewer or the baker'* and would not have been incurred if it could have been avoided. But it could not. And the surprising thing was that management, once it was established, proved to be the most effective contributor to productivity, profitability and growth in what has been referred to as 'the management revolution'.

Management matters but its precise nature often remains obscure. Academic theorists have generally shrunk from any detailed explanation. Smith seemed to think in a company run by hired managers as opposed to owners, the managers should spend their time looking after 'other people's money' with 'anxious vigilance'

Marx, writing ninety years after Smith, thought of managers as the equivalent of an army's officers, responsible for the 'direct and constant supervision' of 'foremen and overlookers'. He may have been right in the sense that they were responsible for the 'esprit de corps' of the organisation, to use Fayol's terminology. However, the army officer analogy captures only the people management part of the role. The aims and tasks of an army are determined for it, war being 'simply the continuation of policy by other means.'[77] The officer ranks are not therefore engaged with formulating policy, whereas managers of an industrial company are responsible for every aspect, strategic and operational, of their autonomous competing organisation.

Business historian Chandler referred to managers as *'administrative coordinators'* which might mean whatever is wanted for it to mean, without shedding much light on what they actually did. Management practitioners themselves have not generally been very good at explaining their role. Most have focused on prescriptions for what they believe in any circumstance will be most effective, but without offering much descriptive analysis of management practice.

More thoughtful practitioners, such as Alfred Sloan, Geoffrey Vickers, Chester Barnard, Wilfred Brown and a small number of others have provided invaluable insights into aspects of the management process, but their main aim has not been descriptive.

Clearly the management task is not simply that of the bureaucrat, operating according to a prepared set of rules which cover all known eventualities, as might have been the case, for example, in a government department. Their responsibility was, and is, to deal with variety and the unexpected, and ultimately to create variety and innovation.

Perhaps Galbraith was right when he claimed that what he referred to disparagingly as 'businessmen' found it difficult to explain what they actually did. Mintzberg's PhD study of managerial work was more enlightening about the allocation of management time to different types of work rather than describing the work itself But it is important to know what management work is and to distinguish between the version of management appropriate for 'the baker, the brewer or the butcher', and the management that developed as large scale business grew up in America.

Adam Smith suggested that every form of labour, so widely defined as to include even philosophers, would be subject to specialisation. The labour of management was certainly no exception. Chandler indicated some of the management specialisations achieved by the American railroad companies. As businesses grew in scale it was imperative for the management process to be so divided.

The process came to full fruition in the big manufacturing businesses of late nineteenth century such as United States Steel Corporation which was not just a steel producer but also manufactured a wide variety of steel end-products. The division of management labour was repeated in every kind of business organisation. And it continues to be repeated today as every successful start-up business progresses towards robust viability. Its aim is for ever increasing efficiency and effectiveness.

The division of management must have started, as it still starts today, when the successful founding entrepreneur, the sole proprietor of the business, found that he or she was no longer able to do everything themselves. Some portion of their workload had to be delegated to another if the business was to survive and grow. That first division of responsibility carried certain unavoidable consequences with it. It was, and is, a big decision.

Firstly, it immediately increased the cost base of the business and necessitated a significant increment in profit if the business was to remain viable. Secondly, the owner manager would be concerned to ensure that the first appointment would not adversely affect the way business was conducted. The established focus on, for example, standards of service and customer relations must not be compromised. And as the business continued to grow and further new appointments were made, it would be important to maintain the internal climate and culture of the organisation so as to preserve and develop its reputation with customers, suppliers and others, critically including potential employees.

Manufacturing, even pin making, remains a useful device for considering the division of management labour as it includes the production process as well as selling and administration. Typically responsibilities for internal operations and those for marketing and sales are the first to be separated, while in the early stages at least responsibility for finance is likely to be held by an external professional on a consultative or part time basis. At the same time a back office administrative role has to be established keeping track of orders being processed as well as basic book-keeping and preparation of accounts. This is the basic division of management discussed in the following sections which occurred when management first emerged and which is still, in broad principle, repeated today.

The division of management labour demonstrates the possibility that management without ownership can be professionally focused on avoiding 'negligence and profusion' and that 'anxious vigilance' would be an inadequate substitute for professional expertise in any business which has grown more complex than *the baker, the brewer or the butcher'*.

The division of management is a variable but continuing process. The division that was appropriate in the eighteenth century was not apt to later times. What was appropriate in textiles may not have been in automobiles or internet firms. Furthermore with each increment in growth the management of a business is forced to consider the possibility of further division, the potential for application of more detailed expertise or newer technology, or simply the division of existing processes among a greater number of hands.

There is no universal truth about the division of management labour. The following is an approximation intended to give some little flavour of the potential complexity and sophistication of management specialisms which goes beyond the simplifications offered by economic models.

Operations Management
The manufacturing process can be accomplished in various ways. Some organisational decisions will depend on whether the items being manufactured are standard products sold on a continuous basis through normal distribution chains, or are items designed and made specifically to the specifications of an individual customer and manufactured and despatched to them in one or more discrete batches. Perhaps the most interesting manufacturing organisation would combine both continuous and batch production. That combination has clear implications for all aspects of manufacture from the receipt and acceptance of raw materials, their storage and control, issue to the manufacturing unit, shop floor operations, production control, the management of quality throughout the whole process and final despatch of finished product.

There is no need here to review any of these different jobs in detail but a summary might indicate the nature of management responsibility. The business process is a continuous cycle but for the present purpose it can be assumed that it commences with the receipt of a purchase order from a customer. Clearly the order has resulted from some prior process which for the moment can be disregarded. The order will require the acquisition of materials necessary for its completion, so the real work starts with the purchase of those materials.

Procurement is one of the critical management support functions. The purchase decision depends on a mix of criteria including price, quality, delivery performance and reliability in all these categories. Moreover, the purchase decision is not simply a one off, but part of a continuing series of such decisions which may be taken on a purely open market basis, or a longer term agreement may be reached whereby both supplier and buyer accept a degree of interdependence in which the supplier is given a contract which excludes other suppliers in return for reliable deliveries which enables the purchaser to minimise their holdings of material stocks. The aim of purchasing management is to minimise the long term costs which arise not only from the prices paid and stock levels needing to be carried but also the reliability of continuous supply and the quality of materials.

When the relevant materials are delivered and their quality assessed and approved they will be accepted into store. Materials control is a basic management responsibility the aim of which is to ensure that sufficient materials are always available so that the factory is never held up for their lack, but on the other hand that there is no more money tied up in stocks than is necessary to assure the sufficiency. Clearly the treatment of materials for standard products in continuous manufacture and for products ordered and made in discrete batches is quite different. For standard products materials will be ordered and received on a regular basis, the most economic order quantities being agreed with suppliers. It may be that each delivery of such items would comprise a four week supply, with deliveries being made four weekly and a safety stock amounting to, say, two weeks supply, being permanently held in store. The safety stock being held to cover for any interruptions to supply so as to ensure the factory is never stopped awaiting supplies. Such a traditional system of materials control, is little different from the modern just-in-time system which operates with more frequent deliveries and without safety stocks.

This summary account of purchasing and materials control is intended only to indicate that there are techniques and procedures which are important to the effectiveness of the company's operations, for which management is responsible and which have no relevance to, or relationship with, matters of the company's ownership. The middle managers carrying these responsibilities are employed to work for the company's good and their performance in that is typically open to regular review.

Similar disciplines apply to the rather more complex processes of production scheduling and control, whose responsibility is to advise the customer of a date for delivery of the finished product and to issue the materials and making instructions onto the shop floor at the appropriate time and to monitor progress through its various work stations to completion. Production scheduling aims not only to satisfy customer delivery requirements but also to minimise the amount of work in progress on the shop-floor and consequently the amount of money tied up, at the same time ensuring there is sufficient work available so that no work station runs out of work and is kept waiting. A key part of the production control function is the maintenance of information as to the stage of the process achieved for all customer orders.

Quality management works hand in glove with the above control systems, in the early days presiding over systems of inspection which were not infrequently in conflict with production management over the required standard of quality to be achieved. Such issues were often heightened by the methods of payment of production workers who may not have been paid for substandard work. The American quality gurus responsible for radically improving quality standards in post second world war Japan, Deming and Juran, changed the practice of quality management. Quality standards were defined precisely in terms of conformance to customer requirements, statistical process control techniques were applied to ensure that variations from those standards were identified before production went out of tolerance limits, and methods were adopted which aimed to build quality into products rather than inspecting it out, as was previously the practice with final inspection systems. Quality standards could be achieved at very little if any cost by eliminating scrap and the necessity for reworking. But as with the other areas of operations management there was a balance to be struck: achieving the customer's requirements could be done efficiently but aiming to achieve quality standards in excess of what the customer required, or was prepared to pay for, may simply have been wasteful.

Although the above account is much oversimplified, it nevertheless indicates that Smith's suspicion of hired managers, on the grounds that they can't be trusted to be vigilant since they are looking after other people's money, is simply misplaced. It is not to deny that his basic contention, especially around a baker's or butcher's shop, might not have some truth, but that it is simply not relevant to the operations of a larger company.

It might be asked how the above account of operations management lines up with economic theory, for example, that quantities of output are set at the level where marginal cost is equal to market price in order to maximise profit. Economic theory does not appear to contribute anything of worth. Perhaps it will be better to review the other components of management labour before considering the relevance of economic theory.

Marketing Management

Whilst the functional expertise in marketing is quite different from that of operations the management concerns to achieve efficiency and effectiveness, avoiding waste and achieving an ever improved competitive position, is just the same. Most businesses start with a product or service for which there appears to be some customer demand and they are initially oriented around that product and the definition of its particular characteristics. As businesses progress they develop their focus more into the processes of production as previously described with the aim of reducing costs and improving quality.

In terms of the division of management labour it is then often the sales responsibility which is the specialism that is first identified and the business becomes sales oriented. But it is quickly recognised that responsibility for sales is not simply a matter of selling, but of marketing. As Levitt pointed out

> The difference between marketing and selling is more than semantic. Selling focuses on the needs of the seller, marketing on the needs of the buyer. Selling is preoccupied with the seller's need to convert the product into cash, marketing with the idea of satisfying the needs of the customer by means of the product and the whole cluster of things associated with creating, delivering, and, finally, consuming it.[78]

The American Marketing Association (AMA) defines marketing as

> 'the activity, set of institutions, and processes for creating, communicating, delivering, and exchanging offerings that have value for customers, clients, partners, and society at large,'[79]

a definition approved by the AMA's board of directors in October 2007 and which bears the certain hallmarks of definition by committee. Kotler more helpfully defined it as *'the science and art of finding, keeping and growing profitable customers.'*[80]

a definition that is so general as to be a little short on specific meaning. Levitt suggested that a business

'must learn to think of itself not in terms of producing goods and services but as <u>buying customers</u>, as doing the things that will make people <u>want</u> to do business with it.'[81] (original emphasis underlined)

Drucker suggested the job of business was to create a customer.

The tools at marketing management's disposal are firstly marketing research which involves whatever techniques and methods are required to identify details of existing and potential customers and markets and technologies. Such research is conducted partly on an ongoing basis so that the company is aware of critical changes, if possible before they occur and at least as and when they occur; and partly on a one off basis when specific researches are designed and executed to find answers to particular questions which may be critical to the further development of the business.

Other mechanisms for which marketing management are generally held responsible, referred to as the marketing mix, are product, price, promotion (of which selling is one element) and distribution, sometimes referred to as placement, or place, in order to comprise '4 Ps'. Each of these variables is controlled by management and none of them are as straightforward as they might first appear.

The concept of the product (or service) is multi-dimensional. It comprises a core benefit or service for which the customer has a need or want. It has a physical existence which is manifest in its price and quality, its performance, specification, design, reliability and longevity. Beyond that there is the question of the service that is involved with the product, such things as its warranty, delivery, after sales service and promotional support. And even beyond that there are psychological characteristics such as the product image and brand and corporate images which are perceived by existing and potential customers.[82] Product analysis goes beyond this level of detail. For example, Garvin has suggested that quality be defined by such additional characteristics as conformance, durability, serviceability, aesthetics and perceived quality[83].

Marketing management's responsibility is to ensure that the product which is delivered, defined in terms of its various attributes as above, is the product which the customers need and want and believe they are getting when they purchase. Moreover it is marketing's responsibility to ensure they understand which attributes are most important to the customer and to ensure that the company does not incur cost delivering levels of attribute the customer does not need or want.

Price is one important attribute of the product and it is interesting to compare how marketers are taught to treat pricing with how economic theory suggests prices should be set. Many different approaches to the pricing decision have been proposed by marketers[84]: premium, penetration, economy, price skimming, psychological pricing, product line pricing, optional pricing, captive product pricing, product bundle pricing, promotional pricing, geographical pricing and value pricing. To this list might be added simple cost plus pricing or even marginal cost pricing. Whatever approach is adopted, the pricing element is clearly only one of many product attributes which need to be complementary rather than contradictory if the product is to present itself as a coherent whole.

Promotion can involve any or all of advertising, internet promotion, personal selling, sales promotion, public relations, direct mail. trade fairs and exhibitions. sponsorship. The management decisions on promotion involve selecting the methods and media to be used based on their efficiency and effectiveness and critically including their compatibility with the other product attributes and existing and potential customer and market characteristics.

Finally, among the marketing mix is distribution, a management decision which is easy to overlook since the most appropriate distribution channels might appear obvious. Distribution could be direct, such as via mail order, internet or telephone sales. Or it could be through an agent who sells on behalf of the producer, or via a wholesaler who sells to retailers, or it could be direct to the retailer who sells to end customers. Innovative distribution decisions could be critical to the success of a particular business.

As with all management decisions those on the marketing mix have to be planned and executed and their effectiveness monitored and adjustments to the original decisions considered. These issues may appear more remote from the business of processing customers' orders than is operations management. But their effectiveness and efficiency are clearly crucial to the company's survival and prosperity. The degree to which the company has absorbed the marketing philosophy is widely seen as a mark of its stage of development.

Economic theory is largely silent regarding any of this. It simply does not engage with the concept of marketing management. It is concerned with what it refers to as commodities whereas marketing is concerned with differentiated products, identifying their uniqueness to differentiate them further from competing products in ways which customers find appealing. Economic theory is concerned with market prices whereas marketing management is concerned to differentiate their product by all means including price in order that it is perceived as more desirable than competing products. Economic theory suggests that corporate ownership is essential to those in control if they are to be *'vigilant'* but ownership is utterly irrelevant to professional marketing management. It is competition, rather than ownership which drives management to efficiency and effectiveness.

Financial Management

The third primary division in the work of management is the finance responsibility. While often headed up by a professionally qualified accountant, it is a management responsibility. Accounting is a distinct sub-division of financial management.

Accounting is concerned with recording management stewardship over past periods and is a tool of management control. It involves the accurate recording of all monetary transactions and the preparation, at the end of each accounting period, of reporting schedules such as the balance sheet, the profit and loss account and cash flow statement. As well as these formal documents, accounting is also concerned with recording and preparing management accounts such as budgets, actual results and reports of variations between the two and the likely import of such variance. Accounting is intended to assist in the effective and efficient internal control of day to day business.

Financial management is a more strategic responsibility, ensuring the business has adequate funding to survive and prosper though not more than is required, that it makes effective and full use of its assets and does not retain underutilised assets and that it invests effectively in its future development.

The planning of adequate funding requires detailed knowledge and understanding of the funds, actual and potential, generated and consumed by business operations and the funds required for the planned business future. This requires an ability to control short term cash conservation and generation from the business, so that sufficient cash is available to fund credit sales, employee wages and any other short term needs such as tax payments. Nothing is quite so strategic as running out of cash. Management is concerned first and foremost with avoiding waste and financial management is responsible for waste incurred by lax control of working capital, by payment of more taxation and dividends than is necessary.

Financial management involves responsibility for generating funds from external sources, usually including shareholders, purchasers of loan stock and banks who might provide short and medium term loans. The mix of such sources of finance is critical to the future viability of the business. While bank loans may be satisfactory for the short and medium term liquidity requirements of the business, its long term structure depends on the mix of shareholders' funding which is rewarded by dividends and the possibility of capital growth as the share price rises, and the long term debt component which is rewarded by interest payments.

Dividends are paid out of profits on which taxation has been paid, whereas interest is treated as a business cost prior to payment of tax. Consequently interest bearing loan stock is generally a substantially less costly form of externally funded capital. Financial management therefore has a fine judgement to make regarding the mix of shares and loan stock it issues to generate funds. If the proportion of debt is too low the company will be paying more for its funding than is necessary. If the proportion of debt is too high the company may be perceived as too risky and the share price will be damaged, thus raising the cost of future increments in external funding. Minimising the cost of the company's capital, (calculating it as the average cost of its different sources, weighted by their proportions in the total capital mix) reduces the return the company has to make on future investments if they are to be profitable. Thus the lower the weighted average cost of a company's capital the more the investment it can afford to make in its future.

Associated with these decisions regarding the capital structure of the business are the more routine decisions as to the level of dividend payments. Dividends impact on the stock market performance of the company's shares, but it is only one such influence. The company's shares, being traded in the freely competitive stock market may be regarded as a product competing with other 'products', and dividends are just one of the product's attributes. Financial management has responsibility for marketing the shares on the market and should use the marketing tools available to it, not simply relying on the one tool, dividends.

Financial management's task is not to maximise the share price on the stock market but to ensure it performs sufficiently to ensure the company's autonomous survival. Distributing more dividends than necessary to achieve this would be just as wasteful as giving the customer levels of quality, or any other characteristic, for which they are not prepared to pay.

This requires the general stock market to be aware of the company's true position and to have that reflected in the current share price as accurately as possible. Given that the market itself is given to 'bull' and 'bear' runs the accuracy is fairly limited, but this only makes it more important that the share price and the company's underlying value do not get too disconnected. If they do the company's autonomy will be threatened because such misleading valuations will almost certainly become apparent at some point.

Financial management is also responsible for ensuring that investment decisions are taken on the basis of rational financial grounds. Non-financial criteria, for example related to the appropriateness of the strategic direction of the investment, may be critical, but properly conducted financial assessment is also necessary to try to ensure the future viability of new investment. These may include the setting of an appropriate interest rate which new investments might be required to exceed if they were to proceed, the hurdle rate being set by reference to the weighted average cost of the company's capital.

This brief summary of aspects of the financial management responsibility is sufficient for the present purpose. Clearly the many and various financial decisions would normally be taken guided solely by the best interests of the company. That is no different from all other management decisions such as those in operations and marketing already considered. However, were financial management to be persuaded that their responsibility was to act solely in the best interests of shareholders, capital structuring and the distribution of dividends might be decided quite differently, subordinating the long term interests off the company to the short term interests of shareholders.

Technical Management

The three primary divisions of management labour appear to be generally applicable in any industrial activity. But the industry specific technical management responsibility is likely to be just as important as the others and may in some circumstances be paramount. Technical management has always been an important management responsibility, right from the beginning of industrialisation. The famous names associated with the first canal, road and rail systems were the engineers such as Brindley, Macadam, Stephenson and Watt. The same is true of manufacturing industries of the initial industrialisation: Arkwright, Crompton, Darby, Kay, Hargreaves and others are all known for their industry specific technological contributions.

The distinction between the technologists and the mere 'businessmen' was made by Thorstein Veblen.[85] He contrasted the engineers and scientists, 'professionals of great skill and productive potential' with the 'profit oriented businessmen'[86]. This appreciation of the technical role, which economists make no attempt to model, adds to the denigration of the 'businessman' which economists from Smith on have claimed to account for. But the 'businessman', synonymous with the capitalist Mr Moneybags, is not management, while the professional technical role is part of management.

Technical management requires knowledge and expertise, relevant to the specific industry, which is normally obtained through graduate education in the particular science or technology. It requires continuous updating as technology advances so that the company's use of technology remains competitive and it oversees the research and development activity which aims to take the company ahead of competition in terms of its use of technology.

The vast majority of inventions and innovations emanate from research and development groups operating within large scale business organisations. The commonplace assertion that big businesses cannot be innovative is patently untrue. But the organisational characteristics which permit organisations to be efficient in their day to day operations can tend to frustrate and inhibit the effective operation of research and development. Protecting the ability to be creative within a large and potentially bureaucratic organisation is one of the responsibilities of technical management.

There has always been some disagreement as to the role of technical management in the initiation of innovations. Marketers can argue that their role is prime, there being no point in producing an innovative new product for which there is no market. The opposing argument holds that constraining research and development to projects approved by marketing effectively rules out the possibility for fundamental step-change innovations for which there is no existing sale and no market experience. The truth is that either markets or technology can initiate innovations, but successful developments will need to satisfy the requirements of both.

The industry specific nature of technical management means that further generalisation on the division of its labour would be problematic, save to note that it may be the most important managerial role in some industrial situations.

The Management Mindset

The division of management labour may continue indefinitely as organisations grow. Mintzberg was quoted as saying he could offer an account of problems an organisation had experienced by reference to the titles of head office departments, many having been created to solve specific issues. The tendency to create bureaucracy as organisations grow and mature is well understood and appropriate counter measures have been prescribed.[87] Some functions, which might be thought of as management, actually are the providers of administrative support rather than being themselves management responsibilities. For example, the personnel or human resource management function was traditionally a line management role with the staff function providing administrative support on such matters as pay and occasionally being asked to provide arbitration when line management and workers were in dispute. The role gained importance in situations where industrial relations were contentious, but among many others Drucker was doubtful whether there should be such a function operating continuously as intermediary between line managers and workers. Such a function might only be indicative of the organisation's personnel problems, and its existence dependent on continuation of those problems.

No matter how management labour is divided there are consistencies of approach amounting ultimately to a management mindset which drives decisions in all such specialist areas. Adam Smith's assertion that it was from the producer's self interest that 'we' - Smith makes it clear he was referring to 'we' as customers - benefit, rather than their 'humanity'. The customers' benefit arises from the fact that producers compete with each other to offer customers a better deal. The cause of this is clearly not because of ownership but competition. The need to avoid losses, or to survive in the face of competition, is what drives management, not the narrow self interest of ownership.

Smith erroneously denied the possibility of business improvement by management without ownership, but management without ownership has achieved massive improvement. Chandler referred to it as 'the managerial revolution in American business; Drucker referred to it as the 'productivity revolution' which had more dramatic impacts on the general population than did the first industrial revolution. The division of management labour demonstrated the means by which this was achieved. It is a technical, professional process rather than simply being based on the subsequently ubiquitous 'greed is good' caricature of Smith's approach.

Management labour may start as described previously or it may take a different route depending on the nature of the business and possibly the personal inclinations of its founding entrepreneur. It does not necessarily imply any particular organisational structure. Perhaps the only generalisation that can be made is that while the business is successful and continues to grow so the division of management labour will also proceed.

Operations management may spawn an industrial engineering function whose job it is to continually improve production methods, ensuring the company maintains its position in available technology. Technical management may set up a separate R&D unit to initiate the development of new products or whole new technologies, such department being quite separate from the main business so that different cultural rules might apply to this essentially creative unit. Marketing may initiate a separate research department devoted to identifying new markets or new applications or new customer wants or needs. Finance may establish a separate treasury function whose job it is to ensure that any short term cash balances the company might accrue are deployed in the most lucrative ways commensurate with their ready accessibility. They may also develop specialist tax expertise whose job it is to ensure the company does not miss any opportunities to reduce its tax payments. Similarly, support systems accounting may establish a specialist credit control function to ensure invoices are paid on time,

The division of management labour is continuous while ever the business grows, and it can contribute substantially to its success.

The management responsibility is for the survival and future prosperity of the organisation and as it grows to find ever better ways of dividing that work so as improve the methods of manufacture (ie to reduce costs, improve yields or improve quality of production), or to improve the products (ie by either lowering their cost, improving their quality or adding more features).

Eliminating waste is invariably the first and simplest way of improving the way things are done. This applies to all the various functional areas of management which have been briefly reviewed in this chapter. The preoccupation is, as Drucker emphasises, with avoiding losses, ie survival, rather than maximising profit:

> *'Nothing shows more clearly how deeply we are still entrapped in pre-industrial thinking than our pre-occupation with "profit". The central fact of industrial economics is not "profit" but "loss" – not the expectation of ending up with a surplus, its justification, and the legitimacy of the claims to a share in it; but the inevitable and real risk of ending up with an impoverishing deficit, and the need, the absolute need, to avoid this loss by providing against the risks.'* [88]

Thus management is a continuously innovative process of improvement, introducing the new, eliminating waste, reducing costs, improving quality, and giving the customer a better deal than competitors. This is the management mindset which drives management across all its responsibilities in operations, marketing, finance and technical management, focusing on ever better use of resources so as to ensure the company's survival and its ability to win in its chosen markets.

The complaint that commercial management seeks to avoid paying, for example, more tax than is absolutely necessary is based on a misunderstanding of the management project. Of course it will seek to minimise its tax payments, just as it does any other expense. It is up to government to set the tax rules without ambiguity. It is not up to management to pay additional unnecessary tax motivated by generosity or patriotism.

It is a paradox of classical economic theory that while it claims to be an objective study, it is based on the concept of the amoral, self-interested individual seeking only to maximise his own utility. Smith knew nothing of large scale industry and its management. His models were the butcher, the brewer, the baker and the pin making workshop. For all his insights, these were the foundation of his theory, which held that hired managers could not be expected to work in the long term interests of the company they managed, but only in their own rather shorter term self-interest. Like much economic theory it may have been appropriate in its own time, but its relevance was not permanent.

7. THEORIES OF MANAGEMENT

The practice of management had been established for the best part of a century before theoretical approaches were developed which might offer guidance to practitioners and short circuit their learning how to make their labour more effective. The first systematic general management text was Henri Fayol's *Administration Industrielle et Générale* which was based on his experience working for a French coal mining company. It was published in French in 1916 and translated into English in 1949 by which time Taylor's 'scientific management' and much of the subsequent 'human relations' work had already been completed. But whereas they focused primarily on the employer – employee relationship, Fayol's aim was more general.

He provided an approach to the structuring of organisations with certain detached guidance on worker relations which he intended should be applicable in all organisational settings as indicated in his preface:

> *'Management plays a very important part in the government of undertakings, large or small, industrial, commercial, political, religious or any other.'* [89]

Concurrent with Fayol's mining management experience, management education and training was being established in America. The first business school, the Wharton School was named after its entrepreneur founder, Joseph Wharton, who had achieved his considerable wealth through the American Nickel Company and Bethlehem Steel Corporation, which coincidentally was home to Taylor's study of the science of handling pig iron. Wharton School was established in 1881 at the University of Pennsylvania with the avowed aim of establishing management as a profession, Wharton's vision being that the school would produce graduates who would become *'pillars of the state, whether in private or in public life.'* [90]

Successive theoretical approaches focused to a considerable extent on how to motivate people at work. The concept of motivation may now be seen as problematic: is the word motivate a euphemism for manipulate, or even exploit?

Is it more the intent to deal with people simply so as to maximise profit? Or is it to make working life more congenial and help people develop themselves further? And if the latter – naïve thought though that may be regarded by some – is it in order to increase the productivity of a healthy, happy work force or is it for the benefit of the workforce with no thought to extract any advantage from them?

In the case of Arkwright it may have been to create a contented workforce with which to combat the Luddite machine breakers as well as to increase productivity. In the case of Owen it was his social idealism, demonstrated repeatedly in his subsequent career, which drove the process of improving the worker's lot, albeit for a profit. Marx included Owen among those he labelled 'utopian idealists', implying they were well intentioned but ineffective. The purposes of management aside, later managers provided a more satisfactory working environment simultaneously with a sufficient return to the employer.

The employer – employee relationship was always an important part of management's responsibility. The potential for the strong employer to exploit the weak worker was apparent from the start of industrialisation. Marx's reference to the 'negotiation' between the labourer and 'Mr Moneybags', after which the latter was 'smirking' his satisfaction at the outcome, did not include any report on the actual negotiation, the act of stealing the surplus earned by the worker. Fred Taylor had no such qualms.

Scientific Management

The application of 'science' to management was timely as it coincided with the blossoming of various branches of natural science and scientific discovery and it was attractive since it appeared to depersonalise the potentially explosive employer – employee relationship. Taylor, the devoted Quaker, was focused on how to bring management and labour together in productive partnership from which both should gain. Taylorism, or scientific management, was concerned first and foremost with business could survive, rather than with how to divide the spoils of industry.

> *"Resolving the power struggle was the end to which efficiency was the means not the other way round."*

The following is Taylor's own account of the scientific management process, including his famous 'negotiation' with Schmidt, as told to a House of Representatives Special Committee investigating his methods. It was subsequently included in 'Scientific Management' published in 1910.

"Our first step was to find the proper workman to begin with. We therefore carefully watched and studied these 75 men for three or four days, at the end of

*which time we had picked out four men who appeared to be physically able to
handle pig iron at the rate of 47 tons [as opposed to the customary 12½ tons] per
day. A careful study was then made of each of these men. We looked up their
history as far back as practicable and thorough inquiries were made as to the
character, habits, and the ambition of each of them. Finally we selected one from
among the four as the most likely man to start with. He was a little Pennsylvania
Dutchman who had been observed to trot back home for a mile or so after his work
in the evening about as fresh as he was when he came trotting down to work in the
morning. We found that upon wages of $1.15 a day he had succeeded in buying a
small plot of ground, and that he was engaged in putting up the walls of a little
house for himself in the morning before starting to work and at night after leaving.
He also had the reputation of being exceedingly "close," that is, of placing a very
high value on a dollar. As one man whom we talked to about him said, "A penny
looks about the size of a cart-wheel to him." This man we will call Schmidt.
The task before us, then, narrowed itself down to getting Schmidt to handle 47 tons
of pig iron per day and making him glad to do it. This was done as follows.
Schmidt was called out from among the gang of pig-iron handlers and talked to
somewhat in this way:*

"Schmidt, are you a high-priced man?"

"Vell, I don't know vat you mean."

*"Oh yes, you do. What I want to know is whether you are a high-priced man
or not."*

"Vell, I don't know vat you mean."

*"Oh, come now, you answer my questions. What I want to find out is whether
you are a high-priced man or one of these cheap fellows here. What I want
to find out is whether you want to earn $1.85 a day or whether you are
satisfied with $1.15, just the same as all those cheap fellows are getting."*

*"Did I vant $1.85 a day? Vas dot a high-priced man? Vell, yes, I vas a high-
priced man."*

*"Oh, you're aggravating me. Of course you want $1.85 a day-every one
wants it! You know perfectly well that that has very little to do with your
being a high-priced man. For goodness' sake answer my questions, and
don't waste any more of my time. Now come over here. You see that pile of
pig iron?"*

"Yes."

"You see that car?"

"Yes."

"Well, if you are a high-priced man, you will load that pig iron on that car to-morrow for $1.85. Now do wake up and answer my question. Tell me whether you are a -high-priced man or not."

"Vell-did I got $1.85 for loading dot pig iron on dot car to-morrow?"

"Yes, of course you do, and you get $1.85 for loading a pile like that every day right through the year. That is what a high-priced man does, and you know it just as well as I do."

"Vell, dot's all right. I could load dot pig iron on the car to-morrow for $1.85, and I get it every day, don't I?"

"Certainly you do-certainly you do."

" Vell, den, I vas a high-priced man."

"Now, hold on, hold on. You know just as well as I do that a high-priced man has to do exactly as he's told from morning till night. You have seen this man here before, haven't you?"

"No, I never saw him."

"Well, if you are a high-priced man, you will do exactly as this man tells you to-morrow, from morning till night. When he tells you to pick up a pig and walk, you pick it up and you walk, and when he tells you to sit down and rest, You do that right straight through the day. And what's more, no back talk. Now a high-priced man does just what he's told to do, and no back talk. Do you understand that? When this man tells you to walk, you walk; when he tells you to sit down, you sit down, and you don't talk back at him. Now you come on to work here to-morrow morning And I'll know before night whether you are really a high-priced man or not."

... Schmidt started to work, and all day long, and at regular intervals, was told by the man who stood over him with a watch, "Now pick up a pig and walk. Now sit down and rest. Now walk-now rest," etc. He worked when he was told to work, and rested when he was told to rest, and at half-past five in the afternoon had his 47 tons loaded on the car. And he practically never failed to work at this pace and do the task that was set him during the three years that the writer was at Bethlehem. And throughout this time he averaged a little more than $1.85 per day, whereas before he had never received over $1.15 per day, which was the ruling rate of wages at that time in Bethlehem. That is, he received 60 percent higher wages than were paid to other men who were not working on task work. One man after another was picked out and trained to handle pig iron at the rate of 47 tons per

day until all of the pig iron was handled at this rate, and the men were receiving 60 percent more wages than other workmen around them.

... The writer trusts, however, that before leaving this illustration the reader will be thoroughly convinced that there is a science of handling pig iron, and further that this science amounts to so much that the man who is suited to handle pig iron cannot possibly understand it, nor even work in accordance with the laws of this science, without the help of those who are over him." [91]

Taylor's treatment of Schmidt was delivered in a world which no longer exists, but the simple outcome was that Schmidt, by following the prescribed methods of working, achieved a 276% increase in output and a 60% increase in his wage. It may be difficult, a hundred years later, to interpret the 'negotiation' and assess its fairness. A contemporary trade unionist, George Preston, General Secretary and Treasurer of the International Association of Machinists expressed his view as follows:

'As one who has devoted the best years of his life to the labour movement I was pleased to have the opportunity of reading in the March issue American the article by F W Taylor, the founder of "Scientific Management".

Any theory of elimination of waste of resources, supplies of labour, from the standpoint of the business world – yes, from the standpoint of society as a whole – is not only worthy of consideration, but should receive the support of all right minded men, irrespective of the class to which they belong. There should be no difference of opinion between us as to the advisability of increasing the output for a given amount of labour especially when that increase is the result of new machinery or of the institution of new methods. It is only by increased efficiency in production that we, the Trade Unionists, can hope to reduce our hours of labour and thereby gain for ourselves a reasonable amount of leisure which is so necessary for our mental, physical and moral wellbeing. ....

*The foregoing systems are beautiful in theory but have been found by those employed under them to be oppressive and often impractical. These so called efficiency systems are not introduced for the purpose of distributing larger earnings among the employees but to more successfully exploit them.
..*

Take his pig iron illustration where one man "who merely happened to be of the type of an ox" and Mr Taylor assures us seriously that "he was no rare specimen" – had by his system been able to move forty-seven tons of pig iron in the same time formerly required to move twelve and one-half tons. Not by the old "rule of thumb method". "Oh no. Such men "of the type of an ox" "are not sufficiently intelligent to properly grasp even the necessity of their obtaining high wages". Therefore it was necessary to have a high priced college student "to train him" or what would be more to the point to watch him work and keep him at it. ....

The more we reflect, the more we are amazed at the possibilities of "Scientific Management". What grand opportunities for employing whole ship loads of "Schmidts" and then consider the avenues of advancement that are opened up for college students. ....

The fact is the system does not count for so much as does judicious management. The highest efficiency can only be reached and made permanent where a fair average day's work has been ascertained under improved methods and a reasonable compensation is given to the employees in recognition of merit so that individual incentive may be stimulated and a true spirit of co-operation between employer and employee may be preserved and fostered, the employee receiving his just compensation and the employer his maximum output and in addition such suggestions from time to time from the employee as will tend to lessen the labour cost in the reproduction of the goods manufactured.' [92]

The 'science' of pig iron handling, and of shovelling, studied by Taylor as well as Frank Gilbreth's later study of the 'science' of bricklaying produced massive improvements in productivity and their system of studying work and work methods was applied to all kinds of manual work and later to clerical work also, as well as feeding into such matters as the layout of factories and the design of mass production lines etc. The aim was to improve both the efficiency and the effectiveness of work by eliminating unnecessary actions and activities, improving methods and building in suitable relaxation breaks and to share the resulting benefit between employer and employee and so remove the distrust between workers and management which had resulted in 'soldiering' or slow working and restricting output intended by the workers to safeguard jobs. Scientific management became a major influence on the management process for decades, in effect raising the factory system to new heights of efficiency, but paying less regard to its dehumanising effects on workers.

The Ford mass production line is the most often cited exemplar of scientific management. Henry Ford's insight was to realise the possibility of a mass market for automobiles if they could only be sold cheap enough. The black Model T and the mass production lines based on the total standardisation of product and production according to scientific management principles was the means to the market end. 'Any color as long as it's black' became the symbolic expression of this mass production standard. Ford is widely cited as the scientific management example because it demonstrated not only the success of the system, but also its ultimate failure. By 1920 the Model T had over 60% of the domestic American market while General Motors with eight different models had 12%. Five years later Ford, still committed to the basic Model T, had been overtaken by GM and ten years further saw Ford's share at around 20% and their survival much in doubt. Scientific management and standardisation clearly had limitations.

Scientific management's foundation was time and motion study which involved the detailed study of work and the assessment of what a normal competent worker would achieve working at normal speed for a given time. The 'science' clearly accommodated some subjective judgment. This was the basis of many and various incentive payment systems which were applied across much of manufacturing industry and became the symbolic focus of industrial disputes through the first half of the twentieth century.

The idea of scientific management spread wider than its origins in the study of work. It became almost a philosophy which coloured the whole of subsequent management practice as well as theory. The idea was to be rational, objective, analytical and scientific in terms of methodology. It led naturally to a more quantitative approach making extensive use of statistical analysis and the new computer based mathematics to produce optimal solutions to specific problems. Management science, otherwise known as operations research, descended directly from scientific management, the titles referring alternately either to the application of mathematical methods or more broadly to a quantitative curriculum for management education which included the social sciences of psychology and sociology as well as quantitative methods of financial and market analysis plus economic analysis and econometrics.

The approach begged the simple question as to whether management was an art or a science. For some the hard quantitative solutions were the essence, while for others the key to management was understanding the irrationalities and inconsistencies of people.

There may still be some debate as to the rights and wrongs of scientific management. It undoubtedly contributed substantially in its day to the productivity of industrial organisations. But equally it did substantial damage to the possibility of a '*true spirit of co-operation between employer and employee*'.

It was the possibility of this co-operation which was the focus of the various studies which came to be known as the human relations school. The human relations approach was to be more or less entirely benign in its impact on working conditions, but was nevertheless subject to interpretation as to its aims, which depended largely on the prior position of the interpreter. Was it all part of the conspiracy to exploit labour? Or was it an initiative which was genuinely motivated to achieve an improvement of the workers lot as well as the company's? The involvement of labour's own representatives in many of the empirical studies went some way to ensure they were genuine researches, observing and learning from the work place and seeking better ways of doing things, better in that they might combine improved economic result with its distribution being fair and just.

Structural Approach

Both Taylor and Fayol were professionally qualified engineers, Taylor a mechanical engineer and Fayol a mining engineer. But while Taylor was essentially a management consultant, perhaps the first ever, Fayol was a manager, serving as Chief Executive of the French mining company, *Compagnie de Commentry-Fourchambeau-Decazeville,* for thirty years from 1888. Not surprisingly their perspectives on management were quite different. While Taylor studied work at the bottom of the organisation, Fayol's view was essentially from the top down with a certain detachment from the shop floor work itself. Nevertheless it was the nature of that work which defined his approach to the management task.

Zola's 'Germinal' [1885] provides a vivid picture of the people, the work and the working conditions that Fayol managed in the French coal industry:

> *'The four pikemen had spread themselves one above the other over the whole face of the cutting. Separated by planks, hooked on to retain the fallen coal, they each occupied about four metres of the seam, and this seam was so thin, scarcely more than fifty centimetres thick at this spot, that they seemed to be flattened between the roof and the wall, dragging themselves along by their knees and elbows, and unable to turn without crushing their shoulders. In order to attack the coal, they had to lie on their sides with their necks twisted and arms raised, brandishing, in a sloping direction, their short-handled picks.*
>
> *Below there was, first, Zacharie; Levaque and Chaval were on the stages above, and at the very top was Maheu. Each worked at the slaty bed, which he dug out with blows of the pick; then he made two vertical cuttings in the bed and detached the block by burying an iron wedge in its upper part. The coal was rich; the block broke and rolled in fragments along their bellies and thighs. When these fragments, retained by the plank, had collected round them, the pikemen disappeared, buried in the narrow cleft.*

Maheu suffered most. At the top the temperature rose to thirty-five degrees, and the air was stagnant, so that in the long run it became lethal. In order to see, he had been obliged to fix his lamp to a nail near his head, and this lamp, close to his skull, still further heated his blood. But his torment was especially aggravated by the moisture. The rock above him, a few centimetres from his face, streamed with water, which fell in large continuous rapid drops with a sort of obstinate rhythm, always at the same spot. It was vain for him to twist his head or bend back his neck. They fell on his face, dropping unceasingly. In a quarter of an hour he was soaked, and at the same time covered with sweat, smoking as with the hot steam of a laundry. This morning a drop beating upon his eye made him swear. He would not leave his picking, he dealt great strokes which shook him violently between the two rocks, like a fly caught between two leaves of a book and in danger of being completely flattened.[93]

Maybe Zola exercised some poetic licence, but this was in essence the work situation Fayol was managing. For him the basic problem was how to get large numbers of unskilled and mostly ill-educated people to do fundamentally unpleasant and dangerous work and do it efficiently in return for wages set low enough for the company to make a sufficient profit to survive and prosper. This was the problem of the 19th and early 20th century, and was not much different from the early years of industrialisation.

Fayol identified various immutable rules that managers should follow if they were to be successful. He referred to these as 'principles of management' and they related to the structure of an organisation as well as what we might now call its strategy and the treatment of its people.

In terms of structure Fayol prescribed the centralization of management decision making from the top, a formal chain of command running from top to bottom of the organization, with management having authority to give orders and have them obeyed, and with each employee having only one boss. Operationally the system was focused on the division of labour and the consequent improvement in skills and working methods and the maintenance of order throughout the organisation.

The focus on strategy was limited but pertinent, emphasising the need for a unity of direction, devised and planned at the top but with all members of the organisation actively engaged in its implementation.

The focus on employee relations was mainly concerned that equity and justice should prevail in terms of pay and general working conditions and treatment.

Fayol emphasised the need for loyalty to 'good' workers, advocating lifetime employment where possible, At the same time he demanded discipline with workers being obedient, focusing solely on the interests of the organisation while at work, and being loyal to the organisation. Finally, he held that it was management's responsibility to establish an *esprit de corps* among all employees.

In summary these principles prescribed a fair but strict management attitude and a hierarchical and rather rigid structure for organisation. This was probably appropriate for Fayol's situation, though certainly not as generally applicable as he had intended. The principles were to guide management in what he regarded as their five prime functions:

> Prévoyance – literally foresight but often translated as examining the future and drawing up a plan of action.
>
> Organisation – building up the structure, material and human, of the undertaking.
>
> Command – maintaining activity among the personnel.
>
> Coordination – binding together, unifying and harmonizing all activity and effort.
>
> Control – seeing that everything occurs in conformity with established rule and express command.

Frequently referred to by theoreticians as a 'theory' it is more accurately described as an approach to management, it having evolved entirely from practice, has been labelled alternatively as the 'classical' or 'structural' theory of organisation. It is commonly characterised as the "command and control" model, implying top down management, the top being assumed to have the knowledge, understanding, foresight and wisdom so to organise the various organisational components as to achieve the best result. It was a system to which most early industrialists would have subscribed. Even the enlightened Owen had a clearly hierarchical concept of how organisations worked. Fayol also recognised the necessity to plan for the future and get everyone contributing to the fulfilment of those plans.

Fayol's approach omits significant reference to the crucial management responsibility of raising and managing capital to finance the organization and its development.

There were several other contributions which became embedded in the structural literature. Mary Follett was widely regarded as a key contributor. In publication terms she was a near contemporary of Fayol's, long before he became known to the English speaking world. Her main thrust was to explicate the notion of hierarchy, emphasising joint responsibilities among partners rather than responsibility and power emanating solely from the top. Like Fayol she believed principles of management were applicable to all spheres of organisation. Her collected writing was published under the title '*Dynamic Administration*' which, though it sounds rather like an oxymoron today, probably contributed the title of the then newly established post graduate business degree, the MBA.

Urwick and Breck, management consultants and writers, developed Fayol's structural principles further, adding the distinction between line and staff management, the staff being professional specialists without line responsibilities acting only for and on behalf of their line boss. They also added the principle that authority should only be commensurate with responsibility and that managers were wholly responsible for the work of their subordinates. Further they added what they referred to as the principle of definition which led to the formal specification of jobs, their duties, responsibilities and authority which should be made transparent to all.

Despite Follett's citing of *dynamic* administration, the structural approach appears to define the rigid, rational-legal bureaucratic form. As the scale of businesses grew the structural principles were applied widely, though unevenly, across all industries. Some confirmation of this was provided by a major empirical study conducted by the Aston Group[94] assessing the degree to which organisations exhibited characteristics of bureaucracy including the specialisation of functions, standardisation of procedures, formalisation of documentation, centralisation of authority and the configuration of role structures, for example, with a published organisation chart. The study found that the larger the organisation, the more it tended to some form of bureaucratic organisation, various forms being identified with only the small personal or family owned organisations not conforming to bureaucratic norms.

Other contributions to the structural approach came mainly from practitioners, Drucker being the exception. Though he was not himself a practising manager, Drucker's contribution to practitioner literature was immense, though his tendency to let incisive prose occasionally take precedence over fact, damaged his reputation among academics. Despite this he contributed to many areas of management practice, not least to the structural approach with his advocacy of decentralisation as conducted at General Motors under the leadership of then CEO Alfred Sloan.

Recognising the dangers of rigid hierarchy and bureaucracy Drucker also advocated the use, throughout a business, of a system he referred to as 'management by objectives' in which individuals were engaged in Follett-like partnership with their line boss, in identifying the three or four key purposes of their job, setting themselves target levels of performance in those three or four main areas and subsequently appraising that level of performance together with their line boss at the end of the relevant time period. MbO became one of the first popular acronyms of modern management and later the foundation of the politically motivated target syndrome which proved so dysfunctional..

Drucker's overriding concern in management was for the support and development of people in their working lives, especially for young and junior managers. This he regarded as a matter of professional management competence rather than simply one of arranging human relations.

Human Relations

While the structural approach of Fayol and others propounded a general system of management, the human relations school exclusively focused on management's relationship with people at work. Barnard suggested that

> *'understanding in the field of human relations ... is of first*
> *importance to the executive; for human relations are the essence*
> *of managerial, employee, public and political relations.'[95]*

The dehumanisation of work on the shop floor, where the imperatives of working with machines had tended to dominate the work of people, had become more evident as mechanisation and automation proceeded, threatening jobs which depended on continually increasing markets.

Elton Mayo and colleagues began their observation of work at Western Electric's Hawthorne Works in 1929 with the aim of identifying any link between working conditions and worker productivity. Their observations were at the time surprising. The so called 'Hawthorne effect' was observed when there were short term increases in productivity in response to experimental changes in working conditions no matter what the changes were. The productivity increases were generally ascribed to the interest and attention being given to the workers by the researchers when working conditions were changed. The Hawthorne Studies served to emphasise the importance of social and psychological factors in the working environment and the recognition of informal organisation structures at work, in contrast to the assumptions of scientific management that motivation was simply a matter of payment by results.

Mayo suggested that workers were motivated by a 'logic of sentiment' and a major task of management was to organise 'spontaneous co-operation' in the work place.[96] This was a direct challenge to the neoclassical orthodoxy, with which scientific management had concurred, that motivation was necessarily based around money as the sole measure of self interest and its maximisation being the human aim. It marks the stage in the development of organisation theory where economic theory and empirical fact became irretrievably separated.

Mayo concluded that the Hawthorne programme

> *'... has come to a clear specification of the relation of working groups to management as one of the fundamentals of large scale industry. It was indeed this study that first enabled us to assert the third major preoccupation of management must be that of organising teamwork, that is to say, of developing and sustaining cooperation.'*[97]

[Mayo had defined the other two preoccupations of management as *'The application of science or technical skill to some material good or product'*, and *'The systematic ordering of operations.'*]

Not surprisingly, for the first thoroughgoing experimental social science study of industrial work, the Hawthorne Studies' conduct and the conclusions drawn there from, have over the years attracted a substantial critique. But, whatever its shortcomings, it opened up a new avenue for study and the possibility of new understanding of how best to manage work. As always the question of what motivated the study itself was never far below the surface. Was it an attempt to find new ways of exploiting the workers, or was it a genuine attempt, *'in the true spirit of co-operation between employer and employee'*, to find ways to improve both their lots?

There is no universal answer. The difference is one of management philosophy, of attitude to people. McGregor expressed the dichotomy as two approaches, Theory X and Theory Y which made assumptions about people at work. Theory X assumed:

1. *The average human being has an inherent dislike of work and will avoid it if he can.*

2. *Because of this human characteristic of dislike of work, most people must be coerced, controlled, directed, threatened with punishment to get them to put forth adequate effort toward the achievement of organizational objectives.*

3. *The average human being prefers to be directed, wishes to avoid responsibility, has relatively little ambition, wants security above all.*[98]

McGregor referred to this assumption as the '*mediocrity of the masses*' and pointed out that while a good deal of lip service was given to people being the most important asset, nevertheless,

> '*a great many managers will give private support to this* (Theory X) *assumption, and it is easy to see it reflected in policy and practice.*'

McGregor used Maslow's expression of the hierarchy of intrinsic human needs in evaluating Theory X, pointing out that though by 1960 employees' physiological needs were largely satisfied, safety needs could be threatened by arbitrary management actions which revealed '*favouritism or discrimination*' which might threaten the employment relationship. Similarly inept management might inhibit the satisfaction of workers' social needs fearing that the development of a '*tightly knit, cohesive work group*' might oppose the achievement of the organization's objectives. Self esteem needs and self actualization would similarly be frustrated by a Theory X style management.

The alternative Theory Y set of assumptions were as follows:

1. *The expenditure of physical and mental effort in work is as natural as play or rest.*

2. *External control and the threat of punishment are not the only means of bringing about effort toward organizational objectives.*

3. *Commitment to objectives is a function of the rewards associated with their achievement.*

4. *The average human being learns, under proper conditions, not only to accept but to seek responsibility.*

5. *The capacity to exercise a relatively high degree of imagination, ingenuity, and creativity in the solution of organizational problems is widely, not narrowly, distributed in the population.*

6. *Under the conditions of modern industrial life, the intellectual potentialities of the average human being are only partially utilized.*[99]'

If people behaved in a way which was consistent with Theory X, McGregor argued, it was because of their experience at work. It was management's responsibility to organize work so that people could achieve their own personal goals by directing their efforts towards organisational aims. Both approaches were to a great extent self-fulfilling.

Theory Y was not a soft option. It required consistent care and understanding if it was to be successfully implemented. It was sometimes naively followed by human relations devotees believing that management was simply a question of being nice

to people and that they would respond in kind. Butr that didn't work. It was not a
management style that could be adopted as and when it appeared appropriate; it
was a fundamental set of beliefs about people to which managements were either
committed or not.

Herzberg's motivation-hygiene theory[100] provided some insights as to what
actually motivated people at work and in so doing explicitly denied the 'economic
man' thesis. He identified factors which led to dissatisfaction at work if they were
unsatisfactory, but which would not be positively motivational. These 'hygiene
factors' were extrinsic to the job and included such things as relations with the
supervisor, working conditions, company policy and pay. The motivators were
intrinsic items such as responsibility, achievement, advancement and recognition,
factors which would tend to be naturally addressed by a Theory Y committed
management.

Drucker agreed that the human relations approach,

> 'freed management from the domination of viciously wrong ideas; but
> it did not succeed in substituting new concepts.' [101]

It focused on individual psychology and interpersonal relations with fellow
workers that determined worker behaviour and effectiveness. For Drucker
therefore management of human relations readily degenerated into a device to
'sell' whatever management was peddling:

> 'it is no accident that there is so much talk in human relations about
> 'giving workers a sense of responsibility' and so little about their
> responsibility, so much emphasis on 'their feeling of importance' and
> so little on making them and their work important.' [102]

The human relations approach suggested a distinct break with the former scientific
management, but it was really a continuation of the divide between traditional and
progressive management, between exploitative and enlightened management,
between systems focusing purely on economic rewards and those that tried to take
account of the whole human being. That dichotomy continues to this day.

The human relations approach provided many new insights into effective people
management during the four decades of its investigation and diffusion. It resulted
in the dismantling of many scientific management based structures which had in
their turn improved productivity but damaged employee management relations.
Nevertheless human relations was focused on that one aspect of management to the
exclusion of all others. Wilfred Brown took a broader view:

> 'Effective organisation is a function of the work to be done and the
> resources and techniques available to do it. Thus changes in

*methods of production bring about changes in the number of work
roles, in the distribution of work between roles and in their
relationship one to the other. Failure to make explicit
acknowledgement of this relationship between work and
organisation gives rise to non-valid assumptions, eg, that optimum
organisation is a function of the personalities involved, that it is a
matter connected with the personal style and arbitrary decision of
the chief executive, that there are choices between centralised and
decentralised organisation etc. '* [103]*

Brown presided over one of the best documented experiments in breaking down a
fully operational traditional system and replacing it with a more progressive
approach. This was at the Glacier Metal Co where he was chief executive for over
twenty years from 1939, during which time he employed social psychologist
Elliott Jaques of the Tavistock Institute of Human Relations to study the
psychological and social forces affecting the group life, morale and productivity of
the Glacier people.

Glacier was a traditionally managed engineering company employing around five
thousand people. The paraphernalia of scientific management was still in place in
1945. Workers 'clocked on' when they arrived at work and 'clocked off' again
when they left. They were paid strictly by piecework ie for each item produced.
Brown and Jacques oversaw the abandonment of piecework payment systems and
the clocking on control procedures.

Despite widespread fears of disaster, the results were largely as predicted by
Theory Y. Brown concluded his case against wage incentive systems such as
piecework and clocking systems,

*'I am convinced that instead of optimising production and
individual satisfaction in work, they are hindering both. ...
operators, supervisors and managers in our Company ... shun the
idea of reintroducing a wage incentive system. '* [104]

He added that other companies which had taken the same route - he
referred to Vauxhall Motors, Lever Bros and F Perkins of Peterborough -
were all of the same view and *'would shun the idea of reintroducing a
wage incentive system'.*

Systems Approach

Writing before and after the second world war Chester Barnard, one time president
of the New Jersey Bell Telephone Company and substantial contributor to the

structural theory of organisation, was the first to conceive of the organisation as including those external stakeholders with which it directly interacts:

> *'an integrated aggregate of actions and interactions having a continuity in time ... (including) the actions of investors, suppliers and customers or clients.'* [105]

This significant advance in the concept of organisation was perhaps influenced by the ideas then emanating from systems theorists whose work in biology was beginning to be generalised to social and other non-biological systems and was later taken up by Elliott Jacques and colleagues at Tavistock studying how social and technical systems interacted under conditions of change.

Underlying all these approaches to organisation and management was an assumption as to the key variables involved. For Taylor it was the productivity of manual and clerical labour, for structuralists it was how the organisation should be organised, for human relations it was what motivated people. For systems it was how to understand the organisation in its wider setting.

Systems theory focused on overall system properties and characteristics which appeared to apply generally to all living systems from a simple biological cell to a complex social organization such as a business organisation. These critical system properties appeared capable of providing an overall explanation of system behaviour and was used in the analysis of industries' chronological development as well as product life cycles.

A very simple explanation of a system was given by Koehler[106], using a candle as his example. At first when a light is put to its wick the candle may spit and sputter and possibly go out several times before the wick achieves the temperature for ignition and is successfully lighted. This birth, introduction or infancy stage is characterised in many systems by volatility and high rates of infant mortality whether we are considering lighted candles, human babies, electronic components, business start ups or new products.

If the candle successfully lights then the flame quickly burns up to its full size. This adolescent or growth stage is again typical of many systems in the speed and continuity of its growth up to a certain ceiling level characteristic of its mature phase.

As the candle reaches this ceiling it again exhibits a generally applicable characteristic of volatility before settling down to a mature phase steady state. The candle's volatility is manifested in a short period of flickering; adolescent human beings exhibit extraordinary volatility as any parent will vouch; the volatility of businesses and products as they move from growth to maturity is also remarkable, for example, as growth predictions have to be permanently downgraded, forcing management's attention on to a different set of problems.

In its mature phase steady state the candle exhibits the general systems characteristic of maximum strength and efficiency. In the case of the candle this is the phase when it burns the maximum wax and gives off the greatest light. It will maintain this maximum energy conversion steady state as determined by its inputs of wick, wax and oxygen and its system characteristics of size and composition of wick and diameter and length of candle. Human beings exhibit similar characteristics, in their maturity being at their strongest and physically most efficient stage. Businesses also appear to be at their most efficient and intrinsically most profitable, cash generating stage.

The steady state will only end when one of the determining factors changes. For example, the wax is used up to the extent that there is no longer a full quantity available for burning. At this stage the system goes into a decline, but again the change from the mature phase to decline is marked by further volatility as the candle flickers and putters and frequently goes out prematurely ie before it has used up all its wax.

One of the intriguing characteristics of this general model is the apparent breadth of its applicability. All manner of systems appear to share these general characteristics and be subject to parallel pressures and influences at the different stages.

A start-up business, for example, is likely to be dominated initially by the need to survive. If it survives this first phase it will be able to turn its attention to growth and the development of competitive strength. As it progresses through adolescence being quick, flexible, opportunistic and focused on satisfying customers' needs. It carries no spare weight, no passengers. It is lean and fit, quick on its feet and builds its strength through constant striving and exercise.

This phase sees the business change from being the creature of the founding entrepreneur with a simple structure, to employing an increasing number of professional specialists concerned either with the firm's technological development or the development of its various management functions.

In a growing market the adolescent business has to run fast in order simply to maintain its market share. If it fails to do this then in all probability it will not survive the first shake out when market growth starts to falter. In a static market there is not the same necessity to grow. Many businesses stay small, providing relatively stable employment for small numbers of people. Nevertheless other businesses are more ambitious and grow rapidly in order to achieve the critical mass at which the new specialists can be profitably supported. Growth in static markets can only be achieved by increasing market share or by moving into new markets, both of which may be problematic in highly competitive situations.

To achieve maturity is the goal of all systems. In the case of a business, maturity is the phase when wealth creation is maximised, when the most surplus cash is generated and when the business achieves its position of greatest power and influence and when the business should be able to focus, with the least inhibition and interruption, on the achievement of its long term objectives.

Maturity is the result of successful infancy and adolescence. The success is usually based on doing the right things right and the business progressively becoming more expert. It learns successful ways of doing things. It finds out what its customers like and gets good at delivering those things. It develops its technological expertise. It uses recipes which work and it becomes efficient. And it becomes effective. All this happens as a result of deliberate management initiatives – it is by no means automatic.

It is difficult, however, for a successful business to make a fundamental change in what has established its leading position. This is especially the case with technology when a successful mature business is likely to have major investments sunk in the old technology. Getting into something new may mean writing off huge capital assets which will weaken the balance sheet and in the short term wreak havoc with profitability. Also there are psychological investments in the old technology. One of the fruits of maturity is the ability to pay top salaries and thus attract top calibre people. Many of these highly qualified professionals may have built their entire careers on the old technology and their very natural response to such a change is likely to be defensive and reactive. Nor is it at all certain that leadership in the new technology will necessarily follow; giving up a leading position should certainly not be done lightly.

A successful mature business, as the systems model suggests, is likely to generate substantial surplus funds which are not required in order to maintain the status quo. How these funds get invested depends very much on the circumstances of the individual business.

Diversification not only adds complexity and confuses strategic direction, but it also creates an alternative focus for future development and an ongoing demand for investment which may in the end result in the starvation of the once successful mature business. Thus diversification leads naturally to the mature business which has lost its direction and failed to keep up investment in its key technologies.

In terms of goal orientation the mature business, like many other systems, seeks to control its environment in order to ensure its own future well-being. The one thing the mature business, with all its heavy investments sunk in the status quo, seeks to avoid is change and instability. It will find it advantageous to invest heavily in preserving the current state of affairs. First of all it will seek to control its own industry, if possible through the achievement of a monopolistic position. In this way it can hope to control prices at a level which ensures its own profitability, and can control the level of business to set limits on the competitive activity which would be profitable for any other business to embark on.

For similar reasons it may well seek to achieve control over its inputs whether sources of raw material or possibly core technologies, if they are in any way insecure. It may seek to achieve this through the exercise of its purchasing muscle in tying up long term arrangements or by acquiring key suppliers.

The systems approach offers a way of understanding business organisations. It is quite different from the other three approaches considered here, but like the other approaches adds to the knowledge and understanding of management. Organisations and particular organisational situations can be analysed in terms of the various interacting systems they comprise. These may be both social and technological.

Members of the Tavistock Institute of Human Relations studied the structure and functioning of organisations at the interface of their social and technological systems under conditions of change. They revealed, for example, the dramatic and previously unremarked social and psychological consequences of technological changes in British coal mining[107] and also the substantial impacts on productivity of changes in social structural arrangements in an Indian textile factory.[108] The work of the Tavistock Institute showed the systems approach could provide invaluable insights into management of people in conditions of rapid technological change as well as the formation of organisational strategy and associated systems of management.

Based on this work, Emery[109] proposed ways in which systems, notably business organisations, could be managed over their long term. This included setting and maintaining organisational direction as prerequisite to survival and prosperity. Similarly, establishing a goal which is demanding but achievable. Management's strategic task was to control the boundary conditions between the organisation and its various environments rather than to exercise rigid control within the organisation. Management's internal responsibility seemed to be more to do with communication to all members, and the establishment of agreements and commitments with them regarding the organisation's direction and progress.

The systems approach to understanding organisation and its management adds new insights not provided by scientific management, the structural approach or human relations. But one of its more significant contributions to understanding was that there was no one best way of managing, that the most effective course of action was largely dependent on the particular system conditions and circumstances which applied. This was the contingency approach.

Contingency

Contingency, usually suffixed with the word 'theory' presumably to give it more significance, is the simple idea that 'there is no one best way; it all depends'. Many theorists contributed to the development of 'contingency' recognising for example that approaches that might be effective in large mass production factories may be completely inept in small professional offices or jobbing shops. Some researchers demonstrated how organizational structure, for example, depended on such contingent issues as the production technology[110] or the demands of the firm's environment in terms of its degree of uncertainty and diversity[111] or the level and pace of technological change.[112]

Tom Burns and George Stalker studied the attempts to implant the fledgling electronics industry in parts of Scotland which had only previously experienced the old heavy 'smokestack' industries of coal, steel and ship-building. The old industries were dying and it was hoped to take up some of the inevitable unemployment with the new high growth high tec industry.

In carrying out their research they identified two types of organisation which have since found their way into fairly common currency: mechanistic and organismic (or organic) organisations.

The mechanistic organisation was suited to stable conditions. In it the job of management was broken down into specialist functions, each with its precisely defined task. There was a clear hierarchy of control, with the reins firmly held at the top. Communications flowed down the line and occasionally back up, but rarely across the organisation. There was an emphasis on loyalty to the company and obedience to one's superior. The result of this bureaucratic system was that individuals in the organisation were not committed to its fundamental business aims, only to obeying the rules and fulfilling their (strictly limited) employment contract and enjoying whatever perks such a regime might offer. Mechanistic organizations were found to be ill-suited to handling innovation.

Croome described mechanistic organisations as demanding that everyone shall have one job, clearly defined and delimited, with responsibility running up to a recognised limit and stopping there. The employee was not isolated, but was part of the organisational machine. In so far as he had to think at all about his relations with other parts of the machine, he saw them as outside 'his' job. They were necessary to the job only as tools are necessary.

> *'For some data needs he can appeal to the slide rule, for others he may appeal to another individual; some tasks can be performed by a tool, others by an order to a subordinate.'* [113]

The clear definition of 'the job' and the simple set of outside relationships, broke down when conditions changed. New situations did not exactly match the traditional frontiers of responsibility. The individual no longer knew just what instructions were needed or where to seek them; he had to consult with, rather than merely give orders to, his subordinates.

The organismic organisation was at the opposite end of the spectrum. It lacked rigid structure, lived by a process of continual adaptation, often involving the redefinition of individual tasks. Communications occurred in any direction as was required at any particular time, and the commitment of employees was open ended and generally dedicated to the achievement of organisational aims. As one might expect, organismic systems were well suited to handling the new and unfamiliar: they were highly effective innovators.

According to Burns & Stalker, the work of the manager under the organismic system was much more exacting.

> *'He must give up his safe, cut and dried, contractual relationship with the firm - a relationship with an impersonal, immutable 'they' - for membership of a body kept going by a shared creative activity; for the limited commitments of the 'nine to fiver' he must substitute the general open ended commitment of the professional'.*

Burns and Stalker did not suggest that there was 'one best way' of organising. If the mechanical system was adequate, then so much the better because it was the most efficient. However, as Croome suggested, when the firm was tackling new tasks, whether commercial or technical, this system of differentiated responsibilities must be 'elastically shared'. Every effort must be made to encourage the sense of the business as a whole with objectives and goals common to all its members, rather than a complex of 'separate jobs'. The stronger this sense, the more there would be resource to lateral consultation. This should be recognised and facilitated, and not regarded as a mere semi-legitimate supplement to vertical channels of command.

Organismic and mechanistic were opposite ends of a continuum. Neither was likely to be met in its full glory, but most companies exhibited tendencies to be closer to one or the other. The more organismic a business organisation was, the better suited it was likely to be to handle innovation and change. This was the basis of the orthodoxy that flexible systems with high levels of participation and open communications were essential for handling change, while rigid, mechanistic, bureaucratic systems were most efficient for handling routine and stable situations.

Thus the contingency approach suggests that any theory of organisation is inevitably complex and contradictory because of the variety of organisations and organisational situations. What works in one circumstance may not be appropriate in another. The most appropriate approach is contingent on the circumstances of the particular situation.

Heavy industry, iron and steel, shipbuilding and other traditional manufactures such as textiles gradually migrated from the developed to the newly industrialising economies. These were the large scale organisations which used rigid, hierarchical organisation structures, formal decision processes and static bureaucratic ways of operating. New electronic and IT based technologies which replaced the old smoke stack firms, had more flexible structures with fast decision making and increased responsiveness to environmental change.

Incomplete though these various theoretical approaches to management undoubtedly were, they nevertheless provided managers insights and understanding to issues that they might well confront in their practical lives. Even though only be encountered as part of an academic management syllabus they could contribute additional knowledge and understanding to support the practical job of management.

8. MANAGEMENT in PRACTICE

The development of large scale multi-business corporations, initially in America and subsequently through the rest of the industrialised world, achieved massive economies of scale but required competent 'administrative co-ordination', to use business historian Chandler's term for management, in order to achieve productivity and profitability. In those terms the resulting management was highly successful.

Chandler propounded the view that business management replaced market forces in *'coordinating the activities of the economy and allocating its resources'*[114] and so became *'the key role in twentieth century wealth creation'*. If it were true that management had usurped the role of market forces it would invalidate classical theory founded as it was on primacy of market forces and the exclusion of management except as a minor friction in the economic system. The truth was less clear cut. A major part of marketing management was the research of 'market forces' so that a business might accommodate to them rather than engage in a vain attempt to defy them. In practice the invisible hand had remained a powerful influence.

However, management's role was not restricted to concerns with the market. Technical, operations and financial roles were of equal importance in 'creating wealth'. General managers, standing at the apex of the management hierarchy, were responsible for the performance of their companies through the post second world war period of unprecedented technological change.

The contrast in scale of American and European production and management practice was highlighted during the second world war when British industry in particular was required to expand armaments production beyond its capacity. This was well illustrated by the single common wartime production project of the Rolls Royce designed Merlin aero engine for the Spitfire fighter aircraft.

> *'British craftsmen "cut out the pieces and fitted them ...,*
> *milling them here, machining them there, and piecing them*
> *together, until a superb engine materialised." [115] The Packard*
> *Company, which took over the Rolls Royce contract, could not*
> *build engines this way. The sketchy British blue prints*
> *befuddled the American engineers. To put the Merlin into*
> *production, they had to tear an engine down and copy it part by*
> *part, in some cases redesigning components for mass*
> *production. The result was a product which, if no better than*
> *the original, could be produced faster, cheaper, and in far*
> *greater numbers.'[116]*

The Rolls Royce approach, without the engineering finesse of Rolls Royce, was no doubt apparent in other British industries which consequently declined after the war, in the face of competition not just from America but also from the resurgent German and Japanese industries which had to rebuild themselves from scratch. The British management which presided over at least the start of this manufacturing decline was still to some extent a class based amateur breed drawn from the public schools and Oxbridge which disdained to provide management education till fifty years after the war.

Traditional industries were migrating from the developed economies to the third world where labour was cheap and where the industrialisation process, for good and ill, could be repeated, apparently with few lessons learned from the earlier experiences of industrialising the advanced economies.

New technologies, developed and applied mainly in America, Europe and Japan, created new industrial problems requiring new solutions, new structures and new ways of managing business organisations.

Management, had evolved from command and control through scientific management to a primary concern for the human relations within organisations and customer relations without. The new conditions led to a concern with shaping the culture of organisation in order to influence the way all people in an organisation behaved. The obvious ambiguity inherent in culture management focused attention on the necessity for integrity in managerial behaviour. And it was the responsibility of general management to provide that integrity and to shape the organisation's culture. These were roles which were necessarily learned on the ground in practice.

New Managers

Individuals holding general management posts might be expected to have won their initial appointment on merit in competitive circumstances, though this was, of course, not always the case. Heredity and the unbalanced influence of the Ivy League in America and public school Oxbridge in Britain continued to frustrate meritocratic entry to management ranks, there being no professional gatekeeper to entry.

Nevertheless, by whichever means individuals gained initial selection, the management training programmes provided by most large companies were themselves prolonged selection processes. Typically in-company management trainee schemes would last for at least one year and often more than two, during which individuals would be given immediate though brief experience in most of the specialist areas outlined in chapter six and more extended experience in one or more of them. They would be subjected to at least some advanced management education and training and not infrequently part-time secondment on to a business school advanced management or degree course where they would be acquainted with, among much else, economic theory and various management approaches such as those outlined in chapter seven.

They could expect during their trainee period to be under continuous observation and assessment and subject to being removed from their traineeship should their performance not meet expectations. They would most probably be enabled to develop as general managers with their spheres of initial control being limited to relatively small scale operations, subsidiary companies or divisions of larger organisations where their mistakes would not be life threatening. Whilst granted substantial autonomy in these limited operations, they would be coached and nurtured as they gained their experience and learned from their successes, as well as mistakes. They would gain practice in key areas of decision making, under conditions of real uncertainty and risk, to make effective use of the resources under their control, notably including their people.

The assertion that large companies inevitably became bureaucratic, frustrating the ambitions and talents of young managers was not necessarily true. Drucker noted in his study of the decentralisation of General Motors:

> *'With the big company safety net beneath them they could display their entrepreneurial talents. And given real authority, they weren't likely to retire on the job or quit out of boredom and frustrated ambition.'*[117]

Thus equipped such trainees might in due course, in the organisation that originally employed them, emerge as senior general managers with responsibility for both the business's day to day operational viability and its longer term survival and development as well as responsibility for effectively balancing those short and long term concerns. In addition they would be responsible for the work and results of all their subordinates, and thus for all the work and results of those specialisms into which management labour is divided.

This general management first came to full fruition in the large scale often diversified businesses of twentieth century America. As these firms established a presence internationally, their approach to management development was adopted more widely. In *The Practice of Management*, Drucker revealed that in the 1940s he could only find two such management development programmes: Sears Roebuck in America and Marks and Spencer in Britain, and only three universities, all American, offering advanced management courses. Ten years later there were over 3000 company trainee schemes and scores of American university programmes. Thereafter the numbers of company schemes and university programmes grew rapidly in both America and Britain. In Britain the 'milk round' became ubiquitous: a cull of bright new graduates to join the management trainee schemes of leading businesses.

Such management training schemes were typical of how large scale businesses supported and developed their succeeding generations of management up to the late 1970s. Many smaller companies followed a similar process and most sought to adopt such development procedures as were within their reach. Management development was therefore achieved through practical in-company training and experience provided by the particular organisation with more fragmentary support from external academic institutions. The managers who emerged from this process were therefore already imbued with the organisation's culture and knowledgeable about its industry, its customers and competitors and understood its technologies. The attractions of management being a completely generalised competence, instantly transferable from one environment to another quite independently of differing industrial environments, had not yet been accepted. The vast majority of senior management appointments were made from within the existing management ranks.

Environments differed radically from one industry to another. Various broad categories were used. 'Smoke stack industries' was a phrase used to describe declining heavy engineering, using 'old' technology to sell into mature markets. Steel and shipbuilding were typical of the category. Such categorisation explained away why advanced economies might cease to be competitive in such activity apart from small high value high technology niches. The continuing application of advancing technology in such apparently mature industries suggests the categorisation may have been misleading.

At the other end of the industrial categories were the then new industries, in electronics, information technology and internet communications which might require a different approach to management from that best suited to the traditional industries.

By the time Henry Mintzberg completed his doctoral study on managerial work in 1973 he was able to reveal that managers actually spent their time working under considerable pressure mainly on tasks which were brief and fragmented.

> '*Half of the observed activities being completed in less than nine minutes, and only one-tenth took more than an hour ... Telephone calls were brief and to the point (averaging six minutes), and desk work sessions and unscheduled meetings seldom lasted as long as half an hour (they averaged 15 and 12 minutes respectively).*'[118]

The great majority of managerial time was spent communicating verbally directly with others, on the phone and face to face, in formal prearranged meetings and in informal spontaneous meetings. This was not the pattern of activities that might be assumed as necessary to the pursuit of command and control managerial functions identified by Fayol and others in less volatile times. But it did seem to fit with the more democratic approach at least partly shaped by 'human relations' inputs and the new imperatives resulting from rapidly changing technologies.

New Technologies

The connection between economic growth and technological innovation was apparent from the dawn of industrialisation. The idea of long wave economic cycles based on innovation was identified by Schumpeter in the 1930s[119]. He attributed the causes of the first 'wave' to the diffusion of steam power, the second to the railway boom and the third to the joint effects of the automobile and electricity. Kondratiev identified similar waves of innovation causing surges in economic growth occurring roughly every fifty years. The first such wave, from 1790 to 1840, was based on coal, steam power and new technology in textiles. A second wave, from 1840 - 1890, was based on railways and mechanisation of manufacturing. The third Kondratiev wave, 1890 - 1940, was based on electric power, the internal combustion engine and advances in chemistry.[120]

Others have identified variations on the Kondratiev analysis. Piatier studied the whole life cycle of technologies, not just their birth and economic growth, but their maturity and resulting economic decline[121]. The first wave of innovations in coal, steel, railways, textiles and inorganic chemistry grew up and grew old together. For Piatier, the great depression of the 1930s was neither a short term economic crisis, nor a crisis of capitalism, but signalled the end of that great wave of major innovations.

Piatier's second conjunction of major innovations causing extraordinary economic growth had its embryonic phase in the 1930s and was based on oil, motor vehicles, aircraft, sheet steel, organic chemistry and synthetic materials. The growth from this revolution was interrupted by the second world war, but was realised in the period of post war reconstruction in the 1950s and 1960s, slowing down in the 1970s, perhaps being brought to premature maturity by the oil price crises of the mid 1970s, but definitely in decline by the 1980s.

A third revolution, which was in its embryonic phase when Piatier was writing in 1984, appeared likely to be based on electronics, information technology, new forms of energy and energy substitute, biotechnology, molecular engineering, genetic engineering, ocean development and possibly new forms of transport or transport substitute.

Freeman tried to identify how these basic innovations caused the economic growth, seeking to identify, for example, the basic scientific advance, invention or innovation, that sparked off the first, steam power induced, Kondratiev upswing of around 1790.[122] Watt had not invented the steam engine, but merely improved it with the external condenser in 1769 and rotational power in 1781. It had been introduced by Newcomen in 1712, or in simpler form still by Savery in 1698. What it was that caused the explosive growth based on the diffusion of steam power in the industrial revolution was unclear. Similarly with the second wave based on the railways starting around 1844. Trevithick had built a locomotive for coal hauling as early as 1804, Stephenson's first locomotive came into operation in 1814 and the first passenger railway in 1825. It was unclear who was the basic innovator. Perhaps it even went back again to the steam engine itself. This lack of clarity was at the root of all such analyses.

Although there were various economic interpretations of the innovation and growth relationship they were not in fundamental conflict. The stimulus to growth was caused or enabled by technological innovation, either in the shape of a single, all pervasive fundamental development, or by the coincidence of a number of basic innovations. On either analysis, the connection was sustainable if not open to detailed measurement. On either analysis, innovation was a contributory cause of economic growth and represented a powerful competitive tool. On either analysis there was a new generation of basic innovations breaking out of their embryonic phase by the late 1970s. At that time only the electronics and information technology strands had reached the stage of substantial commercial exploitation; and even that had only just started. Commercial exploitation was rippling out from a core which was still bubbling with primary innovations.

In part the investigations of innovation and growth sought to explain the real world booms and slumps of business cycles which Say's law had excluded. But they were also interesting in that they recognised the importance of innovation not just at the macro level of the whole economy but also at the level of industries and the individual enterprise.[123] The management of. innovation had therefore become a key focus of research interest by the time Burns and Stalker identified the appropriate characteristics of systems of management, though their simple dichotomy was of limited usefulness to practising managers. Just as industries were not adequately characterised in bi-polar fashion as stable or volatile, so practical management needed to be more nuanced than simply mechanistic or organismic.

Carter & Williams had identified the requirements of 'the technically progressive firm' ie one that was 'keeping close to the best which could reasonably be achieved in the application of science and technology'.[124] Foremost among these were good internal and external communications, a positive approach to the use of science and technology and to the recruitment and training of high calibre technical staff. The broad findings were replicated by subsequent researchers. For example, the lack of external communications in the non-progressive firms, particularly in relation to market appraisal and marketing research, was found repeatedly to be associated with innovation laggards.

Focus on market needs and wants as requirement for effective innovation was confirmed by Myers and Marquis,[125] while project SAPPHO (Scientific

Activity Predictor from Patterns with Heuristic Origins),[126] carried out in
two science based industries, chemicals and instruments, focused on new
product innovation, and identified the following factors as being associated
with success:

1) Understanding user needs
2) More attention paid to marketing
3) Development work carried out more efficiently
4) More effective use of outside technology and scientific advice
5) Individuals responsible for innovation more senior and had more
authority.

Robertson confirmed the SAPPHO findings and summarised the root causes
of innovation failure as 'the neglect of marketing research and preconceived
ideas about market needs'.[127]   Similarly successful innovations were
identified as depending on direct links between research and development
and marketing, planned programmes of innovation and management being
both technically effective and market oriented.[128]   Various other studies
have broadly confirmed the SAPPHO findings in identifying key activities
associated with successful innovation, including:

1) Good contact with the firm's product markets (to know
         accurately user's requirements) and its
         technological environment (to know the state of
         the art).
2) Good internal co-operation and co-ordination between engineering
         (R & D), production and marketing.
3) Careful planning and control.
4) Efficient development work.
5) The will on the part of top management to innovate.
6) Provision of good after sales service and user education.
7) Existence of key individual, such as a product champion,
         business or technical innovator etc.

Holloman identified the essentials of innovativeness as:

1) Technical staff knowledgeable about the state of science.
2) Technical staff fully understanding the strategy and objectives of
         the business.
3) The innovator, or entrepreneur, being organisationally
         separated from the normal day to day business.[129]

Reference is made to these examples of empirical research to indicate that
by the late 1970s, not only was there considerable knowledge of the

economic impact of technological change but a lot of research had been focused on identifying the organisational characteristics of the most effective innovators. These could be summarised as:

1. Open systems and practice of communications internally and externally

2. Emphasis on technical management, science, technology and R&D

3. Focus on understanding customer and user needs and wants

4. Focus on recruiting, developing and empowering high calibre people

This understanding was largely confirmed by the two McKinsey consultants Tom Peters and Robert Waterman in their review of what they referred to as 'excellent' companies. [130] They included in their study twenty four high technology firms, seventeen in consumer goods, six general industrials, seven service industry firms, three in project management and five resource based. They did not consider a single financial sector organisation, focusing instead on wealth creating activity rather than matters of ownership. Peters and Waterman emphasised the people orientation of management in their excellent companies which contrasted with the then traditional rationalist, quantitative analytical approach of the less successful firms they reviewed. Focus on the support and development of people reflected the growing importance of people based resources in an era of rapid technological change.

New Resources

The traditional business resources were land, capital and labour, but labour, largely unskilled or semi-skilled was treated more as though it was a raw material to be bought in, or not, as the need arose. It was essentially a current item, hired by the day and paid by the hour.

More skilled layers of human resource could not be regarded in quite the same light. Craftsmen, professional specialists, scientists and engineers had to be recruited, retained and supported and were a significant part of any company's ongoing resource base. By the early 1960s the idea of a knowledge based business was beginning to diffuse into theoretical literature Drucker writing in 1964 suggested that

> *'Business is a human organisation, made or broken by the quality of its people. Labour might one day be done by machines to the point where it is fully automated. But*

knowledge is a specifically human resource. It is not found in books. Books contain information; whereas knowledge is the ability to apply information to specific work and performance. And that only comes with a human being, his brain or the skill of his hands.[131]

The cliché that 'our people are our most valuable asset' had by then, in that period of rapid technological change, become palpably true for most companies whether or not they realised it. They were not the most valuable asset because of their physical 'labour', but because of what they could, individually and in groups, create. For many companies by the middle of the twentieth century their creation, intellectual capital, had become a vital resource and the means of establishing and exploiting what was referred to as competitive advantage, ie what made the particular company different and in some way better than its competitors.

Intellectual capital comprised such things as patents, copyrights, trade marks and brands.[132] But the knowledge base went well beyond these formal items. It included such things as business processes, collective expertise, innovative capability, entrepreneurial and managerial skills, organisational culture and history and ways of doing things, all items resulting from the combined efforts and brainpower of individuals and groups of people and the way they worked together. These became embedded in the company as what was called structural capital, a permanent aspect of the company remaining in the company when the individuals contributing to its creation left. It was therefore not transitory but permanent and cumulative, even though it was not included with a valuation on any balance sheet.

From time to time attempts were made to establish ways of valuing intellectual capital. Brands were ascribed valuations and league tables of such valuations were published annually, but the valuations were unreliable and not accepted by international accounting standards. Attempts to control 'knowledge work' were also proposed as a way of quantifying and therefore valuing its results. Measuring the output of 'knowledge workers' and improving their productivity were also proposed[133] but, no credible method of evaluation appeared and to this day none seems imminent.

The accounting profession, espousing principles of prudence and conservatism, were rightly suspicious of such dubious valuations of intellectual capital and consequently in the infrequent cases where an intangible item had an identified value, for example as a result of its acquisition, the rule was for its rapid depreciation on the balance sheet no matter how important it appeared to be.

The fact that such resources were not valued on accounting schedules did not in any way diminish their true value. Management had to be aware of their worth and understand how best to nurture, develop and exploit them by combining intellectual and structural property.[134]

Most company resources were relatively easy to copy, and if they appeared to be the source of competitive advantage they almost certainly would be copied by competitors and their potential profitability competed away. However intellectual property, such items as patents, trade marks and brands, was legally protected against competitive copying. Structural capital, as identified here, might also have been valuable as the source of competitive advantage, but it had no legal protection. Nevertheless it was difficult to replicate because it was know-how embedded in the business processes and cultures that had evolved uniquely over time as the business developed.

The care and nurturing of these new resources, which was the responsibility of general managers, required competence beyond the technical and functional, to shape and develop a distinctive organisational culture in which intellectual and structural capital might flourish.

Organisational Culture

The traditional emphasis of management on command and control hierarchy failed when flexibility and innovation became critical. Management's alternative approach was to encourage people to contribute their knowledge, experience and enthusiasm at all levels of the organisation. This change aimed to create a supportive, open, 'democratic' and progressive organizational culture and a substantial amount of research was conducted to establish how this could best be achieved.

Culture explained how people perceive the organisation, and consequently determined how they behaved. It had been defined in many different ways. For example 'the shared values, beliefs and ways of behaving and thinking that are unique to a particular organisation'.[135] But it was not simply homogeneous as was often assumed in such concepts as 'strong culture'.

Organisational culture could be the sum of many subcultures, each of which contributed its own nuances of meaning and its own rituals and images and even in some cases a specialist and exclusive language   Although there was a widely held view that culture was 'the glue that binds organisation together',[136] it was equally clear that culture could in fact be divisive, just as easily as cohesive. In the absence of any dominant super-culture, the various subcultures could well be in conflict with each other. On occasion this conflict might become overt and sometimes highly dysfunctional, but more usually the conflict would be bubbling below the surface. Culture was thus described as a 'melange of cross cutting subcultures', continually reacting against each other in some more or less cohesive, or divisive, not necessarily stable, equilibrium.[137]

Peters and Waterman recounted how,

> 'stories, myths and legends appear to be very important, because they convey the organisation's shared values, or culture. Without exception, the dominance and coherence of culture proved to be an essential quality of the excellent companies.'[138]

The implication was that culture could in some way be controlled to make management's desired culture both coherent in itself and dominant over other subcultures. In the management literature there were many stories, even legends or myths about the great and good, or not so good, originators of such organisations as IBM, Hewlett Packard, NCR, ITT, Macdonald's etc. These businesses all shared 'strong', deliberately established and maintained, coherent, dominant 'cultures'. They had, it was argued, gained the active participation of all their members and their consistent concentration of effort on pushing their organisation further in its intended direction.

The distinctive feature of these strong cultures was that they were hared by all organisation members. The common assumptions about the organisation and the way to behave in it represented a powerful means of getting to the 'hearts and minds' of all organisation members. Thus, potentially, culture offered a way for people in the organisation to focus their efforts, consistently to achieve a sense of direction and achievement, beyond the scope of more orthodox management approaches.

However, the creation of a strong culture was not without problems. Whilst it may have served to replace the control mechanisms once effectively wielded by powerful bureaucracies with something that appeared more congenial, it also replicated the problems created by those control mechanisms. Culture was by definition long lasting, and strong culture may have been particularly so. Thus all the old rigidities and loss of responsiveness that caused mechanistic firms so much trouble when confronted with change, could be equally present in the strong culture businesses. Control was control, whether or not it came in the guise of a nineteenth century bureaucratic structure, or a 1970s strong culture. In either format tight control implied lack of flexibility and ability to innovate.

Nevertheless, one genuine aim of culture management could be to achieve what George Preston (previously quoted) referred to as the *'true spirit of co-operation between employer and employee'.* .

Though Preston was speaking on behalf of labour, his plea surely applied through the organisation hierarchy. Co-operation, rather than calculation or coercion should surely always have been the preferred way forward for both employee and employer, though from time to time co-operation would be bound to break down when interests were so directly competing.

Barnard, after many years himself as a chief executive, had defined what he held to be management's essential functions:

> *'first, to provide the system of communications; second, to promote the securing of essential efforts; and third, to formulate and define purpose.'* [139]

He emphasised the need for management to communicate an in-depth understanding of the internal and external situation of the organisation and its relations with various stakeholders. His emphasis was on communication and persuasion, in order to gain the co-operation of people in achieving the purpose of the organisation. For Barnard this communicative role of management to achieve *'morale'* was paramount, involving the support of *'inducements'* and *'supervision'* as well as *'education and training.'* He recognised the importance of what he referred to as *'communion ie the opportunity for comradeship at work',* as a major motivating force whereas *'material incentives'* were weak once beyond the level of the bare physiological incentives. Though he did not use the term culture he was an early advocate of its management and not just to replace 'control' but to create a workplace where people could achieve some real fulfilment and enjoyment.

Running through the literature on organisational culture, as with most management literature, there was a fundamental ambiguity. Was management learning how to manage in order to exploit the worker and so to maximise profits, or was it done in the 'true spirit of co-operation'? This was not a theoretical question. Through the history of industrial management there have been the amoral exploitative robber barons and there have also been the enlightened, even idealistic, captains of industry. And no doubt coming up through the ranks of junior and middle management there were individuals of both categories. Training and education had given managers the opportunity to be effective, but they were not members of a profession which tied them to any notion of public service and they were not bound by any professional code to ethical behaviour. Managers had always had the choice to behave with integrity, or not.

Management Integrity

From the perspective of labour, economic growth was achieved through the accumulation of capital resulting initially from the dispossession of the working classes and maintained through the profits sequestered from the workers' rightful compensation. It had been management that presided over that inequitable distribution of the economic benefits from industry. The interests of labour and the interest of management appeared therefore to be in fundamental opposition. The early mill owners had employed children from the age of six or seven working all the hours of daylight for just sufficient to survive in poverty. Engels had stood witness to working class starvation to death while the nascent capitalist grew ever more wealthy. Marx reported the smirk on Mr Moneybags' face after his successful wage negotiation. Taylor persuaded Schmidt that a 60% wage rise was sufficient reward for a 276% increase in output. This past, if it were the whole truth would surely have denied the possibility of Preston's *'true spirit of co-operation'* and Robert Owen's *'Village of Co-operation'.* These would certainly have been dismissed as naively idealistic and unreal.

Furthermore, the typical modern mass production plant had become the social reality for many, carrying their *'dreams for equality of opportunity and personal achievement'.* [140] But mass production was the problem. Run by command and control with additional discipline imposed by machines, with the coercion of, for their day, high rates of pay for work produced, it took away worker autonomy, making them wholly dependent for survival on the mass producing organisation. Mass production made it difficult for the worker to achieve any dignity and self respect and for the organisation to build on human strengths. But that was not the whole story. Even within mass production organisations, individuals could find social compensations, comradeship and even fun at work. However, the brute fact of mass production was the dominant theme and it was management who presided over it.

But the idea of co-operation was seductive. Why should the various stakeholders in industry not co-operate with each other for the benefit of all? It would require a degree of trust among stakeholders, even between management and labour. But management could hardly expect to be regarded by labour as in any way worthy of their trust. From labour's perspective it was unlikely that management would be wholly transparent and fair in their treatment of labour. Suspicion and conflict were the general rule rather than trust and co-operation, though there were exceptions.

The establishment of trust between stakeholders in modern organisations had been shown to develop a sense of community and had, for example, encouraged people to work together with less control and hierarchy. [141] In large scale business organisations hierarchy could to some extent be replaced by trust and its reputation.

Jönsson studied the effects of trust on knowledge work. As the value of knowledge work increased and the work itself became more knowledge intensive, so the competence of command and control hierarchies to take decisions over that knowledge work became less feasible and less legitimate unless the decisions were taken in consultation with the relevant knowledge workers.[142]

The development of trust involved being accountable for deviations from the expected performance. So long as those trusted behaved in line with expectations trust would be reinforced as a result of experience and built progressively over time. It did not need to involve belief in the good character or morality of the other party, merely their conformance to agreed action. The replacement of a command and control approach with a more democratic and communicative approach had to be based on establishing trust between the individuals and groups involved.

What worked for knowledge workers was equally important for all other stakeholders including those broadly categorized as labour. If management appeared to be untrustworthy with one group, that perception of untrustworthiness would quickly leak to other stakeholder groups. Maintaining different levels of trustworthiness with different stakeholder groups was shown not to be feasible. The reputation for trust would sink to the lowest common denominator: in the end 'the truth will out'.

Every management transaction with other stakeholders either enhanced or damaged stakeholders' perceptions of management's trustworthiness and this became recognized as a crucial aspect of a company's culture. Peters & Waterman found that one of the eight characteristics of their excellent companies was "hands on, value driven", meaning management in open and regular interaction with other stakeholders governed by the need to develop perceptions of their trustworthiness. This was found to be particularly relevant to the newer forms of more loosely structured organisation where the values driven companies outperformed the more traditional ones that had tighter control and more rigid structures.

And yet, managements were not always trustworthy.

Drucker highlighted the fact that there was much talk about making people feel their jobs were important, but not enough about making their jobs important; too much of the pretence of 'recognition' rather than real recognition of people's contributions to the organisation; much clever technique to make people feel their working lives were meaningful and not enough effort to make their work have meaning. "Management by walking about" (MBWA) became a recognised prescription. Senior managers were to interact with the workforce by visiting the shop floor or offices where the general staff worked. Not only would it cut through the vertical lines of communication in a hierarchical organization structure but it would also motivate by suggesting that senior management take an active interest in the workers. Thus MBWA was a technique to persuade the workers that senior management cared about them despite anything apparent to the contrary.

All such management approaches were shot through with the fundamental ambiguity: is the aim exploitative or genuinely co-operative? Barnard, talking about management's personnel role focused on what he referred to as the 'central consideration' which was the 'development of the individual'. He argued that it was

> 'not merely as a matter of tactics, nor merely or chiefly a
> matter of industrial efficiency. It will ultimately fail if it is
> merely a high sounding fiction for stimulating production and
> good morale. Hypocrisy is fatal in the management of
> personnel.' [143]

Barnard accepted that for most managers and management theorists the main purpose of personnel policies was to 'facilitate the working together of groups of people toward definite ends' but while acknowledging the legitimacy of that aim, emphasised for him the primacy of the development of the individual, the two aims being the entire justification for management in regard to personnel. And the reasons why so little had been achieved in both aims was

*'the lack of confidence in the sincerity and integrity of
management. It is the lack of that confidence ... which
insidiously thwarts the best efforts that are made in the
industrialised world ... that discourages the most promising
developments. And so the advancement of the interests of all is
retarded.'* [144]

The only answer to the apparent ambiguity of management – the *'key role in
wealth creation'* - as it operated at the sharp end of the business:labour
relationship, was to <u>be</u> honest, transparent, consistent and sincere and so
earn the trust of all stakeholders. But, though it was seen as of such
importance to the advancement of all stakeholder interests, neo-classical
economic theory taught something quite different: that it was important for
the economy at large for actors to act in their own self-interest. The
'Keynesian revolution', with the help of the second world war, had achieved
a more equitable distribution of incomes and wealth, but it did not replace
the amoral, wholly rational and self interested 'economic man' as the
fundamental building block of economic theory, which denied the concept of
integrity as the basis for managerial action, regarding all such concepts as
irrational and therefore excludable exceptions.

Keynesian Consequences

Until the general acceptance of Keynesian economics after world war two,
management still operated within a system dominated by neo-classical
theory based on a set of propositions such as the efficiency of markets,
domestic and international trade freed from government intervention, and
the necessity for private property and profit. Keynes himself broadly agreed
with these propositions adding weight to the rather subsidiary contention
that economic progress should result in a progressively more equal
distribution of income and wealth. His model was capitalism plus full
employment.

Keynes' concern to achieve full employment was both moral and technical.
Full employment was the only way a more equitable distribution of income
could be achieved. It was also the way to achieve the fullest sustainable use
of the country's resources including its labour. These concerns were no
doubt dominant at least in part because his experience had been of
depression, war and post-war reconstruction. Depression caused
unemployment while war and post-war reconstruction solved it.

His followers converted his short term analysis into a long run prescription for maintaining economic growth at a steady but sustainable level. This long run 'Keynesian economics' became the established orthodoxy, justifying high levels of public expenditure by national governments continuing after the war both in America and in Britain.

In Britain, unlike America, a left of centre government was established. The Labour party, partly influenced by Marxist ideas, had emerged from the depression concerned that unemployment resulted from automation and that such technological unemployment was unavoidable but could be ameliorated by public ownership and socialist planning to convert unemployment into leisure.

Keynes himself had forthrightly expressed his view on nationalisation:

> *"There is no so called important political question so really unimportant, so irrelevant to the reorganisation of the economic life of Great Britain, as the nationalisation of the railways."*

But 'Keynesian economics' with its justification of ongoing government intervention, facilitated the socialist development of the welfare state and a truly mixed economy with the state taking over ownership and running basic industries.

The war itself had had other unforeseen consequences which impacted directly on management. Before the war work on the assembly line was described as

> *'unnatural, disagreeable, meaningless and a stultifying condition ... devoid of dignity as well as of importance.'* The worker was seen as *'not a human being in society, but a freely replaceable cog in an inhumanly efficient machine.'*[145]

The war had changed that. It substantially raised the role and standing of the individual worker within society as a whole. Drucker cited evidence from Britain that

> *"the war brought the industrial worker a satisfaction, a feeling of importance and achievement, a certainty of citizenship, self respect and pride ..."*[146]

After the war these positive consequences gradually receded as the worker, devoid of value as combatant, resumed their pre-war low status with renewed alienation. But there was a critical difference. The power position of trade unions had been substantially increased by legislative protection and support.

In America this burgeoning influence of organised labour, encumbered as it was with some political intent, was a considerable concern. The continuing advance of communism in the Soviet Union, Eastern Europe, China and elsewhere caused considerable disquiet with mounting suspicions of communist infiltration of the State Department and concerns over the socialist influence in Western Europe and Britain.

Under this pressure the American Taft-Hartley Act was passed in 1947 reversing the trade union protections and advances gained during the New Deal. Unfair labor practices by unions, restrictive practices, wildcat strikes, solidarity or political strikes, secondary picketing, closed shops, and monetary donations by unions to federal political campaigns were all outlawed and union officials were required to formally confirm their non membership of any communist organisation.

It was more than thirty years before any comparable legislation was passed in Britain during which time trade unionism gained substantial influence and power in its relationship with government, business and management.

Keynes foresaw the problem of wage inflation if full employment was achieved and maintained. Especially was this going to be difficult to control when collective bargaining was conducted between the newly powerful trades union movement and less powerful individual employers. But he saw it as a political problem for governments to deal with. He envisaged that enlightened governments would act decisively to control cost-push inflation driven largely by wage demands. He hardly acknowledged that democratic governments were in turn controlled by the market in votes and professional politicians would only be likely to do 'the right thing' if they felt they could persuade their voters to support it.

The classical alternative to the Keynesian approach would have been to let market forces replace the government's commitment to full employment and allow bankruptcy and unemployment to mediate the fight between employers and employed. But classical theory had been replaced by 'Keynesian economics'. While Keynes himself had studiously maintained a balance of approach between capital and labour, the struggle between employers and employed, often driven by political ideals rather than economic considerations, achieved considerable economic and industrial damage in Britain and to a lesser extent in America.

Long run 'Keynesian economics' encouraged the belief that full employment and the affluent society could be maintained for ever and that booms and slumps were things of the past. But it didn't work out that way.

The first OPEC induced oil price crisis in 1973 had a profound effect on the industrialised world, especially on those economies, including America and Britain, which depended on oil imports. In Britain's case the impact of oil price hikes was amplified by a strike of coal miners causing a restriction of industrial output to a three day working week. The wage and oil cost push inflation accompanied by slow, even negative, economic growth was a new phenomenon for which economic orthodoxy was ill-equipped. The prescriptions for dealing with inflation would inhibit economic growth while interventions to deal with stagnation would exacerbate inflation. By the mid 1970s, stagflation ruled and the good times appeared to be over.

The increasingly emboldened trade unions on both sides of the Atlantic were causing concern both within industry and government. Strikes, official, unofficial and wildcat were resulting in ever increasing lost industrial production.

In Britain, the Communist Party, having failed to achieve parliamentary representation focused on developing its presence and influence within the unions in order to influence strikes and industrial action motivated not so much by the best interests of their members as by the progression of their political aims, no matter how unrealistic, for 'regime change'.

The apparent state of the British economy, and especially industrial relations, under the left of centre administration, elaborated by an increasingly right of centre media, brought an end to Labour government for a generation. Subsequently the Carter presidency in America was replaced by the Reagan administration. Keynes had indicated that the problem of wage inflation supported by full employment was a political problem. By the end of the 1970s the Anglo Saxon economies were set to find out if there was a political solution.

PART THREE – FALL

Management's rise as an autonomous category, independent of both capital and labour, placed it in a unique and powerful position. But management was not a coherent group as were the traditional professions. There had always been various routes of entry to management ranks including appropriate education and training as well as ownership through heredity, talent or opportunistic exploitation. Management ranks were therefore mixed, having no agreed agenda, purpose or standards of behaviour.

Some acted in what they considered to be the long term best interests of their company, others combined that concern with a broader concern for the good of the society in which they worked and lived, while some used there power position to maximise their own personal benefit at the expense of others. Thus while the period up to the late 1970s saw the rise in understanding of the role of management, the practical application of that understanding was uneven.

The autonomy which made management such a potentially powerful source of good always attracted individuals who were prepared to exploit their position for ill. The 'key role in twentieth century wealth creation' was not without ambiguity.

This third part looks at how that management role was seduced and reduced as a result of a new focus on matters of ownership disguised as strategy, the renewal of neo-classical free market economics with a more clinical focus on the achievement of wealth and its dogmatic application by government, and the malign effects of management academics and educators in promulgating these corrosive orthodoxies.

Chandler's 1962 account of the development of 'Strategy and Structure' in American industry recorded how diversification, often necessitated by the imperative to grow despite the restrictions of anti-trust legislation which limited market shares, multiplied the complexity of central decision making. It was this complexity which required structural change. Previously most large businesses had adopted a simple multi-divisional structure. The new structures dividing professional specialist staff functions from line management also divided management decisions into two categories:

> 'one – the strategic – dealt with the long term allocation of existing resources and the development of new ones essential to assure the continued health and future growth of the enterprise. The other – the tactical – was more involved in ensuring the efficient and steady use of current resources whose allocation had already been decided.' [147]

The distinction between day to day tactical and long term strategic management implied a hierarchy of responsibilities with the 'strategic perspective' being paramount, distancing top management's primary interest from day to day management concerns.

In due course the top management focus on strategy, notably diversification, caused the development of a new specialism in strategic management. Initially this was driven largely by financial performance, criteria and language. During the late 1970s management's focus was drawn more directly to maximising the performance of company shares on the stock market. This "strategic" perspective, driven partly by the threat from asset stripping share raiders, led to a top management focus on immediate results which could more easily be achieved through mergers and acquisitions, rather than through the assiduous and constant management of existing business.

While management was thus changing its focus, the focus of economic theory was also changing. Keynes had recognised the dangers inherent in his primary concern for achieving and maintaining full employment. Collective bargaining by powerful unions, with government dedicated to full employment, would, Keynes had recognised, lead inevitably to continuously accelerating wage driven price inflation. Keynes had regarded the solution to this economic problem as a political matter, rather than one of economics. In this context, industrial management had been unable to constrain wage inflation, especially during the OPEC controlled oil price hikes of the early 1970s. This failure and the stagflation of late 1970s presided over by Keynesian economists, resulted in government changes in both Britain and America. The new conservative administrations accepted what Keynes had asserted was their responsibility. They dispensed with the commitment to full employment and brought inflation back under control inflicting substantial and symbolically important defeats on organised labour.

In doing so they had returned to neo-classical free market economic orthodoxy, defined by Friedman and colleagues with renewed clarity and zeal. The nineteen eighties earned the label as the 'greed is good' decade. The adoption of the Friedmanite perspective was more or less total in business, government and management education, and it had many implications for industry and for management.

Firstly, the new orthodoxy dictated that management's paramount duty was to maximise shareholder wealth and management were motivated to this end by the adoption of share option bonus schemes the rewards for which were to be dependent on share performance, facilitated by the adoption of the strategic management perspective which focused on 'buy, sell or hold' portfolio type decisions. Thus a combination of management practice and economic theory led to a deal making mentality among top management to exploit whatever short term investment opportunities could be identified.

A further factor influencing the fall of management was the automation and elimination of middle management processes and jobs which further widened the gap between top strategic management and day to day management. Not only did this further dilute commitment to managing existing business but removed the training grounds for junior managers and led to an increased reliance on university based management education in which the economic theory was embedded.

The fall of management went further. Managers were led to focus attention on the 'outsourcing' of any operations that could be outsourced. They became ever more focused on the short term benefits of deal making activity with business organisations more narrowly focused on those few activities deemed to be 'core'. This diminished version of management was then arbitrarily imposed by uncomprehending governments on public sector organisations, with predictably negative result.

These malign effects resulted from the application of Friedman's newly clinical expression of neo-classical theory which had been adopted by business schools and management research departments and promulgated to their undergraduate and postgraduate "customers". From there, neo-classical theory became more firmly than ever embedded in the cultures of business, academia and government, inhibiting attempts in those sectors to correct the worst effects of industry on global resources, pollution and climate.

Management had always been in an ambiguous position. Neither owner of capital nor representative of labour, it had been able to influence the distribution of incomes and wealth between the two, and able to do so with justice and fairness or with destructive exploitative intent. Not being a profession it had no gatekeeper and was not constrained, or inspired, by any code of ethical practice. Management's final descent was corrupted by the neo-classical bribe to accept riches in return for acting exclusively as capital's agent and giving up their autonomy and independence.

9. STRATEGIC MANAGEMENT

Thomas Lombe's first ever water powered silk mill was surely the product of strategic thinking as was Arkwright's cotton spinning mill. A century and a half later Henry Ford's mass production of the Model T, established a virtuous cycle of massively reduced costs through standardisation and mass production, enabling the decimation of automobile prices, thus creating the new mass markets to justify the new factories. More recently Microsoft, Intel, Amazon and Google, just as examples, have similarly blazed new ways ahead which surely represent a strategic approach.

They all did common sense strategy, as have so many other successful entrepreneurs. They did not have, and seem not to have needed, any formal knowledge of strategy as it is now taught in business schools. They were confronted with problems that needed solutions. They were not looking for intellectual challenge for its own sake. And they managed without all the panoply of analytical methods, models and tools and techniques now available.

Chandler focused on diversification as strategy. Successful companies were constrained by anti-trust legislation which limited their ability to dominate their markets, prevented competition reducing acquisitions and sometimes resulted in companies being broken up if they became too dominant by organic means. Growth businesses were therefore forced to diversify into new markets and new activities. Prior to the 1960s, diversification was the only aspect of strategy formally acknowledged in management literature and even then standard dictionary definitions of strategy were still only expressed in military terms as 'generalship' or ' the art of war'. [148]

Subsequently the formulation and implementation of more general strategic plans began to diffuse across industry, such strategy being defined as:

' the pattern of decisions in a company that determines and reveals its objectives, purposes, or goals, produces the principal policies and plans for achieving those goals, and defines the range of business the company is to pursue, the kind of economic and human organisation it is or intends to be, and the nature of the economic and non-economic contribution it intends to make to its shareholders, employees, customers and communities. ' [149]

Strategic management was quickly adopted by leading firms of consultants as well as business school faculty. It was invested with some theoretical ideas and made amenable to quantitative analysis and became fashionable.

But the question remained as to its true substance. Jack Welch, in 2005, on the basis of his forty year career at General Electric including two decades as CEO, expressed his doubts as follows:

'More than a few times over the past three years, I have been on a speaking programme or at a business conference with one big strategy guru or another. And more than a few times, I have listened to their presentations in disbelief.

It's not that I don't understand their theories about competitive advantage, core competencies, virtual commerce, supply chain economics, disruptive innovation, and so on, it's just that the way these experts tend to talk about strategy – as if it is some kind of a high-brain scientific methodology – feels really off to me.

I know that strategy is a living, breathing, totally dynamic game.

It's fun – and fast. And it's alive.

Forget the arduous, intellectualised number crunching and data grinding that gurus say you have to go through to get strategy right. Forget the scenario planning, year-long studies, and hundred- plus page reports. They're time consuming and expensive, and you just don't need them.

In real life strategy is actually very straightforward. You pick a general direction and implement like hell.' [150]

However, picking a general direction and implementing like hell was not widely regarded as an adequate resolution of the strategy problem. It didn't satisfy the early specialist practitioners of the art nor the academic faculty who quickly engaged with the subject. It appeared to be a new and fertile field of management expertise engaging both consultants and academic faculty. By the late 1970s its importance was becoming recognised and it achieved a leading position on the business school curriculum, attracting both high profile faculty and substantial funds for its research. But as an academic subject it lacked provenance of any significance. In the spirit of true academic endeavour, faculty therefore sought to discover both strategy's history and its underlying theory. This discovery research was not carried out with the aim of improving management practice, but of raising the level of strategic management as an academic liberal arts subject within the perceptions of their academic peers.

Strategy's History

The earliest exemplars of writing about strategy date from around the fourth century BC. Sun Tzu was then scratching 'The Art of War' on strips of bamboo when China was divided into eight competing states and a number of minor principalities which were enduring a nightmare of lawlessness and chaos. War was conducted more as a way of life, a purposeless ritual governed by arcane rules and presided over by hereditary amateurs, punctuated by battles resembling disorderly mêlées which rarely produced a clear result.[151]

Sun Tzu recognised the futility of such warfare. He argued that war, which was always costly, should only be conducted in order to achieve a ruler's political aims. Generally these would be related to the survival, security, expansion and/or prosperity of the ruler's state. For Sun Tzu there was no place for war for its own sake, or total war which would only be terminated on the complete destruction of the enemy. Such total war was unknown till the 20th century.

Accounts of Philip and Alexander's strategy at the battle of Chaeronea, around the same time, have also been referenced in the modern strategic management literature.[152] Machiaveli too has received some attention,[153] but the next major contribution was in the early decades of the 19th century when von Clausevitz contributed 'On War'.[154] At around the same time in America the US Military Academy at West Point began teaching the military subject from its then curiously limited experience.

More recently Liddell Hart's 'Strategy' apparently drew the comment from Rommel (German high command in the second world war) that

*"the British would have been able to prevent the greatest part
of their defeats if they had paid attention to the modern theories
expounded by Liddell Hart before the war."*[155]

Military strategists tended to be methodical rather than theoretical, producing
pragmatic and prescriptive guidelines as to how things should be done in
order to achieve victory. Moreover, much of what passed for military
strategy was devoted to what might more appropriately be regarded as tactics.
Bulow defined strategy as relating to military movements which were beyond
the enemy's cannon range or range of vision, tactics being such movements
as were within that range.[156]

Overtaken by technology, the distinction between the strategic and the
tactical or operational remained. Clausewitz argued that strategy was
concerned with using battle for the purposes of war, which was *'simply the
continuation of policy by other means,*[157] while tactics were concerned with
the use of armed forces in battle.

Military strategists produced many much quoted gems concerning the
conduct of warfare, the relations between the sovereign and the general and
the management of armies. Sun Tzu advised generals to be subtle and
insubstantial, silent and invisible.   In order to win you must know when to
fight and when not to, and you must know how to use both large and small
forces. Moreover a successful general must be able to unite all his troops to
focus on achieving the purpose of the war. The prescriptions were
translated in such general terms that they could be readily applied to modern
business situations.

Though winning without fighting was perhaps the most widely quoted of
Sun Tzu's ideas, most were actually concerned with the conduct of battle.
He was concerned that generals should know and understand all they could
about the enemy and the environment as well as the strengths and
weaknesses of his own forces. He emphasised that war and its battles were
conducted only so as to achieve the political objective which was passed
down to the military; it was not for the military to define the strategic
objective.

The parallels between war and competition have been widely recognised and
Sun Tzu's argument for what he referred to as 'moral action' motivated by
enlightened self-interest seen as potent. Moral action drove relationships
between different stakeholders such as the ruler, the general, the officers, the
troops and the local population, not just between states. Such relationships
were built on trust, and Sun Tzu advocated only the pursuit of objectives

which could gain the enthusiastic support of all stakeholders. Such a leader
would have to be 'wise, sincere, humane, courageous, and strict' a
combination of characteristics with which Jack Welch may well have
agreed.

Clausewitz was also concerned with 'such imponderables as the
soldiers' morale and the commanders' psychology' and even
Machiaveli held that, *you will still need the goodwill of the people to
keep a principality'*.[158]   Strategic aims, either an extraneous given, or
a management decision, would not be achieved if the people in an
organisation were not acting in their pursuit. The effectiveness of the
strategy process was dependent on the people in the organisation,
whether an army or a business.

Though military strategy did not offer a coherent body of theory applicable
to modern non-military organisations, it did identify a simple strategy
process, implicit in the writings of Sun Tzu, Clausewitz and others. The
process started with the definition of the aim. This was the starting point for
all the military strategists, given to them by their political masters. Sun Tzu
then suggested success would depend on knowing the enemy, yourself, the
ground and the weather. He emphasised the importance of military
intelligence in gathering all this knowledge and understanding. Finally, on
the basis of this understanding, decisions were necessary as to the
appropriate action to be taken. This then boiled down to a deceptively
simple process which could be generalised as "objectives - external analysis
- internal analysis – action". This four stage strategy process was
subsequently detectable in most published approaches to strategy.

Strategy's Theory

Theory is perhaps a rather portentous term to describe the relatively
lightweight underpinnings of modern models of strategic management which
ranged from practical routines, or even checklists, to those approaches
extracted from microeconomic theory.

The entrepreneurial model[159], for example, rested on the entrepreneur's
originating identification of a customer need that the business was set up to
satisfy in some way better, or at less cost, than existing competitors and the
development of special capabilities to maintain and develop that superlative
mode of satisfying the customer need.

The life cycle model adapted from general systems theory was based on the phases of birth, growth, maturity and decline through which all systems processed. It suggested the purpose of all systems was to achieve and maintain maturity, since that was when systems achieved maximum and most efficient energy conversion. In business terms it was the phase in which most profit and most surplus cash were generated. The objective of the life cycle model would therefore be to ensure a succession of products or businesses which achieved the leadership position in their markets during their maturity phase. To do this would require knowledge of when the life cycle phases were going to occur, in particular when the growth phase would change to maturity. Such directional changes were notoriously difficult to predict; forecasts tending to be based on a continuation of current trends. Understanding therefore of the shape and size of the industry life cycle and the particular company's position on it would be important to deciding the appropriate action to ensure leadership ahead of the change of phase to maturity.

The initial portfolio model introduced by the Boston Consulting Group[160] in the 1960s, also followed the four stage model. Its aim was to achieve a lasting and balanced portfolio of products or businesses. Its external analysis was concerned with the growth rate of the market and the position of the company's leading competitor. Internal analysis was focused on measuring the company's experience, relative to that of its leading competitor, in producing and selling the product. And the actions were focused on decisions to buy, sell or hold products or businesses.

Porter's 'competitive strategy'[161] applied microeconomic theory to what he referred to as 'industry analysis'. Being based on economic theory the model implicitly assumed profit maximisation as the 'strategic' objective. The model was based on the not too profound equation that profit is equal to income less cost. Therefore maximising profit involved achieving either the lowest costs or the highest prices.

His external analysis assessed the extent to which the arcane assumptions of perfect competition applied in a particular market: the intensity of competition between existing competitors; existence of barriers to entry to and exit from the market; existence of substitute products; bargaining power of suppliers and customers. Porter's internal analysis focused on the direct and indirect activities of a firm and assessed the cost of each activity and, as though it was possible, the profit margin which each such activity contributed.

Strategy, for Porter, was then simply a matter of breaking out of the assumed position of competitors in a competitive market, for example by achieving lower costs or higher prices, or by focusing on a less competitive sub-segment of the market where some monopolistic characteristics might be achieved.[162]

Rather more sophisticated application of economic theory to business strategy was achieved by the 'resource based' approach. The weight of resource based strategy was on the acquisition, development and exploitation of difficult to copy resources which might be the source of sustainable competitive advantage. The foundation of this approach lay deep within economic theory, going back to Ricardo, but was initially brought to the knowledge of academic strategists through the work of Edith Penrose[163] in 1959, later developed by Wernerfelt[164] and others in the 1980s and consistently promulgated in the pages of the Strategic Management Journal. As the importance of off balance sheet knowledge based resources increased so the resource based approach has become more pervasive. All it lacked to become the overwhelmingly dominant strategic model among consultants, academic faculty and practitioners alike was some fashionable language and a memorable graphic.

A more widely used and quoted strategy model was that outlined by Prahalad and Hamel which straddled both resource based and market based approaches.[165] This model went beyond the simple economics of profit maximising and acknowledged and responded to the importance of people in the achievement of strategy. The four stage process was implicit in their approach: the strategic aim or intent being to beat competitors, external analysis involving a focus on technologies and competitors, internal analysis focusing on what they referred to as 'core competencies'. The strategic action for Prahalad and Hamel was to develop and exploit the 'core competencies' and create new 'competitive space' by a process of 'leverage and stretch'. This model not only analysed both markets and resources but its strategic action endeavoured to address progress in both, through the motivation, if not inspiration, of people.

The above brief outlines serve largely to emphasis the simplicity of the theoretical background of the main models of strategic management and to confirm their adherence to the generalised four stage strategy process. General systems theory, microeconomics, portfolio theory and resource based theory all provide ample opportunity for interesting complication, but the reality is simple and is not at all dependent on quantitative sophistication or deep qualitative analysis. Practitioners were influenced by these various models with differing, though limited strategic, effect.

The most significant effect of the new focus on strategic management was to disengage top management from the day to day problems of running a business. Day to day management was concerned with the needs and aspirations of employees and customers, and the potential for technologies to satisfy those needs and aspirations. The focus of strategic management was quite elsewhere.

Long Range Planning in Practice

Management's focus on strategy was born of necessity. The most successful of the large diversified companies which had been studied by Chandler, typically, had small central head quarters taking decisions relating to the allocation of scarce resources between business activities, decisions that could not be avoided. Initially this allocation role was achieved through a process of capital budgeting which agreed planned capital expenditures usually over a five year time horizon.

Agreeing how to allocate resources between businesses necessitated those involved in the agreement to have some knowledge and understanding of the relative merits of the different candidate businesses. Business merits might logically include such issues as the inherent profitability of the business, its forecast future growth, the level and rate of its technological development, and some perception of the risk levels involved. Moreover knowledge and understanding must also include some awareness of the relative strengths of the business within its industry in terms of its market or technological position.

The agreement of a 'long range' plan of capital expenditure, critical as it was to the direction of a business, also had other ramifications. Capital expenditure immediately reduced the level of funding available to other business activities. Additionally, though it might have a beneficial impact on a firm's ability to maintain its position technologically and in the market and therefore to survive and prosper in the long term, the short term profit impact of capital expenditure was invariably negative. It was widely held that major capital projects took around seven years before they produced the same level of profitability as an existing business and for completely new diversified projects the delay could be considerably longer.

It was only a small logical step to extend such capital expenditure plans to full five year projections, involving not just capital expenditure but also full forecasts of the profit and loss account, balance sheet and cash flows. Such long range financial plans became fashionable in large diversified businesses during the 1960s. At that time electronic data processing was in its infancy. There were no personal computers and no spread sheet or database type programmes running on mainframes. Research universities, for example, devoted space to 'statistics laboratories' which had suites of physically huge calculating machines, far less powerful than a $5 pocket calculator of today, and which required a trained engineer to reset a machine if a user ever were to divide a number by zero. Computer programmes were still typically entered in machine code on punched cards. Though there were exceptions, for the most part mainframe computer systems were occupied in such administrative tasks as payroll calculation, order processing and inventory control.

Under these circumstances the development of a five year corporate plan for a business of any complexity was a huge clerical task, carried out, or at least supervised by, professional planning specialists then starting to be turned out by America's leading business schools. The completion of the corporate plan based on detailed five year forecasts of all the inputs, showed a projection of profit and cash flow, the 'bottom line' of which may well not at first have been an acceptable result. Changes would have to be made, possibly the growth forecast increased, or capital expenditures delayed, in order to produce an acceptable projection of business performance. The recalculation of the five year plan would involve the same manual accounting labour as the original. Recalculation three or four times or more became an annual nightmare requiring armies of accounting clerks working excessive hours of overtime to achieve rather pointless deadlines. The whole process had little to do with strategy and had limited impact on the way a company developed. The alternative approach, simply to miss out the whole planning process, though equally short on strategic implications at least avoided the substantial costs and wasted time generating the plan.

However the process did have some implications. Firstly, since the plans themselves were written in financial language, the importance of accounting was substantially raised in those companies which engaged with long range financial planning. Secondly, it was not immediately obvious how devoid of strategic impact the plans were. They looked as though they mattered, projecting as they did the company's performance over a five year period. They appeared to flag up potential problems and issues and helped with 'strategic communication' across the organisation. They made the alternative, not planning, seem unprofessional and even irresponsible. Especially was this so as the financial projections were supported by qualitative analysis of the threats and opportunities facing a company and its strengths and weaknesses in dealing with the threats and opportunities. From this SWOT analysis then programmes of action could be specified which went far beyond long range capital expenditures and five year budgets. Thus a complete Ansoffian bureaucracy[166] was created with the inevitable resulting 'paralysis by analysis' identified by Mintzberg.[167]

A further more insidious impact of the new emphasis on long range planning was to move the centre of gravity of management a little further away from the fundamental preoccupations of management with the resources at its disposal, notably its people. Managers who supervised the development, manufacture and marketing of physical products or services appeared to be distanced a little further from the top of large businesses where the important 'strategic' decisions were made. Those that headed up big companies, at least in the Anglo-Saxon world, were drawn not from those with industry specific specialist technological training and graduate level expertise but more probably from those with higher level business school degrees or professional qualifications in accounting or the law. These appeared better fitted for assessing and deciding the sort of deals which the business portfolio approach required.

Portfolio Decisions

The leading management consultancies, such as Boston Consulting Group, McKinsey and Company, Booz, Allen and Hamilton and A T Kearney, were at the forefront of developments in strategic management. While practitioners laboured with the bureaucratic monster their accountants had created the consultancies offered streamlined versions which assisted management to focus on the key strategic decisions which were still seen as related to the allocation of resources.

The first consultancy model to achieve almost global acceptance was that devised by Boston Consulting Group based on its interpretation of learning curve data analysis for twenty four undifferentiated commodities (eg transistors, diodes, crude oil, pvc, etc). Boston found, not surprisingly, that the more of a commodity that was produced by an industry, the lower the cost of its production.[168] They were more precise about the commodities they chose: unit costs reduced by between 20% and 30% every time total cumulative production doubled. In young fast growing industries, total production would be doubled quickly and costs therefore also reduce quickly. In mature slow growth industries the reverse would be true. The competitor with the leading market share of a fast growth industry would enjoy fastest decline in costs and therefore, all things being equal, would be the most profitable in that market.

This was hardly revolutionary. Empirical evidence from the Strategic Planning Institute's PIMS (Profit Impact of Marketing Strategy) database had been published indicating a similar finding:

> 'a business's share of its served market (both absolute and relative to its three largest competitors) has a positive impact on its profit and net cash flow.' [169]

Boston went further, even developing a differential equation for evaluating the net present value of an increment in market share [170], the spurious precision serving to camouflage the crude approximation or fundamental inaccuracy of the basic market share : profit relationship.

Drucker challenged the relationship pointing out that in many industries,

> 'the largest company is by no means the most profitable one
> ... the second spot, or even the third spot is often preferable,
> for it may make it possible for that concentration on one
> segment of the market, on one class of customer, or on one
> application of the technology, in which genuine leadership
> often lies.' [171]

From this simple if dubious foundation, the first portfolio model was derived. It enabled business headquarters to decide the allocation of resources on the basis of just two business characteristics: the growth rate of the served market, and the market share of the business relative to its largest competitor. These two dimensions defined a matrix divided into four quadrants and according to where a subsidiary business was positioned on the matrix so resources would be allocated to it. If it was high growth it would consume a lot of cash just to keep up, but if it had a high share of that market it would generate cash also (Boston labelled such as 'stars'). If it had a small share it would be a net cash consumer ('problem children'). If the business served a mature low growth market it would not consume so much cash, but if it had a low relative market share it wouldn't generate much either ('dogs'), though if it had a large share it would be a net cash generator ('cash cows'). The position on the matrix therefore enabled strategic management to categorise their various businesses: those to invest in, those to draw cash from, those to try to improve and those to be closed down or sold off. Those are the standard portfolio decisions of 'buy' (ie increase investment), 'sell' (ie reduce investment) and 'hold' (ie maintain investment).

These were important decisions for strategic management, and portfolio models – Boston was the first of several similar - enabled them to be taken on purely clinical objective grounds and at the same time cut the bureaucracy involved in the former financial planning system. At least that was how it was intended.

The reality was that it chrystallised the divide between top strategic management on the one hand and day to day operational management on the other. Adoption of the portfolio system announced the rules of a strategy game which were as transparent to the subsidiary business managers as they were to the strategists at headquarters. Managers whose businesses were identified as 'dogs' would naturally wish to change that designation in order to increase financial support from the centre. A simple way to do this was to change the definition of the served market so that it could be seen as a higher growth segment. All subsidiary management strategic effort would therefore be devoted to convincing top management of the new definition. Strategic planning therefore became a field of combat between strategic and operational managers, a dichotomy further exacerbated by the establishment of business school educated elites set up in headquarters' corporate planning departments, who had limited contact with the people and issues of general management and no necessity for talking directly to labour, yet being directly influential with top management to whose jobs they in due course succeeded. The more mundanely educated and industry trained operational line managers thereby lost expectation of succession to the top.

A further reality was that no business could be adequately understood simply through knowledge, even if it was accurate, of just two variables: market growth and relative market share. The decisions based on this partial understanding, or misunderstanding, were therefore likely to be seriously flawed. Nevertheless, the Boston portfolio successfully diffused through 1970s industry, and was the basis of many business divestment and closure decisions. As noted by Drucker and others, many of the divested businesses turned into exciting successes once freed of the portfolio instigated repression.

Adopting the portfolio approach to strategy changed the nature of business itself. The strategic focus was no longer on the development of a coherent business which might satisfy the long term needs of its stakeholders. The new emphasis was on creating, realising, or even 'squeezing out' shareholder value, an ambiguous concept relating both to the firm's market capitalisation and its ability to pay dividends, frequently interpreted as being a short term, even immediate, concept, which certainly did not refer to management's responsibility to be concerned with the survival and long term prosperity of the company as an autonomous entity.

The portfolio management role was to identify and acquire under-valued assets or businesses and 'improve' them by cutting out any costs, such as R&D, which did not have an immediate payback. It might do this, for example, by acquiring another company, divesting 'dog' business units, cutting out surplus assets where possible, and 'improving' the financial performance of retained businesses. The relatedness or industrial logic of such combinations of business units in a portfolio was not of great concern since membership might be only temporary. The centre would limit its involvement in the business units to identifying surplus assets and deploying specialist 'locum' managers to sort out underperforming businesses, or organise their disposal or closure.

Such a portfolio business would minimise the costs of the centre by having only a small corporate staff, with business unit CEOs having a high degree of autonomy, being paid substantial bonuses for achieving clear financial targets with the expectation of low rewards, or loss of position, if targets were not achieved.

Such portfolio based strategic business management was the first of many approaches to strategy promulgated by the consultancies and academic business school faculty. Subsequent models added to the number of input variables and finessed the outputs beyond Boston's simple prescriptions, but the variations were of limited practical significance. Though the models became increasingly complex and apparently more precise in the spirit of Boston's own differential equation valuing market share, in truth the analysis remained crude and inaccurate, creating more the false impression of additional understanding, rather than any genuine new insight, though they clearly increased the interest in mergers and acquisitions.

Mergers and Acquisitions

Mergers and acquisitions (m&a) was the commonly used term, acquisition being where firm A acquired more than 50% of firm B, and merger being where firm A and firm B joined forces to create firm C which was a new legal entity. Though the term m&a has persisted, the vast majority of such transactions have always been in the form of acquisition rather than merger.

Economists noted that new industries quickly attracted lots of small competitors which persisted through the industry's main growth phase. Then when growth slowed and the industry embarked on its mature phase there was a shake out period with some firms leaving the industry and many others consolidating through m&a to form a smaller number of bigger operators. These then continued till the industry went into decline when there would be a further fall out period leaving only a small number of competitors to dominate what was left. The reducing numbers of competitors was referred to as industry concentration. It left the typical mature industry as an oligopoly, a state somewhere between perfect competition and monopoly which defied precise quantitative modelling.

Such m&a had occurred in waves, in America the first being around 1897-1904 seeing a great industry concentration with the formation of, for example, DuPont, International Harvester, US Steel among many other newly formed big businesses. This occurred despite the Sherman Antitrust Act of 1890. A second wave of horizontal industry concentrating m&a lasted from roughly 1916 till the Wall Street crash of 1929. After that m&a activity remained subdued for around three decades till a substantial wave of conglomeration m&as in the 1960s saw the formation of such firms as ITT, Gulf & Western, Litton Industries and others.

Competitors engaging in the process of industry concentration through m&a might be driven by industrial logic. If competition law allowed, firms could achieve an improved market and technological position more rapidly by m&a than by normal organic growth. This would allow firms to achieve economies of scale in production, distribution and promotion as well as add to their financial strength and might also provide access to strategic patents and other intellectual capital. On the other hand, if prevented from that strategy by anti-trust legislation, firms would be forced to pursue their growth by diversifying away from the existing industry and would therefore acquire an established position and expertise in a new industry participating in its concentration process.

Parallel waves of m&a were experienced in Britain where, by the late 1960s, a form of acquisitive financial conglomerate (AFC) was emerging, largely controlled by individuals who had achieved a substantial element of ownership. Companies managed by the autonomous group independent of both capital and labour still prospered but the new AFCs mingled among them. The AFC owner-controllers referred to themselves in the language of entrepreneurship. Their focus was not however on building a lasting enterprise, but rather more on achieving substantial personal wealth at the expense of other stakeholders. They were becoming more sophisticated in their relationship with the stock exchange, learning how to engage in creative accounting to boost price earnings ratios and therefore raise their share's price above sector average levels to better equip them for aggressive acquisitions.

Similar developments were apparent in America where in 1973 the first substantial hostile deal was completed with the merger of Inco-ESB followed by United Technologies hostile acquisition of Otis Elevator and Colt Industries take over of Garlock. By the mid 1970s hostile take-overs had become a substantial part of m&a activity and new ways of achieving hostile deals were being developed, aided by the professional advice and participation of merchant banks.

The first British wave of 'asset stripping' acquisitions was underway from the early 1970s. Slater Walker Securities, for example, was the centre of one network of acquisitive satellites, whose main function was to acquire companies, dispose of disposable assets, frequently for a large proportion of the original cost of acquisition, 'release' the people who worked the assets, and retain, in most cases, just the core of the acquired business held on a tight rein starved of research and development and severely restricted in capital expenditure, before going on to the next big deal. Slater Walker was one of several such AFCs. Jessel Securities, Trafalgar House, Hanson Trust, Lonrho and many others were in the same category. While business success required commitment to an industry, its technologies, its customers and suppliers and to achieving leadership within that setting, AFC success was dependent on having no such commitments but a willingness to move in and out of industries without hesitation if the immediate balance sheet impact was advantageous.

The distinctions between AFCs, and corporations driven by industrial logic was best made by simply identifying which strategy was dominant: wealth creation or wealth ownership. From the macro perspective of the economy as a whole, it was clear that wealth creation was of greater importance.

Provision for health, education, defence and social services were all financed by the proceeds of wealth creation and strategies for wealth creation. By comparison wealth ownership provided few wider benefits. Indeed it was likely that the financial focus of firms driven by wealth ownership was likely to reduce wider benefits. This arose not only from the short term cost cutting focus which led to immediate rises in unemployment, but also to disinvestment and a direct focus on tax avoidance as a major component of corporate strategy and in some cases the prime reason for acquisition, for example Trafalgar's acquisition of Cunard.

AFCs proved to be a short lived means of enriching their founding owner-controllers, rarely outlasting the demise of their founding entrepreneur. Goldsmith, himself a considerable AFC operator in his time, suggested the fate of all AFC's would be to die with their founders.

Similarly the fourth wave of American m&a activity, from 1984-89, had little to do with industry concentration or industrial logic of any kind. It was characterized by 'the use of aggressive takeover tactics, leveraged buyouts and junk bond financing.' [172] The character of this m&a wave, like the British asset strippers of the 1970s, was driven by the accumulation of personal wealth at the expense of the other stakeholders and the destruction of the companies which fell victim to their raids.

This financial and non industrial approach to m&a action, though punctuated by the bear markets of the late 1990s continued through till the collapse of the credit bubble in 2007/8. The means of financing became more sophisticated and the avoidance of taxation more comprehensive, but the fundamental activity, the purchase of company shares funding for which was ultimately charged to the acquired company, the disposal of assets and people and the accumulation of substantial wealth by the business owner-controller-speculators remained fundamentally unchanged since the 1970s.

Drucker made his views clear on the subject of hostile takeovers:

> *"If enough stockholders take what amounts to a bribe, the raider captures the company and quickly unloads on it the debt he incurred in the takeover ... the victim ends up paying for his own execution. ... Fearful of raiders, companies began practicing defensive capitalism ... More and more of our businesses ... are not being run for business results but for protection against the hostile takeover ...The fear of the raider demoralises and paralyzes."[173]*

The changing of management control without ownership to owner-controlling speculator was facilitated by the new top management strategic perspective which emphasised deal making for quick results rather than the painstaking and progressive building of a business for the benefit of all stakeholders. The result was to 'hollow out' many traditional businesses leaving them without the resources which had been painstakingly accumulated over the years, but burdened with massive debt and unable to withstand even small downturns in demand without large scale redundancy. It was in large part justified, and to a considerable extent instigated by, the promulgators of the new neo-classical economic theory. In 1962 its leader, Milton Friedman of Chicago University had, in the classical amoral, wholly self-interested neo-classical spirit famously proclaimed:

> *'Few trends could so thoroughly undermine the very*
> *foundations of our free society than the acceptance by*
> *corporate officials of a social responsibility other than to make*
> *as much money for their stockholders as possible.'* [174]

Friedman's injunction is in curious contrast with Adam Smith's more disengaged assertion of the role of shareholders:

> '[Stockholders] *seldom pretend to understand any thing of the*
> *business of the company; and when the sprit of faction*
> *happens not to prevail among them, give themselves no*
> *trouble about it, but receive contentedly such half yearly or*
> *yearly dividend, as the directors think proper to make them.'*
> [175]

Outsourcing

The deal making mentality and the focus on realising and squeezing out value so as to make as much money for stockholders as possible led inevitably to the possibility of outsourcing 'non-core' activities previously completed within the company. The potential benefit might arise from the activity being completed better and at lower cost by specialists. Moreover it might enable some of the assets involved to be sold and the proceeds either re-invested more profitably elsewhere or returned to stockholders. Drucker himself argued for outsourcing on the grounds that mundane jobs such as cleaning which offered no career structure if done in house, might present opportunities for promotion if conducted by a specialist cleaning business. Outsourcing could therefore be good for the people involved.

Not only that but the new neo-classical economic theory had a sophisticated theoretical argument to support letting 'the market' provide goods and services if they cannot be done better or cheaper in-house.

An early example of outsourcing was to management consultancy. Firms needing special expertise to solve a particular issue would not necessarily wish to employ that expertise permanently just to provide a one off solution. Fred Taylor, possibly the first management consultant, sorted out the best way to move pig iron, but Bethlehem Steel would not necessarily wish to retain his services as a permanent employee.

By 2004, management consultancy had grown to become a £115bn a year global business, Britain alone spending over £10bn. Spending on governmental and not for profit consulting in Europe was £8.1bn, of which £1.9bn was in Britain. Various studies have indicated a high degree of waste involved in this vast expenditure, as much as 60% wasted because it was not implemented or not needed in the first place.[176]

Moreover the waste was not limited to ineffective assignments. The consultants learned a lot on every job they undertook. Their careers developed through these invaluable experiences gained at the client's expense. They came, they learned, they charged and they took all their experience and learning away with them. And they left behind a management that was little the wiser for all the experience generated by the assignment, and probably including a number of key members of the organisation who were more than a little disenchanted by the exercise.

On the other hand, if the assignment had been completed in-house by permanent staff, it would have been an opportunity for the organisation's own people to gain a broader experience than they would ever have gained in their normal daily work. The benefit of this would be difficult to exaggerate: working on just one change assignment would have inculcated a critical approach to work. It would have invited people to challenge the accepted ways of doing things and to develop better ways and, most importantly, of implementing those improvements. That way, not only would the disenchantment have been avoided, but the learning would have stayed in house. Moreover, the prospects of successfully implementing a solution would have been maximised if it was the organisations own people who were responsible from start to finish. Even if the right person, or people, were not available in the company to undertake the project, it would still most likely have been cheaper to recruit than to pay consultancy fees. In that way the skills and capabilities of the permanent staff would have been enhanced and they would have embarked on a morale building virtuous cycle of improvement.

Elements of these positive and negative aspects of outsourcing are inevitably present in most such decisions. The Friedmanite insistence of the unavoidable inefficiency of public provision led in Britain to the mandatory putting out to tender of many public services, notably within the National Health Service. But the problem in such private public provision is predictable in the clash of cultures. Cleaning hospital wards may be done cheaper by a profit oriented organisation, but less thoroughly. The rise in infections such as MRSA which coincided with this outsourcing resulted in the new mega-hospitals becoming, in the public mind, centres of disease and infection rather than being associated with the improvement of health and curing of disease.

Nevertheless there are some real potential benefits from outsourcing. Offloading responsibility for back office activity and getting it done at lower cost by specialists could allow a firm to focus all its attention on the core activity in which the firm has a distinctive competence which is the source of its competitive advantage. But the motivation for outsourcing is confused. The practical costs and benefits may not be persuasive one way or the other. But the opportunity to realise some assets provides a short term benefit for shareholders which often seems to be the main justification.

The danger is that outsourcing can become a syndrome, often with immediate benefits but questionable longer term effects. The decisive issue is the integrity and motivation of those deciding on the outsourcing: is it for short term cash benefit of shareholders, or for the long term best interests of the organisation and its stakeholders?

Automating Middle Management

Most of the specialist areas of management outlined in chapter six have since benefited from advances in IT and computer systems as well as web based facilities. Some functions, such as materials control, production scheduling and control, order processing and quality management and management accounting have been largely automated with the need for discretionary decisions becoming almost peripheral. In other areas, notably in marketing and marketing research IT systems have been largely supportive.

The first steps in this automation process were taken in the 1960s when computers replaced punched card accounting machines in stock control, payroll, maintenance of personnel records and the like. From there it was a short step to envisaging all management information being automated in a single integrated management information system (MIS) which would record, control, simulate and report whatever was asked of it. Such systems proved illusive and the attempts at their implementation were both expensive in terms of both hardware and software development and their operation frequently in excess of hardware capability.

The more practical way forward was to attack sub units of such a system. Initially this was done by systems analysts capturing the essence of existing manual systems which was subsequently programmed as machine code. It was a laborious process, subject to considerable error both of systems analysis and computer programming. Such custom written systems were subsequently replaced, in all but the very largest systems, by standard packages incorporating all manner of facilities which could be accessed for any particular application.

These standard programmes started off in manufacturing with separate stock control and order processing systems. They were subsequently integrated and combined with production planning and purchasing modules to form what was referred to as a materials requirements planning (MRP) system. The aim of such an integrated system was to replicate the management responsibilities of planning the purchase of materials, scheduling production activities, providing delivery schedules to ensure materials and products were available for production and delivery to customers, and consistent with that, maintaining the minimum levels of inventory and work in progress.

Further development of MRP as MRPII saw the added ability to handle monetary quantities including standard cost information which allowed the system to automate product estimates and quotations, analyse and report cost control information and provided the primary inputs to the management accounting system as well as provide business planning facilities.

These computerised systems, so long as the information fed into them was accurate, provided better inventory control and production scheduling which enabled improved delivery performance to be offered to customers. In addition they also offered better quality control information and so improved quality at the same time as optimising inventories and work in progress which reduced working capital requirements and enabled faster production and delivery. But as with all computer systems their success depended on the quality of data inputs: garbage in – garbage out.

MRPII was developed a stage further with Enterprise Resource Planning (ERP) which is still in use in 2008, based on a single common database holding all the information needed for a comprehensive set of business functions including manufacturing, supply chain management, full accounting and financial planning, human resource management and customer relationship management (CRM) vestiges of which are experienced by all customers of modern internet based suppliers such as Amazon.

ERP is a modular software system rather than the originally envisaged management information system which was designed from the beginning as an integrated whole. ERP allows all business departments to store and access data in real-time. Standard ERP modules provide a wide variety of facilities so that any particular business can make use of what ever particular modules or combinations of modules are needed to control and improve the processes of their particular business. Such computer based systems appear prone to error and underperformance which multiplies as the scale of system increases.

This brief explanation shows how progressively, and with mixed results, middle management was to a substantial degree automated out of existence and with it the real training grounds for future top management. Drucker had argued for the decentralisation of large scale business largely so that young managers might be trained and given experience in real decision making and having real responsibility without taking company threatening risks. But the automation of management in these various functional areas destroyed many of these job training possibilities. The ever flattening corporate management of the 1990s left Drucker concerned that the leadership-development purpose of decentralisation was in the course of being lost. *'The flat organisation does not permit managerial farm teams.'* [177]

The consequence was that managers were drawn increasingly direct from business schools and research universities with a management qualification such as a first degree in business studies or an MBA, but limited practical experience. Furthermore the management degrees were taught by academic faculty who themselves lacked practical experience, now being third and fourth generation academic management teachers, subjected to assessment according to academic criteria and who therefore found it necessary to use management texts replete with case studies and 'practical' exercises written by other academics similarly lacking in practical experience. And it was from these ranks that top managers had to be appointed, having had much less contact with real people in the workplace.

Strategic Management Mindset

The change in perspective from general to strategic management was fundamental to management's fall. Paradoxically it resulted in a change of perspective from the long term to the short. Hayes and Abernathy reported in 1980 how American managers' focus on short term costs rather than long term technology, and using analytical detachment rather than hands on experience, was leading to what they referred to as a 'disinvestment spiral' where investment in new technology was delayed or avoided altogether for immediate cash reasons, which only led to a loss of competitive strength either through the lack of product performance or increasing marginal cost of production, which cumulatively led to 'economic decline'.

They cited the portfolio system of central 'control' as inhibiting long term investment in technological innovation. They contrasted technology's achievements, for example, the laser, xerography and transistors, with the trivia such as new shape potato crisps and feminine hygiene deodorant, produced by the new orthodoxy, a risk averse financial orientation to marketing.

The reasons why American managers had adopted this new orthodoxy were several. Firstly there had been a dramatic increase in financial and legal executives getting to the top of American corporations in preference to those with technical or other industry specific experience. Secondly, companies had increasingly hired top management from outside, often from outside their industry. Such managers had necessarily managed their companies simply on the basis of financial information and controlled their development without technical knowledge on the basis of oversimplified decision rules of thumb such as to "invest in businesses which dominate their markets and sell those that don't".

These were the strategic managers and this was their mindset. The consequent focus on deal making, particularly mergers and acquisitions, was therefore not surprising since the top managers expertise was largely limited to finance. But it had done substantial damage to many of America's leading companies as well as Britain's, leading them to neglect their core technologies and rendering them vulnerable to attack by more technologically focused competitors. The automobile industry was then, as now, a prime example.

Since then the short term orientation of top management has been further emphasised. Firstly this was by the explosion in hostile takeovers driven wholly by short term financial aims and justified by the new neo-classical theory; secondly by top management's growing detachment from industry and business arising from the new strategic management led orientation to portfolio management; and thirdly by the seduction of that top management to follow the Friedman injunction to maximise shareholder wealth rather than accepting any broader responsibilities.

10. GOVERNMENT and BUSINESS

Though Keynesian economics had become the accepted orthodoxy after the second world war, in Austria a group of neo-classical economists argued for tight monetary control of inflation and free market capitalism. Ludwig von Mises and Friedrich von Hayek denied the feasibility of Keynes' mixture of liberty and state intervention. For them socialism was the only real alternative to the classical model and that would necessarily replace the autonomous role of management, and create a huge and expensive central planning bureaucracy which could never work as effectively as market forces. Their arguments, supported by Friedman at Chicago university, became the alternative to Keynesian economics, available for implementation whenever governments were so inclined.

By the end of the 1970s, electorates in both Britain and America were ready for change. Keynesianism had resulted in wages push inflation caused by organised labour emboldened by continuous years of full employment and led by increasingly powerful and ambitious trade unions. Keynes had indicated the solution to wage push inflation would have to be political but successive governments had failed to impose one. Inflation combined with stagnating economic growth, 'stagflation', appeared to be the natural result of Keynesian economics. Electorates in Britain and America turned to more conservative administrations for their alternative solution. They were not disappointed.

The new governments turned to the uncompromising Friedmanite restatement of the neo-classical free market model, initially with emphasis on control of the money supply as the lever of economic regulation. Friedman argued that Britain's economy demanded a shock treatment of government spending cuts and tax reductions while controlling money supply, accepting the unavoidable rises in unemployment which he argued would only be temporary. The United States economy being in a less parlous state required a less fierce treatment, but the direction was the same.[178]

Friedman's interpretation of the neo-classical model included the unflinching assertion of the duty of 'corporate officials', quoted in the previous chapter, to accept no social responsibility 'other than to make as much money as possible for their stockholders'. This was voiced in1962, a time when the Soviet Union appeared to be strong and threatening to capitalist systems. The risk that corporations were being weakened by the acceptance of social responsibilities or corporate philanthropy had been highlighted four years earlier in the pages of the Harvard Business Review when Levitt argued that capitalism's future depended on business making money not 'sweet music'[179]; social welfare was not an issue which should divert the attention of industrial management; it was the responsibility of government, paid for out of the taxes from successful business.

Friedman's approach was adopted by governments which were determined and committed to its implementation. Their first priority was to resolve the wage push inflation caused by strong unions and the previous commitment to full employment.

Subsequently free market ideas were focused on the withdrawal of government from direct involvement in the public sector, their aim being to privatise public ownership wherever possible, minimising the state's involvement which had grown up notably in Keynesian Britain. Where it was not politically feasible to privatise, government sought to control through a myopic system of targets intended to mimic what were conceived as private sector performance indicators, a process which tended to undermine any autonomous role for public sector management.

The process gave birth to the mantra of competition and choice. Friedman himself had proposed, as a typical example, the issue of school vouchers enabling parents to pay for their children to be educated at a school of their choice, rather than their local state school. The choice would be influenced by reference to school league tables based on performance against measurable targets, the intention being to introduce competition into the state education sector and so improve performance. The concept of professional school management was reduced to the achievement of recordable performance against quantitative indicators imposed from the remote centre of government.

Friedmanism

The essential planks of Friedmanism were those of neo-classical economics with a heightened emphasis on monetarist control, low taxation and small government.

The monetarist argument stemmed from the 1930s depression which was held by classical theorists to be caused by the Federal Reserve policy of restricting money supply. Monetarists rejected the Keynesian argument for full employment as the best way to stimulate demand and argued that by simply increasing the money supply, market forces would be enabled to do the rest. The inevitable consequent rise in inflation could be controlled by limiting money supply to a level which would support a rate of unemployment which was thought to be sustainable given industrial circumstances. To reduce unemployment further would require an increase in money supply which would lead to accelerating inflation which was not sustainable except in the very short run. The sustainable level of unemployment was a matter for political judgement, a level at which organised labour would be weakened but not necessarily destroyed and forced into covert or open revolt.

However, control of the money supply was no longer straightforward. New technology had added considerable complication. Effective control could only be achieved by precisely the heavy state interference which the Friedmanites argued strenuously against. In later years Friedman accepted that monetarism had never worked as effectively as he had anticipated.

Government needed to be small because it was paid for from the taxation which was a burden on both individuals and on corporations. The high tax burden encouraged non-productive activity, notably in tax avoidance, which Friedman argued would not have been undertaken were the tax rates lower. It was anticipated the lower rates of tax would bring increased revenues to the exchequer by removing the incentive to avoid and evade.

Friedman's predecessors, Smith, Ricardo, Marshall and the rest and including Keynes, all had argued the virtues of a progressive taxation system whereby the richer paid a higher proportion of their income in taxation. Friedman simply argued that tax should be minimized, his followers interpreting this as being against progressive taxation, Friedmanite governments reduced the level of taxation particularly on the richest, thus reversing the more egalitarian trends of the previous fifty years.

Friedman's expectations that lower tax rates would reduce tax avoidance were subsequently disappointed; the tax avoidance industry expanded substantially even though tax rates were substantially lowered.

Friedman's argument was in part political.[180] If non-democratic regimes were to introduce economic freedoms then political freedom would inevitably follow, and conversely, that central control of economic activity inevitably resulted in political repression. Though neither assertion was necessarily true, for Friedmanites, free market capitalism was seen as vital for political freedom to survive and prosper.

Friedman also propounded what he referred to as *'a sort of empirical generalization that it costs the state twice as much to do anything as it costs private enterprise'* [181] Though he provided several examples to support this belief they were not examined in any depth and it was not clear that the comparisons wee fair or that there were not alternative explanations. Nevertheless the 'sort of empirical generalization' informed the philosophy stressing the advantages of the marketplace and the disadvantages of government intervention, and influenced the policies of conservative governments. From the 1980s on Friedman's views on monetary policy, taxation, privatization and deregulation informed the policy of governments around the globe including the Reagan administration in the United States, Thatcher's in Britain, Pinochet's in Chile and many others, as well as of international financial institutions such as the World Bank and International Monetary Fund.

However, his assertion of management's duty to maximise shareholder wealth lacked practical precision, just as did the profit maximisation assumption of microeconomics. The microeconomic model ignored timescale, referring unavoidably to individual transactions, but it was clear that seeking to maximise the profit from an individual transaction, for example the sale of a product to a customer, would compromise the longer term and far greater profit from a lasting relationship with customers. Similar considerations applied to maximising shareholder wealth. Nevertheless, the idea of maximising shareholder wealth influenced management in particular ways in certain situations, for example in the case of a hostile takeover bid.

Before Friedman, management might not unreasonably have construed their duty as being to preserve their company's autonomous survival in the short term and progress its longer term prosperity for the benefit of all stakeholders. But Friedmanism suggested quite different priorities in the event of a takeover bid being received. Then their responsibility would be to get the best deal they could for shareholders, to gain an immediate windfall that would enable them to reinvest elsewhere so as to maximise wealth. The interests of other stakeholders such as employees or customers were not of concern. Thus Friedmanism fundamentally changed the role of management in such situations. Previously, management would have seen its role as to fight, fight and fight again to preserve the company's autonomy in the best interests of all stakeholders and only to accept being taken over as a last resort.

Friedmanism was not just a minor adjustment of direction from Keynesian economics for business, government and academia, but an about turn which had unforeseen consequences. It reversed the previously closing gap between the 'haves' and 'have nots' and created new inequalities. So much was inevitable and the old arguments justifying the inequity of the classical system were used in its defence. It undermined any notion that management might, in its autonomous role, moderate the worst effects of the amoral pursuit of shareholder wealth. The task of industrial management was to pursue shareholder value at all costs. In this practitioners and theorists alike were persuaded to agree.

Economic theorists added to the apparent sophistication of the free market capitalist argument with three sub-plots which directly impinged on the role of management. Firstly, agency theory, not so much a theory as a simple assertion, provided an explanation of the role of management which had previously been missing from economic theory. It held that management were the agents of stockholders and must therefore act in their interests above everything else. This was the prime theoretical justification for requiring management to maximise shareholder wealth. Secondly the development of transaction cost economics was the justification for the existence of firms as opposed to sourcing from the open market. This was used to legitimise the deal making strategies and in particular the outsourcing movement referred to in the previous chapter. Thirdly the definition of a theory of competitive management control, an open competitive market in corporate management, justified what has been referred to as the 'financialisation' of managers and their action to achieve short term gains for stockholders, including those from hostile takeovers.

Together these three explained and justified the pursuit of Friedmanite ideas to their logical conclusions. All three were flawed, if not wholly false, and gave rise to consequences which undermined the role of management, were economically destructive and were inequitable in their effect. Chester

Barnard's earlier comment on the dominance of economic thought in management was pertinent:

> *"Though I early found out how to behave effectively in organisations, not until I had much later relegated economic theory and economic interests to a secondary though indispensable place, did I begin to understand organisations or human behaviour in them."* [182]

But economic theory and economic interests continued to play a primary role in both government and business and continued to obscure understanding of organisations and human behaviour in them.

Conservative Government

Since the second world war the political ideologies which led British and American governments had diverged and only came together again with the almost simultaneous installation of the conservative administrations of Ronald Reagan and Margaret Thatcher, since when a right of centre consensus has ruled on both sides of the Atlantic. Conservatism which was renewed by those governments was essentially Friedmanite in character. In Thatcher's case it replaced the former one nation middle of the road Conservatism which sought to stabilise the economy, exercising control over wages and dividends. In Reagan's it was a renewal of domestic Republicanism after the more international focus of post war administrations.

Thatcher had been instrumental in setting up in 1974 the Centre for Policy Studies, a right wing think-tank to promote Friedmanite free market economics, privatisation of state-owned industries, lower taxation with emphasis moved from direct to indirect taxes, and a reduction of the size of the welfare state.

When she came to power in May, 1979, she had claimed her experience as housewife and daughter of a grocer had taught her the importance of good house-keeping and her duty to make sure that every penny raised in taxation was spent wisely giving good value for money to the taxpayer in return.

Reagan came to power less than two years later with a very similar commitment. Though America's record of industrial disputes had been less stormy than Britain's, Reagan was faced with a critical and decisive strike barely six months into his presidency. The Professional Air Traffic Controllers Organisation (PATCO), despite having a 'no strike' clause in their employment contract felt themselves to be in a powerful position and went on strike for more money, less work and better pensions. Reagan, knowing that all public sector workers would follow suit if PATCO succeeded, ordered them back to work or to face dismissal. The Federal Aviation Administration (FAA) improved its offer but developed a contingency plan for in case it should be rejected. The vast majority of PATCO members did reject the improved offer and were dismissed. Much to most people's surprise the FAA plan worked and over 11,000 PATCO members stayed dismissed and the union was fined heavily for organising an illegal strike. Reagan's handling of the strike impressed the American electorate and other unions alike.

It had also impressed Margaret Thatcher. In her famous claim that there was no such thing as society she was declaring her profound belief in the individual and self help over any collective groups having state support. This commitment would have surely led her into direct conflict with trades unionism anyway, but the ground for such battles was being prepared by the unions themselves.

Industrial strikes had resulted in the loss of office of the previous Conservative government in 1974, had been a continuous aspect of economic life throughout the subsequent period of Labour rule till a final eruption of public sector disputes in winter of 1978-9 were largely instrumental in bringing down the Callaghan government, paving the way for Mrs Thatcher.

The crunch eventually came with the coal miner's strike of March 1984 led by the National Union of Mineworkers whose president was a one time member of the Young Communist League. The strike continued for a full year ending with the miners' defeat. It was probably due to Thatcher's personal determination and stubbornness that the strike was defeated. Two years later the print unions, refusing to accept the implications of new technology, were similarly defeated by News International following their move to new premises at Wapping equipped with new technology. That strike action also lasted, at least nominally, for over a year.

Braverman, in his work on the erosion of craft skills and degradation of work,[183] had noted prior to the Wapping strike (or lock out), that Britain did not de-skill labour in the same way as America; craft skills were broken down, redefined and often protected through trade unions. The Wapping dispute showed Britain in a different light, merely a time interval behind America in its inevitable acceptance of new technology. For Braverman it was not the inevitable progress of technology, but a conspiracy of owners and their hired agents to dispossess and dominate the workers.

The real economic significance of strikes and other industrial action is in dispute. Amateur and incompetent management certainly playerd its part, but the unions were widely portrayed as the major cause of decline in several British industries such as machine tools, automobiles, motor cycles, shipbuilding, coal and textiles. They certainly had a high profile in the largely right of centre media where they were portrayed as crucial. Whatever their real significance in monetary terms they were certainly important symbolically.

It appeared that British management had failed to manage industrial relations effectively. Trade unions were driven on occasions more by political aims rather than simply the pay and working conditions of their members, which management might have found more straightforward to deal with.

Politically motivated union militancy was then broken in both the public and private sectors. The defeats had been inflicted on unions which were fighting for ideas which had ceased to be tenable. Even in 2008 the National Union of Mineworkers website referring to its 1984-5 strike concluded:

> *'The strike had not been about wages, better conditions or any material gain. It had been waged on principle; the principle that miners jobs were held by each generation of workers in trust for those who would come after them, and must not be wantonly destroyed .... This strike had set a new example in working class struggle, marking another milestone in a long road. It had been hard, bitter, painful, and as in 1926, there were those who said that never again would the British trade union movement see such a conflict. As in the aftermath of 1926, only time will tell.* '[184]

Similar sentiments might have been expressed regarding the print workers defeat at Wapping, or about the activities of the Luddites faced with Arkwright's new cotton spinning machinery. The progress of technology is always unavoidable and direct opposition is always bound to fail.

The Friedman ideology which informed the administrations of Reagan and Thatcher succeeded in controlling the money supply, deregulating markets and reducing the power of organised labour. In Thatcher's case too nationalised industries were privatised, elements of the welfare state were reduced and in the short term at least unemployment was allowed to increase rapidly. As a result they succeeded where their predecessors had failed in lowering inflation and reviving the economy. That was in the 1980s. Those same policies were not necessarily appropriate to different situations, but the Friedmanites espoused them as generally valid in all situations, just as the Keynesians had with their opposing prescriptions following the 1930s recession.

So the accumulation and investment of capital resulting in an inequitable distribution of benefits had been successfully re-established. The opportunity had been made available once more for government and for industry led by management to demonstrate some magnanimity in their victory and adopt Preston's *'true spirit of co-operation between employer and employee'*. But the opportunity was not taken.

Since the 1980s governments of all colours, Republican or Democrat, Conservative or Labour, have accepted Friedmanite ideas and used them to shape their tax, monetary, trade and business policies. This universal acceptance was given further impetus with the collapse of communism so that raw free market capitalism was almost universally accepted across the globe as the one best way of organising all economic activity.

Governments had themselves become increasingly involved in promoting international trade in latter day mercantilist ventures. Promoting trade was the unspoken top priority of diplomatic services everywhere. Ex diplomat Carne Ross showed how the whole machinery of government was deployed to maximise business because 'it's the economy, stupid!' He explained it as follows:

> *'It is assumed in places like the Foreign Office and in governments world wide that trade is what their countries "want". But this of course is a very big assumption. The foundation of this assumption is what underpins neo-classical economics, namely that individuals seek to maximise utility through consumption, ie people want more things. Writ on the national scale, this assumption is expressed as more trade and more growth. But there is growing evidence – good hard empirical data too – that this is not in fact the case.'* [185]

The evidence Ross refers to [186] suggests the pursuit of wealth does not result in greater happiness once above a basic level of income. Research among so called neuroeconomists suggested basing economic action not on the simple amoral, self interested utility maximising *homo economicus* assumptions but on what actually goes on in the head of *homo sapiens*. Though more difficult to model, the approach at least indicated that the priority that governments and their civil services gave to the economic interest might be inappropriate. Nevertheless, the orthodox wisdom remained, true or not, that governments must be seen as business friendly if they were to be re-electable.

Political parties of all hues had become nervous in case they should be construed as in any way 'anti-business'. Political leaders were not infrequently drawn to escort groups of senior business people, including tax haven based super rich, on international business jamboreees. Such governmental initiatives were grounded on Friedmanite theory which could even draw governments into unthinking support for apparently dubious, if not wholly corrupt, export activities, such as the British BAE Systems-Saudi arms deal.

Unquestioning acceptance of the necessity to be business friendly was a weakness of democratic government which the business lobby could only be expected to try to exploit. Business would naturally avoid paying taxes if it could, using tax havens where necessary so long as their actions were legal. The role of government was traditionally construed as being firm and fair, for example, closing tax loopholes where the ingenuity of business appeared to defeat the spirit of the law. The business lobby would of course cry wolf – 'they would say that wouldn't they?' - but their real concern would be that they were not disadvantaged compared with their competitors.

Government's traditional task was to provide the level playing field. But under the continuing influence of Friedmanite dogma and business lobby pressure, government lacked the moral conviction and possibly the expertise to resist and fulfil their political role.

Friedmanism made no distinction between the industrial business sector in products and services and the financial sector which though it had begun as the means of arranging debts and loans in support of the business sector, had long outgrown that limited role. The financial sector still depended on real business as exampled in recent years with the emergence of the Chinese sovereign fund as a substantial financial resource. China's traditional problem was how to feed its population. The sovereign fund emerged not from the brilliance of Shanghai's financiers but a bi-product of China's low labour cost manufacturing industries. Without Chinese manufacturing its financial sector would have remained a minor player. Marx would no doubt have remarked on this expropriation from industrial labour and found it surprising in what was still nominally a communist country.

Financial sectors were not concerned with creating new wealth so much as matters of its ownership. Governments, failing to distinguish between business and finance, between creating wealth and owning it, have been anxious to be seen as friendly to Wall St and the City of London as they were to real business. In Britain's case this anxiety led to restricted taxation of financial sector operators for fear they might leave the City and ply their trade elsewhere. It was never clear whether this was a serious possibility or indeed whether their departure would have been significant to the real economy.

Management, Ownership and Risk

The creation of wealth has always been the driving force in growing economies and its distribution the source of aggravation. The financial sector's contribution, originally simply to provide the financing of growth, latterly succeeded in reversing the process, expropriating the wealth accumulated through business operations. The process of expropriation was supported by the Friedmanite theory of an open market in corporate management focused particularly on managements which retained the traditional focus on making things rather than money. The core theoretical prop justifying this reversal was agency theory.

Agency is the assertion that corporate management, in the shape of company directors, are the agents of the stockholders, who are the principals in the relationship. Management must therefore work solely in stockholder interests. But agency theory is palpably false. The principal in this particular relationship is actually not the stockholder, but the company. This was always the case. When joint stock companies were first established they were created as separate legal entities. They were sometimes referred to as "legal persons" as opposed to natural persons. Company directors were empowered to act for and on behalf of the company and acting in good faith, which they were legally bound to do, meant acting in accord with the company's best interests. Directors, like all other employees, had contracts directly with the company, not with the stockholders. It was simply not the case, never was and is not now, that managers or directors were agents of the stockholders.

For agency theory to be valid, it would be necessary to deny the company its legal status.

*'The mechanism agency theory used to break the connection
between the manager and any notion that he or she owed an
obligation to the firm was to argue that the firm itself was a
legal fiction, a ghost of the mind. The organisation
according to early agency theorists Armen A Alchian and
Harold Demsetz[187] was merely "the centralized contractual
agent in a team productive process – not some superior
authoritarian directive or disciplinary power."'[188]*

But in company legislation across the world the company, or the
corporation, is accorded its separate legal existence with rights to make
contracts and behave in many ways like a person, with directors acting for
and on behalf of the corporation. It is not a 'legal fiction' or a 'ghost of the
mind', nor is it merely a centralised contractual agent.

The untruth which is agency theory had unfortunate effects, not only on
perverting the overall objectives of business and its managers, but in more
particular circumstances such as a hostile takeover bid, where the theory can
be used to justify action to the detriment of the company and its employees,
suppliers, customers and other stakeholders.

The effects of the Friedmanite focus on shareholder wealth have been almost
exclusively destructive of the management project and negative so far as the
wider social impacts are concerned. Even though it is based on a flawed
analysis, agency theory remains curiously strong as what Galbraith[189]
referred to as an 'institutional truth', that is not a truth at all, but an
overarching lie which has to be bought into if an individual is to survive and
prosper in a particular setting.

Furthermore, if the company was to be regarded as a 'legal person' then it
could not in the normal sense of private property, be owned by anyone. Not
since slavery was abolished have persons been legally owned. The
stockholders' position is therefore somewhat different from other forms of
ownership. Stockholders own share certificates which give them certain
entitlements, but they do not own a proportion of the company; they may not
go to the company and demand that they take away their proportion of its
assets. Stockholders' ownership position is peculiarly limited compared to
normal ownership rights of private property, more akin to the temporary
ownership of betting chips in a casino. They don't give part ownership of
the casino itself but the right, at some risk, to a potential share of the
surpluses it generates.

The nature of stockholding changed when joint stock companies were quoted on a stock exchanges enabling investors to dispose of their shares and so avoid having their financial fortunes locked into a particular enterprise. They had the freedom of exit at any time. Their financial interests were not restricted to investing in the particular company, but rationally took account of all investment opportunities. Thus a wealth maximising shareholder would readily sell their shares to a hostile bidder for a quick profit in order to invest their newly enlarged capital in other opportunities. Any other response would be irrational. Their interests do not necessarily coincide with the best interests of the company. They have no responsibility, or owe any duty, to the company. If they are dissatisfied with their company's performance they can make representations to the firm's management, they can try to engage the interest of other shareholders at the firm's annual general meeting, or they can sell their shares and invest elsewhere.

Nevertheless the fable, the untruth, remains that stockholders own the business and employ directors and managers as their agents to run it on their behalf. This plugs a gap in the economic theory which could only ascribe to managers the amoral self interested motives which would drive them to maximise their own pay and perks and minimise their inputs. Economic theory does not accommodate the autonomous role of management working in the best long term interests of the company and its various stakeholders.

The problem for Friedmanite economists was how to persuade these amoral self interested managers to make as much money for stockholders as possible. The obvious answer was to convert them into stockholders by remunerating them with share bonuses. They would then act in their own amoral self interest on behalf of shareholders. This would determine how company directors should respond, for example, to take over bids. If the bid resulted in the shareholders receiving an immediate pay back then it should be accepted with the caveat that the directors should endeavour in such deals to ensure the shareholders received the best value for their shares. The directors should not in these circumstances act in the interests of the company itself or of other stakeholders. Remunerating directors in part through share options was to ensure they fully endorsed the Friedmanite injunction and deserted their independent position as professional managers. Those that conformed might quickly join the ranks of the wealthy.

This is a different kind of management from that addressing the tasks and responsibilities described in earlier chapters who were the managers focused on making things rather than money for its own sake. Their prime responsibility was to act in the best interests of the company. Their responsibility to the shareholder would have been best interpreted as managing the share performance, so as to be in the stockholder's best interests while they remained stockholders, but not extending to acting against the interests of the company, much less to sacrificing its independence or its existence altogether, in order to maximise stockholders' financial gain.

The Friedmanite theory and particularly the imperative to act solely for the stockholder had a number of consequences. Firstly the theory was used to justify substantial escalation of management compensation through stock option bonus schemes. These schemes had little effect in terms of raising real management performance,[190] but in conformity to the theory they did serve to convert the manager-as-agent into a shareholder-as-principal and thus, it was argued, to accept the objective of maximising shareholder wealth.

The 'option loaded CEOs had a relatively high likelihood of delivering big losses' because they were encouraged to go for riskier projects because their options had no downside and if all went wrong they were still likely to 'benefit from a lucrative exit payoff if they are fired.'[191]   In 2007 extraordinary examples of such payoffs included the CEO at Merrill Lynch, who presided over an $8bn write down, precipitating the banks ultimate failure, but was given a $161mn payoff, and the CEO at Citibank responsible for $11bn write downs being rewarded with a $100mn payoff.

The same principles applied in industry where director-stockholders were also insulated from the risk attached to any particular strategy and were thus encouraged to adopt high risk high return projects which caution would have prevented them adopting in normal circumstances. This moral hazard was further magnified by the increased pressure to take a short term perspective and so achieve the quick results which would activate the share bonus payments. Under other circumstances management would have been more likely to adopt a longer term strategic view of the business.

The short term perspective and reduced concern for risk reinforced top management's deal making mentality resulting from the 'strategic' approach described in the previous chapter.

The manager turned shareholder is subject to one other potential difficulty. Under current legislation a shareholder who takes advantage of insider information which is not available to all shareholders stands to be accused of the criminal offence of insider dealing. Insider dealing arises when purchase or sale of shares coincides with availability to the shareholder of insider information. The manager-shareholder is by definition an insider and any purchase or sale of shares by them must fall into the category of insider dealing. Similarly the design of any scheme from which they might benefit and which involves any share transactions such as issue, purchase or sale, would appear to fall into that same criminal category. Even more importantly from a management perspective, it succeeds, as it is intended to do, in persuading managers to forsake their all important autonomous, independent role between capital and labour.

The notion that companies exist solely to maximise shareholder wealth has become ubiquitous. Satisfying a customer need is merely an operational means to achieving the overarching goal. So embedded has the notion become that many company directors have the duty formally spelled out in their service contracts, even though this is likely to be in contravention of company law, and certainly against its spirit. Thus the end result for management of Friedmanite economics has been the reversal of the financial and industrial positions. Financiers aggressively attack the industrial sector with the avowed aim of realising, extracting, even 'squeezing out', value that industrial management has been 'sitting on' while they attended to customer needs rather than those of stockholders. The vehicles for achieving this process, the investment banks, private equity funds, sovereign funds and other professionally managed financial resources have little concern for the industrial strengths, capacities and futures of the firms they acquire and deplete.

Governments have remained, naively and gullibly, in thrall to business, failing to distinguish between the wealth creating industrial sector and the wealth expropriating financial sector, fearful that they should be seen as business unfriendly by either. In their final execution of the Friedmanite project governments have sought to impose on the public sector what they conceive as the discipline and efficiency of private for profit business.

Public Sector Competition and Choice

The Friedmanite revolution had a profound impact on the public sector and its management. The overriding idea was that the public sector should be privatised where possible and the parts that remained would be much improved in terms of cost and value for money as well as the quality of its delivery, by imposing on it the management methods, systems and criteria that government believed had worked for the private sector.

This followed Adam Smith's logic of homo economicus which guided the most efficient use of resources in a nation's economy, with public welfare coming as a happy by-product. Today, the Friedmanite Adam Smith Institute, which concentrates exclusively on the free market strand of Smith's contribution, describes itself as

> 'the UK's leading innovator of free-market economic and social policies. It researches practical ways to inject choice and competition into public services, extend personal freedom, reduce taxes, prune back regulation, and cut government waste.'[192]

The first imperative was to privatise whatever could be privatised. The Thatcher government effectively dismantled Britain's mixed Keynesian economy privatising water, gas, electricity generation and distribution, land line based telephones, railways, airports, and nuclear energy plus a number of smaller disposals and secondary offerings disposed of later including British Steel, British Airways and British Leyland.

Initially regulation of the newly privatised industries was done with a light hand and the businesses easily beat their targeted results which were within easy reach. Thereafter regulation tightened. The real impact of privatisation is difficult to assess. Where there was a natural monopoly, as with the utilities, there seemed to be no pressing practical reason to privatise, only the doctrinaire motivation. Where there was natural competition there seemed to be no real reason for public ownership, other than to rescue a lame duck which might have the potential for a long term future. Perhaps the difference between public and private ownership is less significant than widely believed, the critical issue being the degree to which politicians, who increasingly lack non-political experience, engage with detailed management.

A further aspect of Friedmanite thinking was the dogmatic imposition of competition and choice on those areas of the public sector which could not be privatised. And there was the attempt to measure and report the value for money being delivered, usually expressed in terms of league tables of performance against government set targets.

In principle there might seem to be no reason why private sector management principles should not also be applied in the public sector. The division of management labour described previously identifies several specialisations that are equally relevant to public sector organisations, as well as the basic approach of making best use of resources.

But there is a problem. The dichotomy between the public service culture and the commercial is fundamental. Jacobs[193] identified these two moral cultures or 'syndromes', the "commercial" governing the behaviour of people in businesses, which was characterised by competition, honesty, initiative and enterprise, while the other "guardian" culture, governing behaviour of governments and their public servants, emphasised loyalty, tradition, prowess, exclusivity and the distribution of largesse. These cultures had developed over age long practice which had demonstrated the most effective behaviour for their individual situations and circumstances. Jacobs highlighted the incompatibility of the two cultures which Caulkin illustrated with the example of the British government which, in its enthusiasm for imposing private industry criteria on the public sector, included monetary incentives to meet certain targets as part of the remuneration for general medical practitioners (GPs).

> 'the disastrous results of the GP contract can be traced directly
> to the government's determination to turn an essentially
> guardian organisation into a commercial one. GPs have
> responded to incentives in textbook fashion, by finding ways to
> meet the targets. The government had changed their motivation
> from intrinsic (the work itself) to extrinsic (outside rewards).
> But, as a patient, which GP would you rather consult, one
> motivated by money or by doing the best medical job?'[194]

Such an apparent lack of governmental understanding of the guardian culture of its health service employees has been repeated many times over, with inappropriate targets distracting attention from the primary aims of the service. The government's perspective on what motivates people is wholly based on the 'economic man' assumptions; we are all wholly amoral and only interested in maximising our own utility which is defined as money. Friedmanite governments find no finer motivations credible. Yet the existence of the traditional professions and the public areas of health, education and social security are operated by people many of whom are driven by higher motivations than money.

Moreover performances against target all need measuring, recording and reporting, with the costs of the requisite bureaucracy detracting from the health service's primary provision. Friedmanite governments have repeated their doctrinaire prognoses in all public service areas such as education, social services, the police, the fire service and the probation service, with similarly dysfunctional, if not disastrous result.

The critique of the free market approach to public services has became so extensive and so well documented it will not be repeated further. Quality guru Deming held that target setting was hostile to quality because they (ie targets) were goal focused not process-focused; they addressed ends not means. An organisation could resort to any means to accomplish virtually any end wants. For Deming, a *'quota is a fortress against improvement of quality and productivity. I have yet to see a quota that includes any trace of a system by which to help anyone to do a better job'.* As an example Deming cites the policeman who must issue a quota of parking tickets every day. '[195]

Attempts to create artificial markets, competition and consumer choice have generally provided no real benefit and could be disastrous. For example, British governments have expressed the desire to privatise the Post Office for doctrinaire reasons, Friedman having attacked the United States Post Office's legal monopoly in America. But British governments failed to override public opinion in favour of retaining the Post Office in public ownership. So they subsequently sought to introduce competition and choice to various monopoly markets served by the Post Office, with private sector delivery services being encouraged to cherry pick profitable services in which to compete, for example, inter-city deliveries, but not required to provide a universal service including delivery to remote locations. This inevitably reduced the Post Office's overall viability to which the government responded by closing many rural offices which provided a service but no profit. The logical conclusion of this Friedmanite approach is to suspend mail deliveries to the Outer Hebrides, deepest Cornwall and any other unprofitable destinations, or at least to charge the full cost price which would be many times more than the price of city centre postal delivery.

The Post Office in this area, like the NHS, is from the guardian culture, not the commercial. Friedmanite economics don't work in these situations - there is no one best way. Public ownership doesn't necessarily mean direct engagement by the government and the imposition of inappropriate targets which add bureaucratic overhead and non productive cost.

The Friedmanite Legacy

Prior to the Reagan and Thatcher administrations adopting Friedmanism the neo-classical project had been kept alive by a number of dissident academics in various research university departments. The accepted orthodoxy was Keynesian, an elaboration of what Keynes himself had advocated, which justified continuous and significant government control and regulation of the economy in Britain, though less so in the United States, in order to maintain full employment, and which led to wage push inflation and stagnant economic growth.

The Friedmanite version of classical theory, emboldened the new conservative governments to confront organised labour head on. Their victories over union militancy resulted in a prolonged period of much improved industrial relations as measured by working days lost from strikes and industrial action. Organised labour itself appeared subsequently and for the time being at least, to share the view that industrial action was a weapon to be used sparingly and with greater care than previously to avoid doing damage to labour and its cause.

The Friedmanite belief that free market capitalism led to political freedom for the individual ie liberal democracy and that government intervention in the economy led inevitably to tyranny and totalitarianism. This was the basis of what was sometimes referred to as neo-liberalism. It remains a theory, so far falsified by the examples of both China and Russia.

Friedman's belief that private enterprise is good, public delivery is bad because of the *'sort of empirical generalisation that it costs the state twice as much to do anything as it costs private enterprise'* [196] The assertion may have some approximate truth regarding things which are wholly dependent on cost for their justification, but where they are also dependent on non-cost issues the point is valueless. Judging public service by private criteria and vice versa is inappropriate.

Friedman's belief that low taxation would increase tax revenue to the Exchequer was wrong. He argued *it would make it unprofitable for people to resort to the tax gimmicks and loopholes they now use.'* [197] But in fact tax avoidance and evasion has grown substantially since 1977 at the same time as tax rates have been dramatically reduced. The really rich pay expensive tax consultants to eliminate their taxes altogether.

Friedmanism minimised tax and rejected the idea of progressive taxation. It denied the professional culture driven by ethical codes of practice, and the guardian culture of the public sector, and therefore sought strenuously to reduce them to the basic amoral, self interested economic man concept to which all economic actors are persuaded to conform.

The aggravation which inequity causes has been remarked time and again since Defoe's record of peasants pulling up the stakes around new enclosures. The grievance of the poor and excluded is never far below the surface. The 'super rich' of Friedmanite economies have taken inequality to a new level. Drucker had suggested in 1996 that the ratio between the top executive's pay and that of the average hourly paid worker,

> 'could be no more than twenty to one without injury to company morale ... Few top executives can imagine the hatred, contempt and even fury that has been created – not primarily among blue-collar workers who never had an exalted opinion of the 'bosses – but among their middle management and professional people.'[198]

Drucker had quoted J P Morgan as supporting this view. In 1960, the ratio between CEO and average hourly paid pay in America was already far above the twenty to one ideal at 41 times, by 1996 according to a *Business Week* survey it had grown to 209 times, and by 2005 the ratio was 262 times.[199] This inequity, encouraged by Friedmanite governments everywhere, has certainly caused 'hatred, contempt and even fury' and has debased management itself.

A final element in the legacy of Friedmanism arises more from the changing world circumstances. When Friedmanite governments came to power the main concern was how to resume economic growth and the creation of wealth seemed a reasonably appropriate preoccupation. By the turn of the 21st century the notion of wealth creation was widely challenged. Industrial production, it was argued, did not create wealth so much as extract it from the earth's store and convert it with varying degrees of inefficiency. By then it had become plain that the earth's resources were not only finite but were being consumed at a rate which was both unsustainable and accelerating. In addition there was now a more or less total scientific consensus that industrial pollution was adding substantially to, if not the prime cause of, a catastrophic level of global warming.

In these changed circumstances Friedman's injunction for industry not to be concerned with any other social responsibility than to make as much money as possible for stockholders was seen as destructive and dangerous.

Despite these adverse considerations and unforeseen consequences, Friedmanism became the orthodox economic wisdom across the world. And a major source of its success was because it had been promulgated through American business schools and research universities and from there to the rest of world leadership.

11 BUSINESS SCHOOLS & MANAGEMENT EDUCATION

Management has been hugely successful in presiding over the process of industrialisation and the resulting rise in standards of living even if the distribution of industry's surpluses have never seemed equitable. In the early days of the twentieth century management educators saw the role as of heroic importance to the lives of workers and the security of populations. Management had developed a new and decisive role in decision making of unprecedented importance and yet being independent of the traditional rights of private property ownership. It was then neither beholden to capital nor to labour.

This autonomous role of management appeared to lack any traditional form of legitimacy but the overall impact of professionally managed industry was revolutionary. The early doomed attempt to establish management as a profession with its own ideals and standards of behaviour was replaced by the academic attempt to establish it first as a science and secondly as a thoroughgoing liberal arts subject in its own right.

These various approaches to management, led by business school faculty in leading universities, were initially focused on improving its practice but latterly were more concerned with research and the achievement against academic criteria at the expense of management practice.

The promulgation of management as an academic subject was the final piece in the jigsaw of management's fall from good practice and higher ideals. This story is a generalisation and as with all generalisation's there are exceptions. Some managements in all industries operate with integrity for the best interests of their companies and all stakeholders. But in the face of the pressures already described, from the progress of strategic management within and the almost universal acceptance of Friedmanite thinking without, it has become ever more difficult for managers to maintain the values and practical approach of Chester Barnard, Wilfred Brown or Peter Drucker. Such non conformist behaviour on the part of management is not what is learned at business school and might seem to any moderate Friedman influenced individual to be quite puzzlingly irrational.

Why Management Education Matters

Sumantra Ghoshal argued that management theory taught in business schools based on the 'homo economicus' assumption was not only incorrect but in many different ways damaging to management and managed, to industry and to society as a whole.

One example of the damage being done was in the encouragement of management greed and crookedness which had surfaced in corporate scandals such as Enron, Worldcom, Tyco and a hundred others and revealed how the upper reaches of management practice had been perverted. Prior to their downfall many of these firms had featured in 'highly laudatory' business school case studies. Though they were rapidly withdrawn or rewritten and a renewed emphasis laid on the delivery of modules in business ethics and corporate social responsibility, the old Friedmanite ideas persisted as the mainstream orthodoxy.

According to Ghoshal

> *'Many of the worst excesses of recent management practices have their roots in a set of ideas that have emerged from business school academics over the last 30 years.'* [200]

He argued that a refocus of management education was necessary:

> *'Business schools do not need to do a great deal more to help prevent future Enrons; they need only to stop doing a lot they currently do. ... we – as business school faculty – need to own up to our own role in creating Enrons. Our theories and ideas have done much to strengthen the management practices we are all now so loudly condemning.'*

Keynes had pointed out that economic and political ideas were more powerful than commonly understood:

> '*Practical men, who believe themselves to be quite exempt from any intellectual influences are usually the slaves of some defunct economist ... It is ideas, not vested interests, which are dangerous for good or evil.*' [201].

But the ideas of neo-classical thinkers such as Friedman conditioned 'practical men' always to suspect vested interests; to do otherwise would be naïve and naïveté would be an unforgivable error for 'practical men' such as managers.

The teaching of Friedmanite economics supported by the explanations of agency theory, transaction cost analysis and the open market in corporate management, legitimised some management behaviours and de-legitimised others, even for managers who had not personally had the benefit of an MBA education but who had ingested the ideas and spirit of those who had.

The management behaviours which theory legitimised through the Friedmanite injunction to maximise shareholder wealth supported by all the other neo-classical paraphernalia included the exploitation and abuse of employees, customers, the local community and the environment, the grasping of stock ownership for themselves where possible and the manipulation of rewards to stockowners at the expense of the longer term future of the business and its other stakeholders. Drucker exampled the exploitation and abuse of employees when he expressed his contempt for those managers who removed the jobs of employees and paid themselves extraordinary bonuses for so doing.

The management behaviours which theory de-legitimised included the exercise of balance in the distribution of benefits among stakeholders, investment in the local community or environment at the short term expense of stockholders, all long term investment, and the pursuit of social responsibilities and the adoption of any moral or ethical consideration other than maximising shareholder wealth and short term economic gain.

In natural science a theory does not change reality, it is merely an idea awaiting proof. If tested it may be found to be correct at which point it becomes a law; or if found to be incorrect it is disregarded. In social science, theories are not so susceptible to scientific testing. Ideas which are successfully promulgated in social science tend to become self-fulfilling. Despite lack of proof they may be successfully promulgated by sufficient adherents and so achieve a critical mass at which point they present the appearance of a scientific law. But while a scientific law has no impact on reality, merely reflecting it, a successful theory in social sciencecan have a profound impact on behaviour as Keynes, Ghoshal and others have noted.

Today the products of management education have been shaped to a considerable extent by the Friedmanite orthodoxy to act rationally and amorally, to maximise the wealth of their shareholders.

The budding entrepreneur is assumed to be motivated only by a desire to achieve rapid personal wealth – any other consideration would be irrational – so he or she is advised always to have their exit strategy ready; the notion of building a worthwhile lasting enterprise is regarded as fanciful. Consequently the student of management has come to be regarded with cynicism and even contempt. But it was not always so. The notion that a business might be established for the accomplishment of higher ideals was once accepted; management education started out with high aspirations.

The American Lead

The first business school was established in the United States in the late nineteenth century[202] while the first British business colleges were not established till after the second world war and the first university based business schools not until 1965 and Oxbridge did not join the fray till the 1990s. Britain was slow to follow the United States lead. The British schools closely copied the American model, establishing post graduate MBA degrees based around the American curriculum and pedagogic methods and adopting the American management literature.

Khurana's sociological perspective traces the development of American management education from the initial drive to establish American management as a high profession alongside medicine and law. Early management educators aimed to teach not just efficiency and effectiveness but also for management to fulfil its role as a profession for the greater good of society.

As corporate America developed, the economic importance of management and managers was increasingly recognised and the ethically based content of a management curriculum became more appropriate for a university based school. Initially university based management education was delivered by people with practical experience but limited academic standing. So within universities the focus was placed on achieving academic respectability rather than on improving management practice. The need to do research, largely economics based and quantitative, to achieve academic respectability became increasingly pressing.

Management courses, such as the MBA, were not standardised. Schools were variable in quality and reputation and lacked coherent aims. The Association to Advance Collegiate Schools of Business (AACSB) was set up with the aim of becoming the co-ordinating professional body which might act as gatekeeper to the profession. However its ambitions were never achieved and in due course its role declined to that of an accreditation bureau.

Early on business schools adopted economics as the main underpinning theory of business though initially institutional economics, which paid more attention to practical realities, was more flexible and less quantitatively tractable than neo-classical theory, was accepted as more relevant to management education. However, as business school faculty became more academically sophisticated the neo-classical theorists, encouraged by the Ford and Carnegie foundations which funded much business education, gradually became dominant .

The search for academic respectability led business school faculty to try to establish management as a scientific subject: quantitative, rational, technique based, focused on planning, forecasting and controlling. This coincided with the establishment of large scale diversified conglomerate corporations which had resulted from anti-trust legislation which limited the growth of any single enterprise within an industry. Management was then established with a general expertise which was deemed to be applicable to any situation, industry or technology. Finance and accounting provided the common language for managing these diversified corporations and maximising profit became accepted as the single common objective.

The funding foundations favoured the 'scientific' approach to management and encouraged research in economics and business administration, giving priority to schools which focused on the application to management problems of neo-classical economics, behavioural sciences, statistics and mathematics. The foundations funded expansion of doctoral programmes, thus increasing the academic orientation and quality of business faculty. Having developed a scientific basis, management programmes became progressively less concerned with the realities of practice and more with the establishment of academic credibility.

The management generally taught in business schools was focused on tools and techniques, systems, quantitative methods and financial manipulation with little regard for technical competence related to any specific industry situation and little acknowledgement of the value of practical experience. Friedman's focus on maximising shareholder wealth, established within academia long before it extended to government, justified the priority given to short term deal making ahead of long term general management.

Pursuit of shareholder wealth was a core aspect management education. Performance in that regard was monitored and reported and a market in business control was theoretically established such that underperforming managements would be taken over and dismissed.

'If a management team fails to maximise shareholder value, this poor performance will be noticed by observers of the firm and competing management teams will vie to displace incumbents by takeover.' [203]

Whether or not this was realistic, its impact along with the thousands of other such assertions made in mainstream economics texts and repeatedly reinforced by business school faculty, was profound. Despite the legal requirement that directors had regarding the interests of all stakeholders, maximising shareholder wealth became the all pervasive syndrome. Khurana quotes even the Business Roundtable:

'the paramount duty of management and of boards of directors is to the corporation's stockholders; the interests of other stakeholders are relevant as a derivative of the duty to the stockholders. The notion that the board must somehow balance the interests of other stakeholders fundamentally misconstrues the role of directors. It is moreover an unworkable notion because it would leave the board with no criterion for resolving conflicts between the interests of stockholders and of other stakeholders or among different groups of stakeholders.' [204]

In a note on the above quotation Khurana quotes Holmstrom and Kaplan that the shareholder value orientation 'had become institutionalised inside the culture and structure of American corporations' and

'that managers became aware of the potential benefits of pursuing shareholder value by observing the success of LBOs (leveraged buy outs) and takeovers in the 1980s. Helped along by generous stock option programs, management came to endorse shareholder value in the 1990s and to pursue it with vigour.' [205]

Even those who opposed the notion of shareholder value used it to rally objectors and reinforced it as an accepted truth. For example, the anti corporate propaganda film, *'The Corporation'*, asserted that all publicly traded corporations were structured through a series of legal decisions to have a peculiar and disturbing characteristic:

> *'they are required by law to place the financial interests of their owners above competing interests ... even the public good'*[206].

It was not true but it was proclaimed by Friedmanites, taught by business schools, elaborated by others and became universally accepted. It legitimised the asset stripping activities of the financial sector including investment banks and private equity funds which were then able to attract management students who accept their own amoral self-interest as taught.

The business schools themselves were then acting according to the logic of what they taught. They were in the market place, subject to all manner of league tables which determined their market position. Students were attracted on the basis of the return they would get from their MBA degree. One published league table calculated the internal rate of return from MBA courses: the net present value of the additional cash earnings over a life time including pension achieved as a result of having the MBA, less the cost of achieving it. In Khurana's words, business education had taken itself down from its initial aspiration to teach professional 'higher aims' to the production of self interested 'hired hands'.

Management: Science or Humanity

Management struggled to establish itself as a thoroughgoing academic subject worthy of attracting top calibre faculty. It had adopted its underlying neo-classical economic theory. It had produced some interesting empirical research into practice and developed some local theory about organisation structure and human behaviour in organisations. In so doing it had borrowed from psychology and sociology. It had also encompassed some professional credentials in the form of finance, accounting and law. But it did not appear to be an academic subject in its own right.

Based around its economic and quantitative components the attempt was to emphasise its scientific aspect and provide it with a scientific core. This is a problem for social science which has seen repeated attempts to make use of theory from other spheres, notably natural science and mathematics. But the application of mathematical phenomena to explain issues in social science is almost invariably spurious, if not disreputable. Chaos theory, for example, has been a popular mathematical theory applied to the management problem, but its application has no real truth.

> " Unfortunately it is often difficult to find a mathematical model that is sufficiently simple to be analyzable and yet adequately describes the objects being considered. These problems arise in fact whenever one tries to apply a mathematical theory to reality.
>
> Some purported 'applications of chaos theory – for example to business management or literary criticism – border on the absurd. And, to make matters worse, chaos theory – which is well-developed mathematically – is often confused with the still emerging theories of complexity and self organisation. " [207]

There are no examples in the literature of an 'analyzable' chaos model which adequately describes objects in business management. Discussing management issues in terms of chaos, complexity, string theory or any other developing strand of mathematics appears to be insubstantial, once described as 'pretentious froth'.

Game theory has been used to aid understanding of the logic underlying decision processes. For example, Nobel laureate Schelling's insight that a country's best safeguard against nuclear war is to protect its weapons rather than its people, the logic being that an enemy is less likely to strike first if it believes you can strike back after a nuclear hit, rather than simply that you can survive the hit. Examples of game theory models of competition exist but their real contribution tends to be rather more academic than practical. In any case these are fairly slight inputs to management theory compared to the claims of some social theorists to use mathematics and natural science to model social systems.

Game theory apart, the only way in which these mathematical theories could make a useful input to management would be as metaphor. But metaphor is unnecessary when the real thing is at hand. In the case of neo-classical economics models, the mathematical application makes no pretence to be metaphoric. They are mathematical equations which have their own existence quite independently of any pretence to model reality. Nevertheless they embody a pretence to be applicable to real situations and have been so applied with malign effect.

Ghoshal referred to Elster's distinction between the explanations of behaviour in science and the humanities.[208] In natural science the explanation is simply causal: combining a with b causes c. In biological science there may be functional explanations: an organism behaves in a particular way to enhance its reproductive fitness. In the case of management individual actions are largely explained by the intentions of the actor which may be based on some long term aim rather than an immediate result. Management theories, such as the profit maximising model, are assumed to be causal or functional and do not accommodate individual intentions as an explanation of behaviour. The attempt to make management theory scientific therefore meant that moral and ethical considerations had to be excluded as incompatible with the underlying approach.[209] Explanations which could not be reduced to numbers were excluded.

However moral and ethical considerations have been widely acknowledged as essential aspects of management education as demonstrated by the inclusion of 'business ethics' as a standard MBA course and the existence of corporate social responsibility (CSR), a more narrowly defined procedural approach to business ethics in practice, as an even fashionable part of contemporary management. They may be patently necessary aspects of management, but have been added to the curriculum as separate modules which do not infuse or interfere with the basic shareholder value curriculum, and usually offered as options which students may avoid if they so choose. The Friedmanite theories underpinning management education have remained untouched, the core curriculum unaltered.

The alternative of infusing the various management studies subjects with an ethical ingredient would strike right at the heart of the dominant theory and require its substitution with something different and the psychological commitment to the status quo is yet too weighty to make such a modification feasible.

The question of whether or not there should be an element of moral education in management courses has long been debated. Objections are raised that it is not the job of an MBA teacher to proselytize some particular moral perspective to their students, or to try to influence their personal values. On the other hand the promotion of the Friedmanite thesis does just that. And a short course on business ethics hardly offsets the preponderance of business school amorality.

While there may be various approaches in teaching business ethics, there is consensus on three issues. First, that the ethical performance of business needs to be improved. Second, that improvement depends on raising the ethical values of people in business, and, third, it will only be achieved through a process of moral education. Together they are the foundation of the business ethics curriculum.

De George highlights various themes which underlie his approach to business ethics. The first, and perhaps most crucial, of these is that,

> *'business – national or international - can be no more ethical than the persons who run the firms. Companies that act with integrity are a function of individuals within them who act with integrity'* [210]

This is a basic tenet of business ethicists and has long been part of the orthodox wisdom:

> *"What matters most is where we stand as individual managers and how we behave when faced with decisions which combine ethical and commercial judgments."* [211]

The approach of business ethics is therefore personal, the intention being to inform, educate and indoctrinate so that the ethical standards of the individual recipients are raised and the business organisations in which they operate are therefore also 'improved'.

Ethicists can tend to be unrealistic suggesting, as they often do, that managers can't be genuinely ethical unless what they do in no way serves their own interests, ie ethics must hurt. Stark reported the following assertion:

> *'To be ethical as a business because it may increase your profits is to do so for entirely the wrong reason. The ethical business must be ethical because it wants to be ethical.'* [212]

Such statements may be regarded as idealistic or simply wrong headed, but their unworldliness stems from their theoretical roots in moral philosophy. They contribute little to the practice of business management. A typical business ethics course covers, at a necessarily superficial level, aspects of moral philosophy, such as utilitarianism and universalism, and defers to Mill, Bentham, Kant and others as well as the ancient Greek philosophers, all of whom are totally innocent of modern business and the dilemmas it poses.

The idea that the ethical performance of a business depends on the moral values of its managers would be a major limitation. Managers are temporary post holders, whereas the integrity which the business needs its stakeholders to perceive, is permanent. It needs to be built into the culture of the business so that it not only survives changes of senior managers, but is robust and impervious to any who might either deliberately or inadvertently put the company's reputation at risk.

The practical application of ethics to business practice is also problematic. Several different vehicles have been tried. Corporate philanthropy was advocated, but the object of the philanthropy, according to ethicists, must not be associated with the activities of the business. Otherwise it would not be philanthropic, but merely self interested publicity. Whether or not such considerations have any value they appeared to weaken the appeal of corporate philanthropy as a management initiative.

CSR is another approach which has established itself as a fashionable management routine which has penetrated deep into the reporting of business practice:

> *'It would be a challenge to find a recent annual report of any*
> *big international company that justifies the firm's existence*
> *merely in terms of profit, rather than "service to the*
> *community". Such reports often talk proudly of efforts to*
> *improve society and safeguard the environment.'* [213]

In the pursuit of CSR some businesses have invested in schools or health facilities as, for example, Shell have done, in the delta region of Nigeria to partially mitigate the adverse impacts their operations have had on the local population. In Shell's case the net impact of its Nigerian operations on corporate reputation has nevertheless been overwhelmingly negative.

Despite all this the basic Friedmanite philosophy remains dominant.

> *The proper business of business is business. No apology*
> *required.* [214]

It is government's responsibility to guard the public interest, to regulate business so as to protect its citizens and to attend to the demands of social justice, to provide public goods and collect the taxes to pay for them. Governments tend sometimes not to be good at discharging these responsibilities. But that does not mean business should pay voluntarily instead. Friedman's insistence that business must seek to maximise shareholder wealth and Levitt's warning not to make 'sweet music', express the dominant fear that free market economy businesses risk being sidetracked into ineffectiveness by business ethics and CSR.

From the academic perspective, business ethics has considerable attractions. It brings to management educators the provenance stemming from the great and ancient philosophers which is helpful to management faculty in establishing their credentials to their academic peers.

Academic Criteria

In both America and subsequently Britain great investments were made in raising the academic standing of business school faculty and the academic quality of business school research and publication. Inevitably this strengthening of the academic focus resulted in a divorce from management practice. As DeGeorge expressed it forthrightly about business ethics,

> *'the legitimacy of business ethics as an academic field does not depend on its ...being effective in changing the climate of business in the United States. As an academic field it stands or falls on the quality of the research done in it, on the body of knowledge developed, and on its success as an academic liberal arts subject.'* [215]

University departments, including business schools, are formally assessed as to their 'quality of research' - by which is meant very largely the number of publications in academic journals of appropriate standing. And they are publicly funded accordingly. Faculty members are therefore driven to achieve against the academic criteria of research and publication rather than to impact on management practice. Harvard Business School, for example, proclaimed on its 2007 web page:

> *'Each academic year, the faculty authors or co-authors about thirty-five books, produces more than 300 academic papers, and writes a broad array of articles for general business publications.* [216]

Practice is similar in Britain where the Higher Education Funding Council for England is responsible on behalf of government for the allocation of research funds to universities. It sets criteria and establishes procedures by which to evaluate universities' research activities, ie publications, and funds are allocated according to the ratings which result. The funding is important. In Britain there is much less private benefaction and endowment of university activity than there is in the United States. Public funding of £4.6Bn is provided for teaching students which is the basic university support and on top of that a further £1.5Bn is targeted at research universities according to the quality of their research which is assessed primarily on the amount and quality of their publications.

Consequently the primary purpose of management educators, since this system of assessment and funding was first instituted in the 1980s, has been to publish academic papers rather than contribute to the improvement of management practice. Business school faculty now tend to have limited practical management experience other than as occasional advisors or consultants with no line responsibility for results. Nevertheless they dominate the mainstream subject area aimed at practitioners. This is exampled by the Financial Times supplements on Mastering Management[217] which contained 55 articles by management specialists. Of these contributions 51 were by academics, 2 by consultants and 2 by practitioners. Parallel supplements on Strategy[218] contained seventy eight articles by strategy specialists. Of these contributions, all bar two were by academics and the two exceptions were by 'educators' (one on-line and one consultant); not a single contribution was from a practitioner. This dominance by academe is of prime importance in the promulgation of theoretical ideas to the practical and political worlds.

The need for business school faculty to publish their research is facilitated by the publication of academic journals. The EBSCO database on which 'academic institutions worldwide depend ... as their core resource of scholarly information' contains full text for more than 2,000 journals, including more than 1,550 peer-reviewed titles, covering virtually every area of academic study. Its business database 'includes nearly 1,100 business publications, including full text for nearly 500 peer-reviewed business publications'. Most of these journals comprise articles written by academics and are edited by academics and whose readers, if any, are also academics. The purpose of such journals is not to be read but to be vehicles for the allocation of research funding. Their relevance to management practice is incidental.

The quality of such academic journals is variable as is the calibre of the academic peers who review contributions. All have a vested interest in the publication of journals and journal articles, irrespective of their limited readership and lack of relevance to real world practice.

The subject matter of management being clearly determined according to academic, rather than practical, criteria, has led it into abstruse and problematic areas which offer the opportunity to contribute an article on a subject which has not previously been exhausted. Such abstruse topics serve academic ends, for example, the reputation building of young faculty plus perhaps the provision of some intellectual challenge against which students can be tested in order to achieve their educational qualification. They have little practical interest or content.

Mis-Educated Managers

Espousing the stark Friedmanite version of the dismal science, so useful in establishing the academic worth of management studies as a fully fledged social science subject, management students are led inexorably to the denial of moral or ethical considerations. Business school 'educated' managers are thereby freed from a sense of moral responsibility in their subsequent management practice. So the theory is self-fulfilled.[219]

Management has been perverted from its original higher aims. It provides access at its top to unimaginable riches, but the inequality it exploits only brings its practitioners into public contempt. This is a far cry from anticipations of Chester Barnard and Wilfred Brown whose practice was efficient and effective within a tough but ethical frame which respected all people and sought to deal fairly with them and ensure their equitable rights were honoured.

Instead managers were taught by new models of strategic management how to maximise short term shareholder gains by hollowing out the resources which manufacturing businesses and mutual societies had managed to accrue over many years. They learned the quick benefits of deal making as opposed to managing. With no professional affiliation or commitment, subverted by business school education, led to short term shareholder value maximising decisions, legitimised by reference to Friedman and colleagues, they largely ignored more profound longer term impacts.

And these longer term impacts were considerable, including the depletion of the earth's resources, the pollution of its atmosphere and destruction of its climate. Industry and its management were not only the prime cause of these ills, but also the only real hope for their solution. But while under Friedman's baleful influence there would be little reason to expect management to fulfil these heroic responsibilities.

PART FOUR – MANAGEMENT RENEWAL

Just as management first came into existence from necessity, an additional cost but an overwhelming benefit, so now its renewal is also necessity. It presents the best, perhaps the only, opportunity for the earth's resources to be conserved and its climate protected. Continuation along the Friedmanite route is leading to disaster.

Management's competence is specific: cost minimising, efficiency maximising, profit oriented, technologically innovative and competitive. Of themselves these characteristics will not resolve the problems referred to above. The global playing field must not only be level but it must be slanted against the polluters in favour of the environmentally fiendly. Free trade capitalism may remain the foundation, but government intervention to regulate markets, to fund appropriate projects and outlaw others, will have necessarily to be accepted as legitimate.

Management's aspiration to create the new is continually demonstrated by the development of start-up enterprises and by the innovations of established businesses. Willingness to take risks in the interests of improvement are demonstrated by the high mortality rate among new enterprise and by the totality of R&D investments in private enterprise. Small and medium sized enterprises (SMEs) continue to play a hugely important role in the developed world. Even in Britain, 99% of enterprises were SMEs in 2005, accounting for around 58% of employment and over half of business sales revenue.

The continuing vitality of technological innovation within the commercial and business setting, overseen by management is demonstrated in a thousand different industries. Every industry has the capacity to respond to new situations such as climate change, if effectively managed to use its creative vitality for the greater good as well as the individual enterprise.

Corporate legislation reasserts the autonomous position of management with the responsibility to act even handedly between all stakeholders in the best long term interests of the enterprise. Economies in this twenty first century will need to be managed, as Keynes himself would have done, increasing government spending and possibly reducing taxes to increase demand when in a slump and then prodding it to remain prospering at full employment. But when, if wage push inflation gets out of hand as it inevitably will, using the only political solution that has been seen to work, allowing unemployment to rise, and if necessary bankruptcy, to bring it back under control. To run a balanced budget in the longer run, allowing deficits to arise when in slump, repaying them when in full employment.

Other aspect of Keynes, and of Adam Smith, Ricardo and Marshall before him, are likely to be implemented such as the establishment of a progressive income and inheritance taxation system to achieve a more equitable distribution of incomes and wealth and what Galbraith referred to as 'social balance', bringing the Friedmanite super rich back into society's fold where they will no longer be the source of 'hatred, contempt and even fury'.

These ideas are replacing more dogmatic versions of free market capitalism among opinion formers in research universities and business schools where there is increasing awareness of the extent to which managers have been corrupted, and management educators misled, by 'bad theory'.

12 NEW RESPONSIBILITIES

In 2008 it was still possible, and in fact common practice, to separate thinking about economic growth from thoughts about the damage being done to the planet by economic activity. Media reporters, in their perennial search for disaster stories, turn from the dire consequences of a reduction in GDP growth rate projections, to reports of the more dire consequences of the melting of the polar ice caps, to reports, for example, of the planned opening of a third runway at Heathrow to accommodate projected growth in air travel which, without the third runway, might go elsewhere. The topics are treated as separate and unrelated, as though the thought that they might be connected is too uncomfortable even to be entertained.

For Friedmanites it may be too uncomfortable. To misquote the man himself: few trends could so thoroughly undermine the very foundations of human life on this planet as the acceptance by corporate officials of no other social responsibility than to make as much money for their stockholders as possible. Friedman's assertion of management responsibility has to be refuted and reversed if humanity is to survive and prosper.

The fall of management from its higher aims resulted from a combination of causes: its development of 'strategic' thinking which paradoxically resulted in a shorter term, deal making orientation, the rampant progress of Friedmanite free market capitalism which seduced management from its autonomous role into becoming the agents of shareholders and the puppets of neo-classical, amoral self-interest. The result was measurable in terms of generally, though not universally, higher living standards, increasing inequality of wealth and income, massive pollution and the unsustainable depletion of the earth's resources.

This economic refocusing was sparked by a group of academic economists, firstly in Vienna and subsequently in Chicago with their re-interpretation of neo-classical economics. Like all paradigm shifts it took a long time to replace the Keynesian orthodoxy.

Management's renewal might be achieved by the different ideas being researched and starting to be taught in research universities and business schools. These include a modification of the fundamental 'homo economicus' idea by what has been labelled 'behavioural economics'. This is based on empirical studies of real human behaviour. It is unlikely to provide a mathematically sophisticated model of economic activity, but its importance lies in its rejection of the dismal reductionist version of human motivation necessarily assumed by Friedmanism.

The achievement of this paradigm shift will also take some time. But its nucleus of academic researchers and promulgators has already been at work for half a century. The adoption of Friedmanism, following a long slow period of incubation, was achieved after a recognizable tipping point, signaled in Britain by the 1978-9 'winter of discontent' which ushered in the Thatcher government, and in the United States with the swearing in of the Reagan administration. From that point the paradigm shift was swift. The credit crunch of 2007-8 with its outrageous beneficiaries such as the erstwhile CEOs of failed banks, the super rich morally hazardous, may be another such tipping point.

A more equitable model of free market behavioural economics incorporating some notion of social balance both within and between existing populations but also between this and future populations, might quite rapidly emerge as the new economic orthodoxy. This will require different economic theory and a different management curriculum to be taught in business schools and research universities.

Business, Resources and Pollution

When the Republican administration came to power in the United States in 2000 it was possible to deny the reality of climate change and the global warming impact of human activities. Public perceptions may respond only slowly to the weight of published evidence, but the position has changed radically over the past few years.

> *"In 2002, Watson (now the British government's climate change tsar) was ousted as Chairman of the Intergovernmental Panel on Climate Change (IPCC) after pressure from the Bush administration. Lobbyists from the American oil industry*

reportedly pressed the new president to replace Watson at the earliest opportunity for a heinous crime: claiming that humans were contributing to climate change by burning fossil fuels, and then getting a 2,500-strong group of experts to produce influential and carefully constructed scientific reviews to prove it.

The oil men hoped to change the course of the IPCC, and stop the world waking up to some of the awful truths about climate change. Five years on they must feel a little dejected: a series of reports by the IPCC this year [ie 2007] *unequivocally linked climate change to human activity.'* [220]

Bush's opening position on climate change was not long tenable. In his second term he was forced by the weight of scientific evidence and opinion to reverse his former denial.

Industry causes, directly and indirectly, the vast bulk of man-made climate change which is contributing to global warming with as yet unknown, but generally believed to be catastrophic, result. Industry must also produce the solutions. Until governments internationally intervene to provide the necessary regulatory framework it will be difficult for individual businesses to take decisive action, even with their own carbon footprint, because of the probable response of competitors.

Industry's activities have always polluted the environment and consumed limited resources and in the past companies have rarely paid the full price for these 'externalities'. Sometimes it has been because the adverse impacts were not known or not fully understood. Businesses have usually been reluctant to admit the extent of the damage they were doing, and when whole industries were involved they have typically tried every means of avoiding paying for the consequences of their activities. Early industrialisers polluted without restraint, doing grievous damage to the local communities and to their local environment. And such damage is being repeated, especially in the underdeveloped and emerging economies where the pressures to raise standards of living are greatest.

The asbestos companies provide an example of the polluting process and its outcome. They responded only slowly to the increasing awareness of their health impacts. In many cases they carried on operations almost regardless of consequences for as long as they could. The reputation of the major operators was destroyed and the cost of compensating the damage they had caused bankrupted the industry.

While asbestos had a particular virulence the impact of industry as a whole on the earth's climate is a more serious proposition. Hardly any industry has a clean record. Global resources such as water, oil and various metals, are being used up. Air is being contaminated; land and oceans are being polluted with chemicals, toxins and heavy metals, and ever more waste is being created with no apparent means of its safe reprocessing. Biodiversity is being lost in both vegetation and animal species on land and in the oceans. And all these problems are going to get worse before they can ever start to get better.[221]

Pollution in general, and the level of greenhouse gas emissions in particular, are in a state of flux. Projections from the US Energy Information Administration, for example, indicate that world coal consumption is expected to grow by 74% over the 25 years to 2030 during which time coal's share of international energy consumption will have marginally increased from 26% in 2004 to 28% in 2030.

China, already the world's largest coal consumer and enjoying GDP growth around 10% pa, is a major cause of the increase in coal consumption and greenhouse gas emissions. But China's per-person energy use and greenhouse gas emissions remain far below levels found in richer countries, for example, roughly one-eighth of that in the United States.[222]

> "Even if we were to stabilise the concentration of greenhouse gas emissions at today's levels, which is impossible, we would still see a further half degree or so just built up on past emissions ... It's absolutely inevitable we're going to see 1.5C°, so our challenge is to try to limit it as close as possible to 2C° above pre-industrial (1850). Some level of adaptation is going to be needed and, clearly, to limit at 2C°, you need significant global action to reduce the projected emissions over the next 50-100 years." [223]

The scientific consensus is that the problems are real, are becoming ever more dangerous and are caused at least in substantial part by human activity. As time passes the gravity of expected outcomes becomes more and more alarming. Strict pollution control will in due course have to be imposed if life on the planet is to prosper.

When disaster has been predicted in the past, for example Malthus' prediction that population growth would outstrip food supply, it has been technology, rather than government, that comes to the rescue. And it is apparent that technology is the only feasible means of resolving the current environmental threat. Ensuring that polluters are taxed and the necessary technology is subsidised is a substantial global political problem.

Company managers are today charged with the legal duty to, quoting the British Companies Act of 2006 which is fairly typical, 'have regard to the impact of the company's operations on the community and the environment'. The severity of punishment for polluting is bound to increase as the climate change threat becomes more severe and the probability of punishment will also increase as public interest becomes more pervasive. Whatever are today's incentives not to pollute, they will substantially increase over time.

The problem represents a substantial opportunity and motivates green innovations in products, processes and services. This is illustrated by, for example, developments currently being worked on in the internal combustion engine, a basic technology that is more than a hundred years old. Hybrids using new battery technology may be a stop gap solution to more fuel efficiency. Superchargers made feasible by today's more robust engines enable the same power output from engines of half the size thereby reducing fuel use and carbon emissions. Fuel injection and variable valve timing have already improved engine efficiency but replacing their mechanical control by electronics and hydraulics enables part engines to be shut down when not needed and for the normal four stroke cycle to be varied according to need, radically increasing fuel efficiency as well as the construction of powerful but small two and three cylinder engines. Other innovations include the ability to switch from petrol to diesel fuels according to performance needs. The combined effect of the above developments would be to double the efficiency of that ancient technology, car engines. Other innovations in the application and use of cars could multiply that improvement several times over.

It is difficult to see a limit to the potential of technological innovation, but the possibility of an economic return would be essential for it to be accomplished.

The reward for fuel efficiency is clear when fuel prices are high. On the other hand, the application of technology to reducing pollution does not provide this promise of economic return unless governments intervene to punish polluters and reward green products and processes and fund green R&D. Such intervention and regulation might be anathema to Friedmanite free traders, but will be essential to future development.

Similarly corporate legislation directly contradicts the Friedmanite contention but is vital to the future development of industry.

Directors' Legal Responsibilities

The British Companies Act of 2006, like most corporate legislation right across the globe, confirms the status of the joint stock company or corporation as a separate legal entity, thereby totally invalidating the application of agency theory and thus much of the dismal science's perspective on business and management. Both shareholders and management have contracts with the company, but there are no contracts directly between management and shareholders, defining one as the agent of the other.

The shareholders' contract with the company has changed quite radically from the time when they invested in overseas expeditions and were effectively locked in till the expedition's safe return. Today their contract is simply related to the purchase of share certificates for which there is no guaranteed return of value. Their investment is known to be risky and as a consequence there is an expectation of an appropriate return, but no legal contract. Shareholders' liability on behalf of the company is limited to the their initial investment and beyond that they have no responsibilities to the company. They are free to come and go as they please.

Management's contract with the company is defined in corporate legislation referring to the duties and responsibilities of company directors. Directors' transactions with the company are dealt with in some detail as there may clearly be a conflict of interest between the director acting in his or her own interest and when they may be acting for and on behalf of the company. Such conflict of interest may well arise in the case of a hostile takeover. The general injunction in such cases is to be completely honest and transparent. There is also specific legal constraints on how a director may act for the company in a situation where they know it to be insolvent. Accepting payments under such circumstance is fraudulent and the director may well face legal action. These apart, directors' duties tend to be identified rather tentatively and in some cases even ambiguously. There are indications that so long as directors act in good faith they may be unlikely to face legal action. Nevertheless, corporate law in the English speaking world suggests a more enlightened approach to business and management than is suggested in mainstream management education.

The 2006 Companies Act introduced the concept of "enlightened shareholder value" (ESV) suggesting that achieving success for the company involves a balance between short term and long term as well as sustaining good relationships with employees, customers and suppliers and others and also maintaining the company's reputation and being careful of its operations' impacts on the local community and the wider environment. The Act actually charges directors with the following:

> *'to promote the success of the company for the benefit of its members as a whole, and in doing so have regard (amongst other matters) to—*
>
> *(a) the likely consequences of any decision in the long term,*
>
> *(b) the interests of the company's employees,*
>
> *(c) the need to foster the company's business relationships with suppliers, customers and others,*
>
> *(d) the impact of the company's operations on the community and the environment,*
>
> *(e) the desirability of the company maintaining a reputation for high standards of business conduct, and*
>
> *(f) the need to act fairly as between members of the company.'* [224]

The meaning of the "success of the company" is not defined in the act but a ministerial statement suggested

> *'For a commercial company, success will usually mean long term increase in value.'* [225]

This broader view of management's responsibilities is not new. As far back as 1844 legislation charged company directors with responsibility for

> *'the direction, conduct, management, or superintendence of a company's affairs'* [226]

By direction was meant the framing of policy

> *'so that action can be kept consistent with the desired ends and that long term objectives and the general welfare of the company shall not be sacrificed to some short term or temporary advantage.'* [227]

The legislation indicates that the company has explicit or implicit contracts with all its stakeholders: customers, employees, suppliers, shareholders, bankers, tax authorities, local community, environment (as proxy for future generations) and it is management's job to work for the best long term interests of the company, balancing these various stakeholder interests.

Directors are legally charged with acting for and on behalf of the company in its transactions with all its stakeholders. They occupy positions on both sides of any company : director transaction, both acting for and on behalf of the company and necessarily also acting as independent stakeholders in the company. There is therefore the potential for substantial conflict of interest. As well as indicating how directors should promote the success of the company the Act flags up special requirements on the way directors should conduct themselves [Part 10, Chapter2 of the Act]. These include the duties not to exceed legal powers, to exercise independent judgement, reasonable care, skill and diligence, to avoid conflicts of interest, not accept benefits from third parties and to declare any interest in proposed transactions or arrangements. These last would presumably include any projects that might influence any bonus issues or payments.

Responsibilities to Other Stakeholders

The company's other prime transactions are with its shareholders, its employees and its customers. Shareholders are not just the recipients of dividends and share price sensitive news. The company's shareholder communications include its annual and half yearly reports, publicity through financial and general media, brokers' reports etc, product news and other items using the traditional and internet media resources. Some of these are directly controlled by management, others may be influenced by management, yet others may be beyond management's control or influence. Moreover, the messages that find their way to shareholders may be planned and deliberate or they may be unplanned, completely inadvertent and wholly unwelcome.

Similar considerations apply to transactions with all stakeholders. With customers, for example, transactions go far beyond the simple matter of delivery of product and receipt of payment and includes a wide array of communications, not simply advertising and publicity, but third party publicity which may well be hostile, after sales follow up and service and including financial communications such as credit control etc. The interactions themselves may be continuous or one-offs, formal or informal, written or verbal, corporate or personal and controllable or not.

In each case communications may be with past, present, future and potential stakeholders, communications with one category being likely to be received by the others.

Interactions with employees are especially rich and varied. Employment contracts vary hugely, some being largely informal, others detailed and formalised. The form and level of payment of wages and salaries, the nature of the work involved and the variety of forms of payment whether or not by results are all subject to great variety. Transactions critically also depend on the degree to which the work done is measured as a basis for payment, or simply for the building of, for example, quality. Payment for work done is the basis of the employee relationship and can clearly be accomplished in many different ways, but employee communications include the way people are treated on a day to day basis, how they are supported and given opportunities for their personal development. The potential variety of employee interaction is almost infinite, including planned and deliberate, unplanned and inadvertent and wholly unwelcome communications with past, present, future and potential employees.

The company's suppliers represent a broad category including not only suppliers of raw materials, finished parts and consumables, but also suppliers of various services that might have been outsourced, suppliers of technology, advisors and consultants, the providers of loan capital and financial services, banks and venture capitalists. Similar variety and considerations apply to these groups of stakeholders as to the ones previously discussed.

Directors also have legal duty to have regard to 'the impact of the company's operations on the community and the environment' as discussed above. Finally every company interacts with offices of local and national governments, including tax authorities, and the laws and regulations they enact, enforce and protect. This political:legal context is shaped also by various non-governmental organisations (NGOs) and pressure groups and where they are relevant to the company's operations, management maintain open communications also with these less direct stakeholders.

Management finally has a legal responsibility for 'maintaining a reputation for high standards of business conduct, and, the need to act fairly as between members of the company'.[228] This suggests interactions with all stakeholders need to maintain that reputation, be positive and supportive of the company's activities. An inappropriate interaction with one set of stakeholders will quickly be communicated to all others with potentially catastrophic effects on the business

Reputation takes long to build because it is the result of continued interactions with stakeholders which result in positive feedback. It cannot be simply created by some corporate publicity campaign – the most effect publicity or advertising can have is a marginal change in direction or emphasis.

Some aspects of reputation are newly decisive. The damage done to the environment has made pollution, perhaps measured as a company's 'carbon footprint', more important. Investors may shun buying shares in a company which has a poor environmental record, despite its financial performance to date. Partly this may be on the perfectly rational grounds that a poor environmental record today is going to adversely affect the company's future financial performance. And partly it may be on the, to an economist, irrational grounds, that the investor simply doesn't wish to be associated with, or seen to support, a polluter. Similarly, valued employees would, all other things being equal, prefer to work for a clean and green company rather than one which pollutes. Knowledge of the environmental record of the company is likely to impact on how the company is perceived by all stakeholders, some significantly, others less so.

Being perceived by all stakeholders as part of the green vanguard, so long as it is real, will have a lasting positive effect on a company's reputation. An ever increasing number of major industrial concerns, led early on by American GE, are recognising this and the opportunities for growth it represents.

In carrying out these legally defined responsibilities, management may well be acting in the interests of the company, the local community and the environment, but it would not be following Friedman's injunction. Galbraith offered an alternative more Keynesian approach which would have been compatible with corporate law and the imperatives of climate change.

Social Balance Economics

According to his fellow economists, Galbraith was the most famous, most widely read and most popular economist of his time. And yet, he appears not to have left a substantial imprint on economic theory. His time coincided with Friedman's, being born four years earlier in 1908, while both lived till 2006, but the Friedmanite legacy was more substantial in their own life times.

Galbraith feared for the fragility of economic growth which he saw as increasingly reliant on the production and purchase of goods which were not needed but for which demand was created artificially through sophisticated corporate advertising. The "goods" which were in genuine demand were the public goods, such things healthcare, education, a clean and healthy environment, increasing leisure and the public facilities for its enjoyment. Today he would no doubt have added a livable and sustainable climate. He identified the problem as one of social balance.

At the start of his examination of the theory of social balance Galbraith quoted from R.H. Tawney:

> 'It is not till it is discovered that high individual incomes will
> not purchase the mass of mankind immunity from cholera,
> typhus and ignorance, still less secure them the positive
> advantages of educational opportunity and economic security,
> that slowly and reluctantly, amid prophesies of moral
> degeneration and economic disaster, society begins to make
> collective provision for needs which no ordinary individual,
> even if he works overtime all his life, can provide himself.'[229]

Writing four years before Friedman's Capitalism and Freedom, Galbraith pointed out that classical economic theory had been born and applied to a world of poverty and was inappropriate to a world of affluence. He contrasted America's affluence in the late 1950s in terms of privately produced and advertised goods, with its inadequate provision of public goods, most of which were fundamental needs.

He fully accepted that the balance between different private goods, such as cars, steel, fuel and insurance, would be best maintained through the operation of market forces. Any attempt to plan such a balance would be likely to result from the inevitable cock-up, in imbalance. But he was concerned with the balance over the whole area of products and services both private and public. Thus increased production of privately produced cars would require more publicly funded roads and if they were not provided in appropriate proportion the economy would suffer eg through congestion and the consequent waste of fuel and time.

> 'The city of Los Angeles, in modern times, is a near classic
> study in the problem of social balance, Magnificently efficient
> factories and oil refineries, a lavish supply of cars, a vast
> consumption of handsomely packaged products, coupled with
> an absence of a municipal trash collection service which forced

*the use of home incinerators, made the air nearly unbreathable
for an appreciable part of each year.*[230]

The following half century saw the problems of Los Angeles becoming more general and global. In 2008, for example, the Beijing smog, pollution and precipitation, had to be artificially held at bay for the duration of the Olympic Games.

Galbraith's social balance economics stood in contrast to the Friedmanite stance on private and public goods. Friedman had argued that public provision of goods and services was twice as costly as similar provision by private enterprise. This simple but fundamental statement, which is intuitively appealing to any who have experienced bureaucratic inefficiency, was fundamental to Friedman's focus on eliminating the public provision of goods and services. Where that was not possible their supply would be minimised and organised and managed as nearly as possible according to the Friedmanite version of private sector practice emphasising competition and choice.

Friedman's idea was clear and simple as an idea whereas Galbraith's were less clear cut and led to some unattractive implications. The lack of social balance in America at that time was seen by Galbraith in the inadequate provision of health, education, public law enforcement and housing as leading to social dysfunction, increased crime and drug and alcohol abuse. This argument appeared to have some truth and the argument for achieving social balance between private wealth and public squalor was appealing. But Galbraith combined that argument with the simultaneous observation of the private wealth embedded in the subtle marketing of private goods of no great social value such as dubious media products, films, television, comic strips, pornography etc. In this the argument was straying into judgements of taste and in advocating an increased role for government, risked becoming a justification for what is now referred to disparagingly as the 'nanny state'.

Galbraith's view that the power of advertising could create an artificial demand for products that were not needed or wanted, substantially overstated the power of advertising. Friedmanite corporate officials might have yearned for such a tool but none was available. Vance Packard's '*The Hidden Persuaders*' came out the year before Galbraith's '*The Affluent Society*' was published and ideas about sinister new methods of advertising were then prominent which may have influenced Galbraith's argument. He was prone to expressions of his own personal patrician tastes and was also criticised for his ill informed and naïve explanation of how large enterprises were actually managed.[231]

And yet, the idea of social balance remains appealing. After thirty years of Friedmanism the disparity between what Galbraith referred to as 'private wealth' and 'public poverty' has only widened. The throw away shopping culture has developed apace while the richest nation on earth still lacks a universal healthcare system and leaves its poorest citizens in slum dwellings and tenements unfit for human habitation.

Galbraith also made the positive case for social balance. A community – a term with which Friedmanites might have some difficulty – would have been better rewarded by having better schools, parks and recreation facilities than simply, as an example of private wealth, bigger cars. Galbraith argued that the private investment in marketing bigger cars influenced the choice of citizens away from the unpromoted public goods such as better schooling or hospitals. In the Friedmanite world, the engineer or scientists who focused on developing a new device to make cars go better was a hero, while a public servant who proposed a new public service was regarded as a 'wastrel'. In that Friedmanite world public expenditure was by definition bad, private provision good. Friedman himself was given to quoting Adam Smith:

> 'There is no art which one government sooner learns of another than that of draining money from the pockets of the people.'[232]

Galbraith's social balance seemed to require the state's imposition of subjectively based tastes and values. But the truth was that it really only demanded that the public sector did those things which the private sector did not, or could not, do. The public sector's base task was to provide universal healthcare, education, social security, defence, and support for minimum standards of living, including critically housing. Arguments could also be made for the public provision of services which were natural monopoly necessities, such as gas, water and electricity. But as Keynes had pointed out there was no reason why there should be any benefit from the state being involved in industries such as the railways, or for that matter steel, coal, ship building, cars, aero engines, except in the short term to support of lame ducks which had long term potential or industries with strategic importance such as defence.

Galbraith also raised the consequent concern of social balance economics in the investment balance between material and personal capital. The distinction was fundamental. Public investment in material capital such as a school or a hospital was an increase in capital formation and a national asset. Investment in schooling increased the supply of educated human beings, of scientists and technologists on who the nation's intellectual capital depended. But capital formation in human beings was 'off balance-sheet' and did not show up in any census of public capital formation. It was nevertheless of prime importance to a nation's future development and would be especially so in an era of high technology when solutions were sought to global warming and resource depletion and the most powerful resources were various forms of intellectual capital which were all dependent on the calibre of the people generating them..

Despite Friedman's quest to minimise government intervention and regulation it was from time to time essential to stabilise the economy, for example, to end the mass unemployment of the great depression of the 1930s or more recently to provide banking support during the 2007-8 'credit crunch'. Keynes advocated such interventions in order to maintain full employment and Galbraith additionally advocated the maintenance of social balance to improve society which in so doing would help address the 'hatred, contempt and even fury' engendered by the Friedman induced disparity of income and wealth between the average earners and the highest paid.

Behavioural economics might encompass both the Keynesian and Galbraithian amendments to free market economics applied pragmatically to maintain economic stability. The political problem was to address this change of economic orthodoxy in a global context when Friedmanite free market globalisation appeared no longer sustainable, and getting global acceptance of the necessity to exclude competitors which did not conform to global standards regarding pollution as well as human rights and minimum worker pay and conditions.

Curriculum Change

The fundamental lesson of the Friedmanite curriculum was that management took place within an economic system which was dependent for its success on managers ignoring all social responsibilities other than to maximise shareholder wealth. This underpinned all management teaching.

A discrete module on business ethics did not challenge that fundamental, but ignored it in favour of reference to the ancient Greeks and moral philosophy. Teaching corporate social responsibility on the other side of the curriculum failed to upset the fundamental Friedman idea which was invested with the long standing authority of neo-classical economics supported by agency theory, transaction cost analysis and the concept of the open market in corporate management.

Homo economicus teaches that people are opportunists, prepared to lie and cheat to achieve their self interest, and that to prevent them exploiting the others, management must monitor and control, reward and punish. But, as with McGregor's Theory X, the result is that mistrust becomes endemic and opportunism is increased. The combined effect of agency theory with transaction cost theory produces the worst possible outcomes, mistrust multiplies, monitoring and attempts to control increase and become more bureaucratic, repressive and costly.

But, even though this dominant model did not work and was obviously 'bad theory', it would not be easily overturned. The barriers were high. From the structure of PhD training, to the requirements of publishing in top journals, the criteria for faculty recruitment and promotion, were all built around the dominant model. Yet there are suggestions of an approaching crisis. The current interest in behavioural economics, the review of Galbraith's concept of social balance and the imperative to re-enact Keynesian interventions in the 2007-8 credit crunch, all suggest the dominant theory is being questioned.

Business school faculty are returning to a position of pluralism, allowing the free market model to apply with some necessary regulation and subject to the maintenance of a supportable level of employment which itself regulates wage push inflation, facilitating the inclusion of social balance and not undermining the idea of corporate social responsibility and corporate integrity.

The newly imposing disciplines of global resource depletion and climate change are pressuring governments to regulate markets and technologies and new global infrastructure will require conformance from national governments. So much is inevitable. Management can energise this change or frustrate it according to how they are taught to behave.

The management curriculum is also subject to other contradiction. The Newman – Locke debate was between a liberal education and the teaching of specific skills and competences. The Newman argument was picked up by Barnard who argued for mental practice and challenge. But management is intellectually simple. And educators who seek to give mental challenge to students using management problems as the vehicle only serve to confuse, for example, by teaching the usefulness of microeconomic models of the firm. It may be better to provide a direct challenge to train the mind through mathematics, physics or philosophy or even literature. And to provide the skills and competences outside of university or in a skills and competencies module delivered in concert with industry practitioners to augment the practical experience gained on corporate management trainee schemes.

The management issue in the 21st century is how to recruit, retain support and develop highly skilled and educated people, working in smaller numbers with a high degree of autonomy and with their rates of pay no longer the main cost drivers, but their individual and team contributions crucial to organizational survival and prosperity. The emphasis has moved from control of labour costs to innovation and the development and exploitation of technology.

These changes are happening already. It remains to be seen whether they happen fast enough and go far enough.

EPILOGUE

This brief history of the emergence, honourable rise and corrupted fall of management, is less definitive about its renewal. This epilogue is even more conjectural in identifying ways forward which appear probable having regard to the historical context. The 2007-8 bursting of the credit bubble might turn out to be a tipping point when the Friedmanite neo-classical economic orthodoxy was supplanted by a less dogmatic, neo-Keynesian behavioural social balance model which might facilitate the renewal of management in its semi autonomous professional role. Whether it turns out to be so will only be certainly known in retrospect. There never was one best way, the most appropriate and effective way of managing a company, or an economy, is contingent on the circumstances at the time. The Friedmanite shock treatment had some beneficial effects in the 1980s and beyond, but its extreme dogmatic and continuous application is not appropriate to a world dominated by fears of the industrial effects of resource depletion and climate change.

The crude 'economic man' assumptions may apply properly to some people, but not to all. Some managers have always behaved ethically, driven by altruism and ideals, others have been motivated by simple greed. That has always been so. But it is only under Friedman's influence that managers have been taught that the economy depends on them identifying their interests wholly with maximising their own utility and therefore shareholder wealth, so even those who start out with ideals are undone and persuaded to conform by business school teaching.

'Economic man', the mathematical workings of microeconomic models of 'the firm', the subtle dishonesty of agency 'theory' and transaction cost analysis are among the falsehoods of the Friedmanite orthodoxy. They bear little resemblance to practical reality. As academic research develops ever more detailed versions of the emerging models, they become ever more distant from real situations. Better to accept some broad generalisations and disregard the detailed nonsense.

Professional management was motivated by higher aims than simply getting 'filthy rich' (as a British Labour party spokesman put it). But the dominant Friedman based culture seduced management into ownership through spurious share option 'incentive' schemes which ensured a focus on short term shareholder wealth instead of focus on the long term survival and prosperity of the enterprise for the benefit of all stakeholders. But such management-owners are not in a position to avoid the crime of insider dealing.

Management's legal duty is to act in the best long term interests of the company bearing in mind the interests of all stakeholders. Their ownership of shares undermines their independence and inhibits their acting in the best interest of the company.

As share owning beneficiaries management not only have insider information not available to all shareholders and make use of it, but actually decide the relevant projects and strategies. They could not be more "inside". TO avoid criminality management would have to be debarred from share ownership in their organisation. Owner-directors of publicly quoted firms would have to have their shares held in trust while they remained part of the executive management of the firm in question.

The problem for management created by their unequal remuneration was referred to by Drucker as *'a denial of justice and fairness'*

> *'The resentment against the big salaries of the top executives poisons the political and social relations within the plant, aggravates the difficulty of communications between management and employees, and reduces management's chance to be accepted as the government of the plant.'*[233]

That was over half a century ago when the problem of income disparity was much less than it is today. By 1997 Drucker's comment on exorbitant executive salaries referred to 'the hatred, contempt and even fury' they caused.

That was before the later outbreak of super exorbitant salaries multiplied by the wealth accumulated from perverse share option incentive schemes. The reversion to pre Friedmanite progressive systems of taxation would ameliorate this problem and might serve to reduce the 'contempt' and 'hatred'. It was never made clear what the justification was for eliminating progressive taxation. The broad argument was to reduce taxation and so reduce the burden on industry, but that could be done without eliminating the progressive element. Adam Smith and his successors, prior to Friedman, had all accepted the concept of progressive redistributive taxation to compensate the fundamental inequity of the capitalist economy.

Smith recognised the worship of the rich and powerful and the despising of the poor and mean, curiously common in his day, was a corruption of society. It is equally true today seen not just in the celebrity culture but more importantly the approach of Friedmanite governments' accommodation of the super rich and taxation of the relatively poor.

More progressive and redistributive taxation would ensure the super rich, no matter what their detailed arrangements, always paid more tax than the standard rate tax payer and could be welcomed back as a bona fide member of modern society, rather than remain as the outcast financial abuser.

The falsehoods of neo-classical theory still taught in business schools include the denial of the joint stock company as a legal entity. The company is set up so far as is possible as a legal person in its own right. As such its ownership is different in nature from that of other private property. Ownership of company shares is a different and more limited entitlement, limited as to rights and limited as to risk. Currently ownership of the majority of shares enables that owner to act as though the company is their personal property to do with as they like. The legal limitations of company ownership should be protected against abusive and destructive ownership just as even a slave had some legal protections against abuse.

To protect the company against shareholder predation, the legal rights of other stakeholders could be protected by reflecting their position in granting voting rights on certain specific issues, such as mergers and acquisitions. For employees, for example, to be bale to exercise a proportionate influence over such items as merger and acquisition, they might be allocated, say, 25% of voting rights on such occasions.

Government interference in markets should be restricted to ensuring competition is open and free and no markets are 'cornered' or unduly influenced so as to reduce the effects of free and open competition. This is a particular problem in the market for management with cross directorships operating to frustrate good practice as specified by law or in voluntarily accepted codes of practice. For example, cross directorship representation

on corporate remuneration committees can frustrate and pervert
remuneration practice.

Directorships of quoted companies could be restricted so that no individual
could occupy more than, say, three executive positions in quoted companies,
membership of remuneration committees counting as an executive position.

The autonomous role of management without ownership is already limited
by the corporate reporting and disclosure procedures required by law. It
could be further extended by requiring every company director to submit a
brief personal report annexed to the annual report of the company and
presented to the AGM which might include details of other directorships,
salary, bonuses (in all forms), other compensation, job title, functional
responsibility, total responsibility (numbers of people reporting), annual
budget spend, and a brief statement on their annual contribution to corporate
development.

It is now recognised as essential that pollution be eliminated, resources
conserved and green activity encouraged. Governments will necessarily
become more aggressive in taxing polluters, subsidizing green activity and
funding green research. But this is a global imperative. If industries from
other economies do not follow similar practice then their trade could be
refused. This would be a necessary limitation on the free operation of global
markets, but free trade can no longer afford to be blind.

The analogy has been made elsewhere between managing the economy,
within which enterprise management operates, and driving a car. Progress is
best achieved smoothly rather than by violent acceleration and braking and
swift changes of direction. But the economy is not very like a car; there are
no very direct precise controls, there is not one driver and the economy is
not a single entity nor the road very clear in its direction, nor very well
surfaced or signed.

An alternative analogy would be a flock of sheep infiltrated by a small
number of feral felines. The general aim is to move the flock from A to B
where there is fresh pasture. Under normal circumstances the flock moves
progressively along in the desired direction requiring only the occasional
bark from a sheep dog to keep it going. Under these circumstances the
shepherd is hardly required to intervene at all beyond the occasional
whistled instruction to the dog. This is equivalent to the Keynes's full
employment special case of the classical model. However, the individual
sheep may act individually; the flock is not necessarily a coherent whole
though it may frequently act as though it is. This mirrors Marshall's

distinction between elements of the economy, for example the different industries with their individual characteristics and circumstances which produce partial equilibria, rather than a single general equilibrium.

Should an individual member of the flock head off in the wrong direction it will need to be brought back into line individually by a sheep dog, rather than the shepherd taking action which would affect the whole flock. If the whole flock should deviate from the desired steady progression, for example by slowing down, stopping or even turning back, then the shepherd should take action to correct that deviation. This would be the equivalent of a slump or depression requiring short term governmental intervention to get the economy moving in the right direction again. Another risk might be that the flock starts to run at an unsustainable rate threatening to get out of control and run over a cliff edge. This would be the equivalent of a developing bubble boom which is inevitably going to lead to a bust.

Analogies can clearly be taken beyond their useful limits, but with the above analogy there is one other issue to consider: the feral felines. Normally they feed on the lame and sick members of the flock and so perform a useful task for the flock as a whole and their numbers stabilise around the level which the flock can support in this role. This was the situation when a small number of financially oriented businesses focused on the opportunities for asset stripping and so kept industrial management on their toes aware of the necessity to satisfy shareholders as well as their other stakeholders.

But the risk is that the felines breed to excess and so have to attack healthy members of the flock for their own survival. Once that starts it is difficult to predict where the process would end. This was the case when the deregulated banking system including the newly freed investment banks, private equity organisations and sovereign funds, joined the asset stripping game removing the accumulated wealth from the companies they acquired and leaving them saddled with the debt it was necessary to raise in order to acquire them in the first place.

At some stage it may be that the flock is abused by the felines which multiply in number, even becoming dominant with just sufficient sheep being maintained so as to feed the felines. If that happens the shepherd has clearly lost control and is no longer able to drive the flock, which is now led by some cats that have become fatter than the others. The parallel with the raiders, speculators and investment banks of Wall Street and the City of London is obvious.

The question as to what the shepherds might do in those circumstances seems worth consideration. The urgent necessity is to reduce the numbers and strength of the felines and revive the flock of sheep. It doesn't appear that a gradual, evolutionary solution would work. Shock treatment is probably necessary in the form of a violent cull of the felines.

Again the analogy could become too fanciful, but the equivalent of a violent cull of the financial parasites has become urgent together with the rebuilding of productive industry led by an autonomous management focused on the development of their enterprises and responding to the needs of all stakeholders including their community and environment's needs for clean technologies and conserved resources.

In 1955 Drucker commenced 'The Practice of Management' with the following words:

> 'The manager is the dynamic, life giving element in every business. Without his leadership 'the resources of production' remain resources and never become production. In a competitive economy, above all, the quality and performance of the managers determine the success of a business, indeed they determine its survival. For the quality and performance of its managers is the only effective advantage an enterprise in a competitive economy can have. '[234]

Despite the seduction by Friedmanite theory into the pursuit of personal wealth, Drucker's words remain true. Only now, it is not just the success of a business which depends on the quality and performance of management.

INDEX TO BE COMPILED

REFERENCES

(Not yet fully compiled)

[1] *The Visible Hand: The Managerial Revolution in American Business* (1977), Cambridge, Mass: The Belknap Press of Harvard University Press, p1.

[2] Ibid, p490

[3] Ibid, p491

[4] Smith, A, (1776), An inquiry into the nature and causes of the wealth of nations' , Book 1, Chapter 2.

[5] Ghoshal, S., (2005), 'Bad Management Theories Are Destroying Good Management Practices," *Academy of management Learning & Education*, Vol 4, No 1, p79

[6] Friedman, M, (1962), *'Capitalism and Freedom'*, Chicago: University of Chicago Press

[7] Smith, A., (1776), *'An Inquiry into the Nature and Causes of the Wealth of Nations'*,Book 4, Chapter 2, Part II, republished in the Oxford World's Classics imprint by Oxford University Press of Oxford in 1993, p292.

[8] Smith, A., (1759), *'The Theory of Moral Sentiments'*, Part VI, Section I, republished in the Dover Philosophical Classics imprint by Dover Publications Inc of New York in 2006, p213.

[9] Smith, A., (1776), *'An Inquiry into the Nature and Causes of the Wealth of Nations'*,Chapter 11, Part II, republished in the Oxford World's Classics imprint by Oxford University Press of Oxford in 1993, p152.

[10] Veblen , T, (1899), The Theory of the Leisure Class: An Economic Study in the Evolution of Institutions. New York: Macmillan.

[11] Maslow, A, (1943), 'A Theory of Human Motivation', *Psychological Review,* Vol 50.

[12] Murray, H.A., (1938), *'Explorations in Personality'*, Oxford: Oxford University Press.

[13] Atkinson, J.W., (1964), *'An Introduction to Motivation'*, London: Van Nostrand.

[14] McClelland, D.C., Atkinson, J.W., Clark, R.A. & Lowell, E.L, (1953), 'The Achievement Motive', London: Van Nostrand

[15] Alderfer, C.P., (1972), 'Existence, Relatedness and Growth', New York: Free Press

[16] Adams, J.S., (1965),.'Inequity in social exchange'. *Advances in Experimental Social Psychology,* Vol 62, pp 335-343

[17] Defoe, D., (1722), *'A Tour through England and Wales, vol 2'*, J.M. Dent & Sons Ltd, Everyman edition published in 1928, p15.

[18] Mingay, G.E., (1968), *Enclosure and the Small Farmer in the Age of the Industrial Revolution*, Studies in Eonomic History Series, London: Macmillan, p51

[19] Ashton, T.S., (1955), 'An Economic History of England: the eighteenth century', London: Methuen & Co, p71.

[20] Ashton, T.S., (1955), 'An Economic History of England: the eighteenth century', London: Methuen & Co, p78

[21] Phillips, J, (1792), '*History of Inland Navigation*', p87, quoted in Ashton T.S., (1955), 'An Economic History of England: the eighteenth century', London: Methuen & Co, p85.

[22] William Pitt the Younger, parliamentary speech introducing 1792 budget, quoted in Galbraith, J.K., (1987), '*A History of Economics*', London: Hamish Hamilton, p61.

[23] Smith, A, (1776), 'An inquiry into the nature and causes of the wealth of nations', Book V, Chapter 1, Part First. Republished with an introduction and notes by Katheryn Sutherland in the Oxford World's Classics imprint by Oxford University Press of Oxford in 1993. In references from Wealth of Nations page numbers will be quoted from this Oxford edition.

[24] Plato, '*The Republic*', translated by D. Lee, Penguin Classics, Part II, Book II, p57

[25] Petty, W., (1691) 'Political Anatomy of Ireland' based on his experience in 1672 and published posthumously.

[26] Hughes, J., (1711), 'Nihil largiundo gloriam adeptus est', *The Spectator* No 232, 26th November, available at:
http://meta.montclair.edu/spectator/text/1711/november/spectator232.xml

[27] Mandeville, B., (1728), '*The Fable of the Bees*', Vol II.

[28] Hume, D., (1729), '*A Treatise of Human Nature*'

[29] Smith, A, (1776), '*An inquiry into the nature and causes of the wealth of nations*', Book 1, Chapter 1.

[30] Smith, A., (1776), '*An Inquiry into the Nature and Causes of the Wealth of Nations*', Book V, Chapter 1, Part III, Article II: Of the expense of the Institutions for the Education of Youth, p429.

[31] Smith, A., (1759), '*The Theory of Moral Sentiments*', Part VI, Section I, republished in the Dover Philosophical Classics imprint by Dover Publications Inc of New York in 2006, p3

[32] Smith, A., (1776), '*An Inquiry into the Nature and Causes of the Wealth of Nations*', Book V, Chapter 2, Part 2, Of taxes, Article I: Taxes upon the Rent of House.

[33] Smith, A., (1776), '*An Inquiry into the Nature and Causes of the Wealth of Nations*', Book I, Chapter 10, Part 2, p129.

[34] Ricardo, D., Galbraith p84

[35] Sismondi, J.C.L. de ,(1819), *Nouveaux Principes d'économie politiqu, ou de la Richesse dans ses rapports avec la population'*.

[36] Smith, A., (1776), *'An Inquiry into the Nature and Causes of the Wealth of Nations'*, Book V, Chapter 1, Part 3, Article 1.

[37] Galbraith, J.K., (1987), *'A History of Economics'* London: Hamish Hamilton, p71.

[38] Mantoux, P., (1961), *The Industrial Revolution in the Eighteenth Century*, Loondon: Jonathon Cape, p233.

[39] George, C S, (1968), *The History of Management Thought*, Englewood Cliffs, New Jersey: Prentice Hall, p 52.

[40] Engels, F, (1844), *'The Condition of the Working Class in England'*, republished in 1969 with an introduction by Eric Hobsbawm by Panther Books, p59.

[41] Engels, F, (1844), *'The Condition of the Working Class in England'*, Page numbers following the extracts refer to the Panther Books edition referred to in previous note.

[42] Owen R., (1847), *'Life of Robert Owen Written by Himself'*, Republished: London, 1922 edition to which page numbers refer, p42.

[43] McGregor, D, (1960), *'The Human Side of Enterprise'*, Tokyo: McGraw Hill Kogakusha, International Student Edition, p48.

[44] Bentham, J., (1789), *Introduction to the Principles of Morals and Legislation.*

[45] Mill, J.S., (1861), *Utilitarianism*, Chapter 2, paragraph 2, quoted in Warnock, G., (1967), *Contemporary Moral Philosophy,* London: Macmillan.

[46] Galbraith, J.K., (1958), *The Affluent Society*, London: Hamish Hamilton, p65.

[47] Marx, K, & Engels, F., (1847), *'The Communist Manifesto',* New York: Modern Reader Paperbacks (1964) p10.

[48] Marx, K, (1867), *'Capital',* Volume 1, Chapter 25, Section 4, Oxford: Oxford University Press, p362

[49] Marx, K, (1867), as above, p181.

[50] Marx, K, (1867), as above, p113/4.

[51] Marx, K, (1867), as above, p292.

[52] Marx, K, (1867), as above, p203

[53] Briggs, M. and Jordan, P., (1967), *Economic History of England*, sixth edition, Foxton: University Tutorial Press Ltd, p539.

[54] Briggs, A., (1983), *A Social History of England,* London: Weidenfeld and Nicolson, p280

[55] Smith, A., (1776), *'An inquiry into the Nature and Causes of the Wealth of Nations',* Quote is from Book I, Chapter 10, part 2, p129 in the Oxford

World Classics edition, edited and introduced by K. Sutherland, Oxford: Oxford University Press,.

[56] Levy, A.B., (1950), *Private Corporations and their* Control, London: Routledge & Kegan Paul Ltd

[57] Griffith, S B, (1963), *'Sun Tzu: The Art of War '*, London: Oxford University Press, p111.

[58] Galbraith, J.K. (1958), *The Affluent Society',* London: Hamish Hamilton, p49.

[59] Sumner, W.G., (1914), *'The Challenge of Facts and Other Essays',* Ed A.G.Keller, New Haven: Yale University Press, p90, quoted in Galbraith, J.K., *'A History of Economics'*, London: Hamish Hamilton, p123.

[60] Hofstadter, R.A., (1959), *Social Darwinism in American Thought,* New York: Braziller, p45

[61] Veblen, T., (1899), *'The Theory of the Leisure Class: an economic study in the evolution of institutions'*, New York: The Macmillan Company. P167-8.

[62] Galbraith, J.K. (1958), *The Affluent Society',* London: Hamish Hamilton, p53.

[63] Ibid p249

[64] Chandler A.D., (1965), *'The Railroads: the nation's first big business'*, NY: Harcourt, Brace & World Inc (The Forces in American Economic Growth Series), p21/2.

[65] Ibid p7

[66] Ibid p9

[67] Berle A A & Means G C, (1932), *The modern corporation and private property*, NY: Macmillan, p119.

[68] Ibid p121

[69] Pearson, G, (1995), *Integrity in Organizations: an alternative business ethic*, Maidenhead: McGraw Hill Book Co.

[70] Khurana, R., (2007), *'From Higher Aims to Hired Hands'*, Princeton NJ: Princeton University Press, p

[71] Ibid p46

[72] Newman, J.H., (1854), *The Idea of a University: Discourse 7. Knowledge Viewed in Relation to Professional Skill.*

[73] Keynes, J.M. (1936), *'The General Theory of Employment, Interest and Money',* London: Macmillan & Co, p372.

[74] Ibid, p378

[75] Skidelsky, R., (1977), *'The Political Meaning of the Keynesian Revolution'*, in 'The End of the Keynesian Era', (Ed: R Skidelsky), London: Macmillan, p34.

[76] Cairncross, A., (1978), *'Keynes and the Planned Economy'*, in 'Keynes amd Laissez Faire' (Ed: A P Thirlwell), London: Macmillan Press, p36.

[77] Von Clausevitz, C., (1830), *On War*, currently available in the Wordsworth Classics of World Literature series, based on the translation by J.J. Graham, revised by F.N. Maude, abridged and with an introduction by Louise Willmot. The quotation is from Book 1, Chapter 1 section 24.

[78] Levitt, T., (1960), 'Marketing Myopia', *Harvard Business Review, July / August,* now accessible at http://www.dallascap.com/pdfs/MarketingMyopia.pdf

[79] http://www.marketingpower.com/AboutAMA/Pages/DefinitionofMarketing.aspx

[80] Kotler, P., (1999), *Kotler on Marketing*, New York: The Free Press, p36

[81] Levitt, T., (1960), 'Marketing Myopia*', Harvard Business Review, July / August*

[82] Pearson, G., (1999), *Strategy in Action,* Harlow: FT Prentice Hall, p59

[83] Garvin, D.A., (1987) Competing on the eight dimensions of quality, *Harvard Business Review, November / December.*

[84] Marketing Teacher at http://marketingteacher.com/Lessons/lesson_pricing.htm

[85] Veblen, T, (1904), *'The Theory of Business Enterprise'*

[86] Galbraith, J K, (1987), *A History of Economics*, London: Hamish Hamilton p172.

[87] Pearson G., (1999), *'Strategy in Action'*, Harlow: FT Prentice Hall, chapter 12.

[88] Drucker, P F, (1949), *'The New Society'*, New York: Harper & Brothers, p52

[89] Fayol, H. (1949). *General and Industrial Management,* translation by Constance Storrs, London: Pitman Publishing Company, p3.

[90] Quote is from the Wharton School website:
http://www.wharton.upenn.edu/whartonfacts/history/

[91] Taylor, F, (1910), *The Principles of Scientific Management,* this extract available at http://www3.niu.edu/~td0rafl/labor/Story%20of%20Schmidt.htm

[92] The Letter is archived by the Samuel C Williams library of the Stevens Institute of Technology, Hoboken, New Jersey, and can be seen in full at http://stevens.cdmhost.com/cdm4/document.php?CISOROOT=/p4100coll1&CISOPTR=442&REC=1

[93] Zola, E, (1885), *Germinal,* Chapter 4.

[94] Aston Group studies (Child, Hick, Hinings, Pugh et al – a few words of explanation.

[95] Barnard, C., (1948), *Organization and Management,* Cambridge, Mass: Harvard University Press, P199.

[96] Mayo, E., (1933), *'The human problems of an industrial civilisation'*, New York: Macmillan.

[97] Mayo, E., (1949), *The Social Problems of an Industrial Civilization*, London: Routledge, quoted in 'Organisation Theory', London: Penguin p357.

[98] McGregor, D, (1960), *The Human Side of Enterprise*, New York: McGraw-Hill, pp33-34.

[99] McGregor, D, (1960), *The Human Side of Enterprise*, New York: McGraw-Hill, pp47-48.

[100] Herzberg, F., Mausner, B. & Snyderman, B.B., (1959), *The Motivation to Work*, New York: Wiley

[101] Beatty, J, (1998), *'The World According to Drucker'*, London: Orion Publishing, p116.

[102] Ibid p117

[103] Brown, W., (1960), *Exploration in Management*, London: Heinemann, p42.

[104] Brown, W., (1962), *Piecework Abandoned*, London: Heinemann, p93.

[105] Barnard, C., (1948), *Organization and Management*, Cambridge, Mass: Harvard University Press. P112.

[106] Koehler, W., (1938), *Closed and Open Systems*, included in Systems Thinking, F E Emery (Ed), Harmondsworth: Penguin Books, Penguin Modern Management Readings.

[107] Trist, E.A. & Bamforth, K.W., (1951), 'Some Social and Psychological Consequences of the Longwall Method of Coal-getting', *Human Relations*, Vol 4, No 1, pp6-38.

[108] Miller, E. J. and Rice, A. K., (1967), *Systems of Organization: Task and Sentient Systems and Their Boundary Control*, London: Tavistock Publications

[109] Emery, F.E., (1969), *'Systems Thinking: Penguin modern management readings,* Harmondsworth: Penguin Books Ltd.

[110] Woodward, J., (1965), *'Industrial Organisation: Theory and Practice'*, Oxford: Oxford University Press.

[111] Lawrence, P.R., & Lorsch, J.W., (1967), *'Organisation and Environment'*, Harvard: Harvard University Press.

[112] Burns, T & Stalker, G.M., (1961), *'The Management of Innovation'*, Oxford: Oxford University Press,

[113] Croome, H., (1960), *'Human problems of Innovation'*, Department of Scientific and Industrial Research pamphlet, Problems of Progress in Industry, No 5.

[114] Chandler, A.D., (1977), *'The Visible Hand'*, Cambridge Mass: Belknap Press of Harvard University Press, p1

[115] Nelson, D.M., (1946), *'Arsenal of Democracy: The Story of American war production,* New York: Harcourt Brace & Co., p226

[116] Gillingham, J., (1991), *'Coal, steel, and therebirth of Europe, 1945-1955',* Cambridge: Cambridge University Press, p82.

[117] Drucker in *'Concept of the Corporation'* quoted as summarised by Beatty, J, in 'The World According to Drucker', London: Orion Business Books, p57

[118] Mintzberg H., (1973), *'The Nature of Managerial Work',* New York: Harper & Row, p33.

[119] Schumpeter, J.A., (1939), *'Business Cycles: a theoretical, historical and statistical analysis of the capitalist process',* New York: McGraw Hill

[120] Kondratiev, N.D., 1935, 'The Long Waves in Economic Life', the Review of Economic Statistics, November.

[121] Piatier, A., (1984), *'Barriers to Innovation',* London: Francis Pinter. A study carried out for the Commission of the European Communities, Directorate-General Information Market and Innovation.

[122] Freeman, C. 1978, 'The Kondratiev long waves, technical change and unemployment', OECD

[123] Rothwell, R., (1980), 'The Role of Technical Change in International Competitiveness: the case of the textile machinery industry', *Management Decision,* Vol 15, No 6.

[124] Carter, C.F. and Williams, B.R., (1956), *'Industry and Technical Progress - factors governing the speed of application of science',* Oxford: Oxford University Press.

[125] Myers, S. and Marquis, D.G., (1969), *'Successful Industrial Innovations: A Study of Factors Underlying Innovations in Selected Firms',* National Science Foundation.

[126] Project SAPPHO, (1972), *'Success and Failure in Industrial Innovation',* Science Policy Research Unit, University of Sussex.

[127] Robertson, A., (1973), 'The Marketing Factor in Successful Industrial Innovation', *Industrial Marketing Management,* Vol 2.

[128] Chisnall, P.M., (1985), *'Marketing: A Behavioural Analysis'* 2nd Edn, Maidenhead: McGraw Hill.

[129] Holloman, J.H., (1967), *'Innovation and Profitability',* Science of Science Foundation.

[130] Peters, T.J., & Waterman, R.H., (1982), *In Search of Excellence',* New York: Harper & Row.

[131] Drucker, P F., (1964) *'Managing for Results.* Oxford: Heinemann Professional Publishing, p104

[132] Stewart, T.A., (1997), *'Intellectual Capital: The New Wealth of Organizations',* London: Nicholas Brealey Publishing.

[133] Davenport, T.H., (2005), *'Thinking for a Living: How to Get Better Performance and Results from Knowledge Workers'*, Harvard Business School Press.

[134] Edvinsson, L & Sullivan, P., (1996), 'Developing a Model for Managing Intellectual Capital', *European Management Journal* Vol. 14, No. 4, pp. 356—364.

[135] Child, J., & Faulkner, D, (1998), *'Strategies of Co-operation'*, Oxford: Oxford University Press, p230

[136] Deal , T. & Kennedy, A., (1982), *'Corporate Cultures: the rites and rituals of corporate life'*, New York: Addison Wesley.

[137] Gregory, K.L., (1983), 'Native-View Paradigms: Multiple Cultures and Culture Conflicts in Organisations', *Administrative Science Quarterly*, September.

[138] Peters, T & Waterman, R.H., (1982), *'In Search of Excellence'*, New York: Harper & Row

[139] Barnard, C I, (1938), *The Functions of the Executive,* Cambridge, Mass: Harvard University Press, p217.

[140] Drucker, P.F., (1949), *'The New Society',* New York Harper & Brothers

[141] Misztal, B.A, (1996), *'Trust in Modern Societies: The Search for the Bases of Social Order',* Cambridge: Polity Press

[142] Jönsson, S., (1996), 'Decoupling hierarchy and accountability: an examination of trust and reputation', in R.Munor & J Mouritsen (Eds) *'Accountability: Power, ethos and the technologies of managing'*, London: Thomson Business Press

[143] Barnard, C I, (1948), *'Organization and Management'*, Cambridge, Mass: Harvard University Press, p8.

[144] Ibid p11.

[145] Beatty, J, (1998), *'The World According to Drucker',* London: Orion Business Books, p47.

[146] Beatty, J, (1998), *'The World According to Drucker',* London: Orion Business Books, p47.

[147] Chandler, A.D., (1962), *'Strategy and Structure: chapters in the History of the American Industrial Enterprise'*, Cambridg, Mass: The MIT Press, p383.

[148] Concise Oxford Dictionary third edition, (1964), p1273.

[149] Andrews, K R, (1980), *'The Concept of Corporate Strategy,'* Chicago: Irwin.

[150] Welch, J., (2005), *'Winning'*, London: HarpurCollins Publishers, p165.

[151] Griffith, S B, (1963), 'Sun Tzu: The Art of War', London: Oxford University Press.

[152] Mintzberg, H. & Quinn, J. B., (1996), 'Te Strategy Process: concepts, contexts and cases', third edition, NJ: Prentice Hall International.

[153] Machiavelli, N., (1521), *The Art of War,'* currently available from De Capo Press, New York (1965) with an introduction by Neal Wood.

[154] Clausewitz, C., (1997), *'On War,'* abridged version with a useful introduction by L Willmot, Ware: Wordsworth Editions Ltd

[155] Liddell Hart, B.H., (1967), *'Strategy,'* second revised edition, London: Faber & Faber.

[156] Paret, P, (Ed), (1986), *Makers of Modern Strategy,* Oxford: Clarendon Press, p186.

[157] Clausewitz, C., (1997), *'On War,'* abridged version with a useful introduction by L Willmot, Ware: Wordsworth Editions Ltd, p22.

[158] Machiavelli, N., (1521), *'The Art of War,'* New York: De Capo Press, New York, p27.

[159] Pearson, G, (1985), *'The Strategic Discount'*, Chichester: Wiley.

[160] Boston Consulting Group, (1968a), *'Perspectives on Experience'*, Boston: Boston Consulting Group

[161] Porter, M.E., (1980), *Competitive Strategy – techniques for analyzing industries and competitors,* New York: Free Press.

[162] Porter, M.E., (1985), *Competitive Advantage - creating and sustaining superior performance,* New York: Free Press

[163] Penrose, E T, (1959), *'The Theory of the Growth of the Firm*, Oxford: Oxford University Press.

[164] Wernerfelt, B., (1984), 'A Resource Based View of the Firm', *Strategic Management Journal,* 5: pp171-80.

[165] Hamel, G. & Prahalad, C.K., (1994), *'Competing for the Future'* Boston: Harvard Business School Press.

[166] Ansoff H I, 'Corporate Strategy – page of mess diagram

[167] Mintzberg, H., paralysis by analysis

[168] Boston Consulting Group, (1968a), *'Perspectives on Experience'*, Boston: Boston Consulting Group

[169] Schoeffler, S, (1977), '*The PIMSletter on Business Strategy, No2',* Harvard: The Strategic Planning Institute.

[170] Boston Consulting Group, (1968a), *'Perspectives on Experience'*, Boston: Boston Consulting Group, p102-107.

[171] Drucker, P F., (1964), *'Managing for Results',* New York: Harper and Row

[172] Gaughan, P.A., *'The Fourth Merger Wave and Beyond'* in 'Readings in Mergers and Acquisitions, (Ed P A Gaughan), Cambridge Mass: Blackwell Publishers, p3.

[173] Drucker, P F. (BEATTY, p158)

[174] Friedman, M., (1962), *'Capitalism and freedom'*, Chicago: Chicago University Press

[175] Smith A, (1766), *'Wealth of Nations',* Book 5, Chapter 1, Part 3, Article 1.

[176] Craig, D., (2005), *'Rip Off: the scandalous inside story of the management consulting money machine,* London: Original Book Company.

[177] Drucker, P F in Beatty P57.

[178] Friedman, M, (1977), *'From Galbraith to Economic Freedom',* Occasional Paper 49, London: Institute of Economic Affairs, pp48-51

[179] Levitt, T., (1958), 'The Dangers of Social Responsibility', *Harvard Business Review,* September - October.

[180] Friedman, M, (1962), *'Capitalism and Freedom',* Chicago: University of Chicago Press.

[181] Friedman, M, (1977), *'From Galbraith to Economic Freedom',* Occasional Paper 49, London: Institute of Economic Affairs, p57

[182] Barnard, C I, (1938), *The Functions of the Executive,* Cambridge, Mass: Harvard University Press, pxi.

[183] Braverman. H., (1974), *'Labour and Monopoly Capital: the degradation of work inth twentieth century',* New York: Monthly Review Press.

[184] http://www.num.org.uk/?p=history&c=num&h=13

[185] Ross, C, (2007), *'Independent Diplomat: Dispatches from an Unaccountable Elite',* New Yok: Cornell University Press, p116.

[186] Layard, R., The Lionel Robbins Memorial Lectures of 2003 at London School of Economics under the title *'Happiness: Has Social Science a Clue?'*

[187] Alchian, A.A. & Demsetz, H (1972), 'Production, Information Costs, and Economic Organisation', *American Economic Review,* Vol 62, p778.

[188] Khurana, R., *'From Higher Aims to Hired Hands: the transformation of American Business Schools and the unfulfilled promise of management as a profession',* Princeton: Princeton University Press, p469

[189] Galbraith, J.K., (1989a), *"In pursuit of the simple truth",* Commencement address to women graduates of Smith College, Massachusetts.

[190] Jensen, M. & Murphy, K.J., (1990), 'Performance Pay and Top Management Incentives', *Journal of Political Economy,* Vol 98, pp225-264.

[191] Caulkin, S., (2007), 'Buccaneering bosses are the worst of all options', *The Observer, Business & Media Section*, 18th November, 2007, p10.

[192] See http://www.adamsmith.org/

[193] Jane Jacobs, J. (1992), *'Systems of Survival: A Dialogue on the Moral Foundations of Commerce and Politics'*, New York: Random House.

[194] Caulkin, S., (2008), '198 reasons why we're in this terrible mess', *The Observer, Business & Media Section*, 9th March, 2008, p10

[195] Beatty, J, (1998), *'The World According to Drucker'*, London: Orion Publishing Group, p112

[196] Friedman, M, (1977), *'From Galbraith to Economic Freedom'*, Occasional Paper 40, London: The Institute of Economic Affairs, p57.

[197] Friedman, M, (1977), *'From Galbraith to Economic Freedom'*, Occasional Paper 40, London: The Institute of Economic Affairs, p50.

[198] Beatty, J, (1998), *'The World According to Drucker'*, London: Orion Publishing Group, p83

[199] Mishel, L, (2007), *'CEO-to-worker pay imbalance grows'*, Economic Snapshots web site: http://www.epi.org/content.cfm/webfeatures_snapshots_20060621

[200] Ghoshal, S., (2005), 'Bad Management Theories Are Destroying Good Management Practices," *Academy of management Learning & Education*, Vol 4, No 1, pp75-91.

[201] Keynes, J.M., (1953), *'The General Theory of Employment, Interest and Money'*, New York: Harcourt Brace Jovanovich, p306.,

[202] Khurana, R., (2007), *'From Higher Aims to Hired Hands: the social transformation of American business schools and the unfulfilled promise of management as a profession'*, Princeton: Princeton University Press.

[203] Besanko, D., Dranove, D. & Shanley, M. (2000), *'Economics of Strategy'*, New York: John Wiley & Sons Inc, p210.

[204] Ibid. p321.

[205] Holmstrom, B & Kaplan, S.N., (2001), 'Corporate Governance and Merger Activity in the United States: making sense of the 1980s and 1990s', *Journal of Economic Perspectives,* Vol 15, No 2, pp132-133.

[206] The Corporation

[207] Sokal, A. & Bricmont, J., (1998), *"Intellectual Impostures"*, London: Profile Books, p135.

[208] Elster, J., (1983), *'Explaining Technical Change '*, Cambridge: Cambridge University Press

[209] Ghoshal, S., (2005), 'Bad Management Theories Are Destroying Good Management Practices," *Academy of management Learning & Education,* Vol 4, No 1, p79.

[210] De George, R.T., (1993), *'Competing with Integrity in International Business,*, New York: Oxford University Press, pv.

[211] Cadbury, A., 'Final Report of the Committee on the Financial Aspects of Corporate Governance', published by Gee, South Quay Plaza, London, 1987

[212] Anon quoted in Stark, A., (1993) 'What's the matter with business ethics?' *Harvard Business Review*, May June.

[213] Crook, C., (2005), 'The Good Company', in 'A survey of corporate social responsibility', *The Economist*, 22nd January, 2005

[214] Economist, The, (2005), 'The Ethics of Business', in 'A survey of corporate social responsibility', *The Economist*, 22nd January.

[215] DeGeorge, R.T., (1991), *'Will success spoil business ethics?'* in 'Business Ethics: the state of the art', Freeman, R.E. (Ed), Oxford: Oxford University Press, p45.

[216] http://www.hbs.edu/about/pioneer.html

[217] Pickford, J, (Ed), (2001), Financial Times Mastering Management: Your Single Source Guide to Becoming a Master of Management, London: Financial Times Prentice Hall.

[218] Dickson, T, (Ed), (2000), *Financial Times Mastering Strategy: the complete MBA companion in Strategy*, London: Financial Times Prentice Hall.

[219] Gergen, K.J., (1973), 'Social Psychology as History', *Journal of Personality and Social Psychology,* Vol 26, No 2, pp309-320.

[220] Jha, A., (2007), 'Facing down the heat', *The Guardian Society Guardian Environment,* 24th October, 2007

[221] Esty, D.C. & Winston, A.S., (2006), 'Green to Gold: how smart companies use environmental strategy to innovate, create value, and build competitive advantage', New Haven: Yale University Press, p287.

[222] Bradsher, K., (2003), *'China's Boom Adds to Global Warming Problem'*, 22nd October, 2003: http://healthandenergy.com/china_burning_more_coal.htm

[223] Watson, R., (2007), interview reported in Jha, A., (2007), 'Facing down the heat', *The Guardian Society Guardian Environment*, 24th October,

[224] Companies Act 2006, Part 10, Chapter 2 para 172

[225] Goldsmith, Lord, (2006), Statement to the Lords Grand Committee, 6th February, 2006, column 255.

[226] Read, A., (19971), *'The Company Director: His Functions, Powers and Duties'*, London: Jordan & Sons Ltd, p3.

[227] Read, A., (19971), *'The Company Director: His Functions, Powers and Duties'*, London: Jordan & Sons Ltd, p10.

[228] Companies Act 2006, Part 10, Chapter 2 para 172

[229] Tawney, R H, (1931), *'Equality'* London: Allen & Unwin, pp134-5

[230] Galbraith, J K, (1958), *'The Affluent Society'*, London: Hamish Hamilton, p210.

[231] McFadzean, F.S., (1968), *'Galbraith and the Planners'*, Glasgow: Strathclyde University Press.

[232] Friedman, M, (1977), *'From Galbraith to Economic Freedom'*, Occasional Paper 49, London: The Institute of Economic Affairs, p14.

[233] Drucker, P F., (1950), *'The New Society'*, New York: Harper & Brothers, p93

[234] Drucker, P.F., (1955), *'The Practice of Management'*, London: William Heinemann, p13.